"I fear that our children face numerous threats and pressures in this complicated world. *Raising Positive Kids in a Negative World* gives real insight into how we can avoid these modern pitfalls. It was a joy to read."

PAULA HAWKINS
U. S. Senator

"Illustrates with rare understanding why bringing up children today is far more difficult than it was a generation or two ago, and how we can avoid or cope with the special problems and gaping potholes on the road to successful parenting today."

PEGGY MANN

"Our experience in teaching our positive attitude course to over 3 million kids proves beyond any doubt that these concepts work, not just for kids, but for the whole family."

MAMIE McCULLOUGH
President of Positive Life Attitudes
for America

"Not only does he describe the problems many of us have in our own homes, but he also gives us tangible, easy steps that will help us have a better family unit."

ROGER STAUBACH

RAISING POSITIVE KIDS IN A NEGATIVE WORLD

Zig Ziglar

BALLANTINE BOOKS • NEW YORK

Grateful acknowledgment is made to the following for permission to reprint previously published material:

Fleming H. Revell Company: Excerpts from ONE HUNDRED NINETY-NINE QUESTIONS PARENTS ASK by Grace Ketterman, M.D. Copyright (c) 1986. Reprinted by permission of Fleming H. Revell Company.

Victor Books: Excerpts from HOW TO REALLY KNOW YOUR CHILD by Dr. Ross Campbell. Reprinted by permission of the publisher, Victor Books, a division of Scripture Press Publications Inc.

Scripture quotations are from the NEW KING JAMES VERSION. Copyright © 1979, 1980, 1982, Thomas Nelson, Inc., Publishers.

ISBN 0-345-36188-1

This edition published by arrangement with Thomas Nelson, Inc.

Manufactured in the United States of America

First Ballantine Books Edition: September 1989

Dedication

To the four most positive kids I know:
Jean Suzanne Ziglar Witmeyer
Cindy Ann Ziglar Oates
Julie Ann Ziglar Norman
John Thomas Ziglar

Contents

Thank You

Of all the efforts I've expended in the writing of a book, this one has been the most challenging, exciting, and rewarding. As always, a project of this kind is never handled by one person alone. In this particular case, the contributions made by others—including the numerous authors who were willing to permit the use of their writing and research—have been invaluable.

My deep thanks go to my friend Walt Clayton for his in-depth research; my wife, Jean, for her support, proofreading, and help editing; my daughters, Suzanne, Cindy, and Julie, and my son, Tom, for their insight and suggestions.

I would also like to express my special appreciation to Dr. Forest Tennant for his help in the area of keeping our kids off drugs, to psychologist Dr. James Dobson and to psychiatrists Dr. Grace Ketterman and Dr. Ross Campbell for their willingness to let me quote from their marvelous books, as well as to Dr. J. Allan Petersen, who shared some valuable insights from his monthly publication "Family Happiness is Homemade."

For their practical advice and persistent encouragement, I am especially grateful to Mrs. Mamie McCullough, the "I CAN" Lady; Anne Ezinga and Karen Roossien, corporate wives; Victor Oliver, my publisher; Laurie Magers, my administrative assistant; and Kay Lynn Westervelt as well as Leola Stone, who filled in so capably during Laurie's vacation and work overloads.

To all of these loving, faithful people, I give my heartfelt thanks.

Dear Reader

When I consider reading a book, my first step is to identify the author and his qualifications for addressing the subject. Since I am best known as a motivational teacher and sales trainer, you will undoubtedly have an interest in my qualifications for addressing the subject of raising positive kids, which is *possibly* the most important subject in America. (Kids don't make up 100 percent of our population, but they do make up 100 percent of our future.)

My book, *See You At The Top* (over 1.5 million copies in print), is the textbook for the ''I CAN'' course developed by Mrs. Mamie McCullough. This course is currently being taught in over five thousand schools in America, and over three million kids from kindergarten through college have benefited from its concepts. This is possibly the largest laboratory with the most comprehensive measurable results *ever* made available to an author. The results have been dramatic: improved grades and attendance; diminished drug usage, violence, and vandalism; improved self-image, dress codes, and moral behavior; and a host of other positive benefits. (Data are available upon request.)

Raising Positive Kids in a Negative World takes these same principles taught in the school and adapts them for parental use in the home. Results should be even better because of individual attention, ease of adaptability, more flexibility (the book deals directly with the subject matter as it applies to your child), and even greater love for the student (your child).

In addition to this, it was my privilege to work in the direct sales world for sixteen years, and I have been in thousands of homes—homes that represent every racial, religious, and socioeconomic group in our land. I saw firsthand the good, the bad, and the indifferent methods and steps for raising kids. To this add the fact that my wife and I successfully raised four of our own, and it boils down to one basic fact: What you are about to read is not theory; it is current, valid information gleaned from the "University of Life."

Sincerely,

Zig Ziglar

Foreword

The following letter represents a moving experience in my life and led me to commit anew my determination to encourage our kids to believe in themselves, use the ability they have, and become the winners they were born to be:

"Dear Zig: My name is Scott Allen. I met you at the Roswell Street Baptist Church this year. I am 12 years old. You looked at me and turned me around and checked me over. You said, 'Yes, I can see you are going to be a winner.'

"Since my mom was going to your seminar, I wanted to let you know how I am doing. My grades are better and my teacher likes me more. I guess I am going to be a winner. I have lots of friends now. Thank you for caring. I will see you at the top. Love, Scott Allen."

Scott's mother delivered this letter to me on December 15 when I was doing a seminar in Atlanta. Later, I overheard her tell my goddaughter, Dana Jones, that I must have spent a full minute looking Scott over, but mostly looking him in the eye. She said it was almost as if I really could see that Scott was a winner. At that point I interrupted her and assured her that, indeed, I could see "something" that clearly showed Scott was a winner.

In all candor, I'll confess that I truly believe that in every child there is a spark that, when ignited, can release the giant that lives within him or her. As Ethel Waters said, "God don't make no junk." In Scott's case, I'm truly grateful I saw that spark because later I learned he had been abused when he was two years old, and he needed lots of encouragement. That encouragement is easy to give when you truly believe that every child, including yours, was BORN TO WIN.

I'm convinced that every child can be number one. Now obviously, I don't believe that every child can be the biggest, fastest, strongest and smartest. I do believe each child can be number one if we teach him to start every day with the promise to himself that he is going to do his very best that day. He is number one if, at the end of the day, he can look himself in the eye and say that he has given this day his best shot. He's number one with himself in his integrity and commitment, and with those two qualities combined with his best effort every day, he will soon be number one in every area of life that really counts.

No Guilt Trip, Please

Now before we go any further, let me emphasize that I will have failed in my purpose for writing *Raising Positive Kids* if, when you've read the last page of this book, you put it aside with, "If only I had done this or that" and off you go on a guilt trip.

I'm convinced that the overwhelming majority of parents deeply love their kids and want the very best for them. Any mistakes we've made—and *all* of us have made lots of them— have by and large been mistakes of the head, not the heart. We made those decisions and took those actions based on the information we had at that time. We did the best we could—and that's all anybody can do.

A number of parents who deeply loved their kids have gone above and beyond the call of duty and still lost (at least temporarily) their kids to drugs, sex, booze, rebellion, etc. If that includes you, let me remind you that God was the perfect parent and yet Adam and Eve both rebelled. Let me also state that I believe with all my heart that the information in this book, when lovingly and consistently applied, will stack the odds heavily in your favor that you can and will raise positive, morally sound, drug-free kids in a negative world.

But if the worst comes to pass, you must not assume personal guilt. To do so, according to Dr. Spiros Zodhiates, will make it more difficult for your child to repent from his own sin.[1] ·

Now let's dig in with some information, love and inspiration that will make our tomorrows better than our yesterdays.

Your Unasked Question

In answer to your unasked question, no, my wife and I did not do all the things I'm suggesting when we were raising our three daughters and our son. (Anyone can tell it like it is. I want to tell it like it should be.) We did follow most of the principles mentioned in this book and were, we feel, successful in raising four happy, healthy, productive, well-adjusted, morally sound, positive kids. If I did not firmly believe the validity of that last statement, you can rest assured this book would never have been written—at least, not by me.

Introduction

When the proud new mama and daddy hold their seven-pound bundle of joy in their arms, it's difficult to imagine that someday that little package of helplessness could be a six-foot, two-hundred-pounder or a five-foot beauty who will make major contributions to the world. Positive parents, however, have the capacity to "see the future," to use their imaginations, to visualize that baby growing up to be a successful, creative, positive adult. Just as Michelangelo saw the mighty Moses in that block of granite before he struck the first blow, so we parents (1) can confidently project an image of the fine young man or young woman who will emerge from that tiny "block" of humanity and (2) can nurture that helpless babe through successive growing stages into positive adulthood. Of course, the nurturing process is not exactly a piece of cake. Remember, a well-baked cake consists of various ingredients subjected to just the right amount of blending and heat for the proper length of time. The result? A finished delicacy. To raise positive kids we've got to use many essential ingredients—love, discipline, forgiveness, and many other qualities all wrapped in an abundance of care and commitment for our children's eventual well-being. Raising positive kids is not an easy trip by any stretch of the imagination, but it can be fun, exciting, and tremendously rewarding. However, before all those good things can happen, "balance" is required. Grace Ketterman, M.D., helps parents achieve that balance through her marvelous books, such as *One Hundred Ninety-Nine Questions Parents Ask*.[1] I admire Dr. Ketterman because of her professional competence but I appreciate her because she was genuinely pleased when I told her I thought of her first as a mother and then as a psychiatrist. Here are some of her guidelines:

We need to give our kids:

1. Enough attention and protection to establish trust, but not enough to stifle growth toward individuality and independence.
2. Enough limits to offer security, but not enough to prompt rebellion or promote the despair of helplessness.
3. Enough work to teach the pride of achievement, but not so much that life becomes a grim drudgery.
4. Enough discipline and training to teach a sense of responsibility, but not so much that it destroys a sense of healthy freedom.
5. Enough laughter and play to keep life joyful, but not so much that pleasure becomes a goal in itself.
6. Enough consistency to make life predictable, but not so much that it makes life unbearably rigid.
7. Enough pride to teach the happiness of being productive, but not so much that it makes a child an egomaniac.
8. Enough love to make each day tender and warm, and to motivate the painful efforts to grow—for a lifetime!

I love the way Dr. Ketterman sums it up: "Few people can resist optimistic, outreaching, unconditional love. Even the prodigal son returned to his father. And sure enough, the father was waiting, looking far down the road to glimpse the first sign of that return. So even if your children stray, don't give up your commitment."

CHAPTER 1

Raising Positive Kids
Is Simple—But Not Easy

> *The first step in raising positive
> kids is to become a positive parent.*

New Glasses for a Challenging Opportunity

In the spring of 1984 I went to see my optometrist friend, Bob Vodvarka, to be examined for some bifocals. Bob took advantage of modern technology in the form of his computer and was able to write the ideal prescription for my glasses. Ten days later he fitted me with the glasses, pronounced me ready to see everything I needed to see, and bade me farewell.

My car was parked about fifty feet from the door of his office. As I walked out with those new bifocals, I picked my feet up extremely high. I was unaware of this until I got to the curb next to my car and saw the reflection in the window. My foot was up in the air about two feet. I quickly looked around to see if anybody was watching. (You know how you feel when you do something that is not overly bright!) When I saw that nobody was looking, I laughed, thinking how ridiculous I must have looked.

Then a sobering thought hit me. I, too, am an optometrist. I travel our country on a regular basis, fitting people with a very special custom-made pair of glasses—not rose-colored glasses, but ones that are unique in that they magnify your potential as a parent. These glasses do even more than that—they turn outward to help you see the love, hope, intelligence, personality, genius, integrity, and all the other positive qualities that your child possesses. In other words, these glasses will help you see the tremendous potential represented in your child. That's where this book begins—by urging you parents to *look again and see what that special child of yours can be in the future.*

Two Principles for Raising Positive Kids

Throughout *Raising Positive Kids* I state two principles a number of times. I do this because they are so important that if we can own them, they will simplify our entire educational and parenting process.

The Way You Think Is the Way You Perform

The first principle is, *You are what you are and where you are because of what has gone into your mind*, and you can change what you are and where you are by changing what goes into your mind. In other words, your thinking directly affects your performance, and what you put into your mind affects your thinking.

Talking about performance, several years ago I agreed to buy a computer because I was convinced it would be a key factor in helping our company grow into the 1980s and better achieve our objectives. I was tremendously excited about this computer. As a matter of fact, when you understand that I'm from a small town in Mississippi and that I get excited about buying anything new, you can understand my enthusiasm for something as significant as a computer. I went all over the country telling audiences about that marvelous computer and all of the wonderful things it was going to do—check the payroll, take care of the inventory, do the mail-outs, make the coffee, clean the kitchen. I mean, that computer was going to do everything!

Some People Could Foul Up a Two-Car Parade

Six months after I bought the computer, I put it on the market and tried to sell it for a lot less than I had originally paid for it. You talk about a fouled-up affair; we really had one! Here's an example. We do a mail-out to subscribers for our bi-monthly *Top Performance* magazine. It keeps our customers informed about what's new in personal growth, management, sales training, etc. We had a Dr. and Mrs. William B. Jones on our mailing list, and they got one of the bulletins. So did Dr. and Mrs. William Jones, and so did Dr. and Mrs. Jones. Additionally, *Mr.* and Mrs. William B. Jones got a bulletin; Mr. and Mrs. William Jones got one; and so did Mr. and Mrs. Jones. Not only that, but *Mrs.* William B. Jones got one! Well, I think you get the picture. We were overbilling, underbilling, late-billing, and early-billing customers; and you cannot believe how upset some of them got when we tried to collect the same bill the third time!

> *You are what you are and where you are*
> *because of what has gone into your mind.*
> *You can change what you are and where you are*
> *by changing what goes into your mind.*

Now you readers who've had an encounter with a computer won't have any difficulty relating to what I'm saying. When the full impact of what it was doing to us hit me, I really was up in the air. I told our people, "Sell it! Get rid of it! Move it out!'' It was ruining us! Fortunately we could not find a buyer. I say ''fortunately,'' because today, without a doubt, it is critical to the success of The Zig Ziglar Corporation.

Question: What is the difference between the computer we *had* and the computer we *have*? Answer: None, except that the first two groups we had running it could have fouled up a two-car parade. Then one day Dave and Marilyn Bauer walked in our front door and said to me, ''Mr. Ziglar, we can make that computer of yours laugh and talk and whistle and sing. Why, we can even make it work!'' I said, ''Come on in!''

Just the other day I was back in the computer room talking to that thing, and I'll tell you, it is the most excited computer I've ever seen. It was laughing and talking and whistling and singing and *working*! The natural question is, What in the world did we do? And the answer is simple! *We changed the input. And when we changed the input, we changed the output.*

If You're Tough on Yourself, Life Will Be Easier
The second principle is, *Life is not easy—as a matter of fact, it's tough*, very tough. This is true whether you're a household executive or a corporate officer. It's true whether your are an athlete or a coach. It's true no matter what you do in life. To be winners, parents and children must survive in a tough world. And that requires learning to be self-disciplined.

If you're not pleased with your child's output, try changing the input—especially from you.

Parents, I have found that if you are tough on yourself, life will be much easier on you. That's why it's so important for parents to train children at an early age to be self-controlled. Not to be disciplined is tantamount to disaster, because when a child gets out into the world, he will quickly discover that any discipline he has not been given by loving parents will be meted out to him by an unloving world. Developing self-control often requires painful learning experiences, but the result is well worth the effort.

Success Doesn't Come Easily

One example I often use to emphasize that life isn't easy has to do with my speaking engagements. One day I met a woman who, with some reluctance and without looking me in the eye, asked me: "You kinda make a nice little ol' fee for the speeches you make, don'cha?" I smilingly looked at her and said, "Oh no, ma'am. I don't know where you got your information, but it simply is not true. I really make a great big ol' fee for the speeches I make!"

What I did not tell her, however, was that before I ever received a fee of any kind, I had made many, many free speeches at Lions Clubs, prisons, Rotary Clubs, drug rehab centers, Jaycees, church groups, garden clubs, and to various office and sales groups. On countless occasions I have driven many miles in an evening, at my own expense, to speak to a group of a dozen people and then returned home that night because I did not have enough money to pay a motel bill. Why did I do it? I hung in there because I believed that I had something to say and knew that if I learned how to say what people needed to hear, in a way they were willing to hear it, eventually I would be paid for saying it.

I also believed that Steve Brown from Atlanta, Georgia, was right on target when he said that anything worth doing was worth doing poorly—until you could learn to do it well. *That* is an incredibly important principle parents need to learn—and then teach to their children.

> *Teach your kids:*
> *You gotta be before you can do*
> *and you gotta do before you can have.*

Choices Make the Difference

We go through life making thousands of choices and every choice has an end result. For example, for twenty-four years of my adult life by choice I weighed well over 200 pounds. I say "by choice" because I have never accidentally eaten anything. The reality is that when I choose to eat too much today I have chosen to weigh too much tomorrow. If a twenty-year-old chooses to smoke one package of cigarettes every day he has chosen to die seven and one half years early.

Every choice, to repeat myself, has an end result. Obviously babies and small children do not have the option of making many choices, so the choices we teach them to make in their lives will be tremendously important. The choices we make for our children initially will have a direct bearing on the types and kinds of choices they will make later in life because choices are primarily based on what we know, believe and feel.

To expand on what I said earlier in the computer example, I want to emphasize that the choice is yours as to what you feed into, or permit to be fed into, the mind of your child.

The right choices lead to positive results and the wrong choices can lead to tragedies. The next two stories illustrate the point.

Two Choices—Two Different Results

At age fifteen, Ben Carson was a poor black teenager from a broken home in inner-city Detroit.[1] He had a pathological temper that was out of control and when someone infringed on his rights, he took whatever steps were necessary to go after them. "One day," he says, "I tried to stab another teenager with a camping knife. He had on a large metal belt buckle and it broke the knife. It struck me then that if he hadn't had that belt buckle on, I would be on my way to jail or reform school and he would be on his way to a hospital or dead."

Ben said he sat in the bathroom on the edge of the bathtub for several hours and thought about his temper. He asked God to take that temper away. Please understand, here was a young boy living in an environment which literally screamed that he couldn't do anything with his life, but fortunately he had a mother who put an end to those kinds of thoughts very quickly. Ben said you might say she brainwashed him and his brother into believing that they could do anything. By the eighth grade, Ben did so well that he won a prize as the best student in his class. This infuriated his white teacher, who chastised the rest of the class for letting him be number one. Needless to say, Ben never forgot that particular day.

In high school, he briefly drifted with the wrong crowd. Fortunately, his mother stayed after him and convinced him he was going nowhere fast and he made another wise choice. He graduated and won a scholarship to Yale. From Yale, Ben Carson went through medical school and into a series of prestigious posts. Today, he is the Director of Pediatric Neurosurgery at the Johns Hopkins Children's Center. He has gained international respect and acclaim for some of the miracle surgeries he has performed. He says, "The big difference between people who succeed and people who don't is not that the ones who were successful don't have barriers and obstacles. Everyone has barriers and obstacles. If you look at them as fences that don't allow you to advance, then you're going to be a failure. If you look at them as hurdles that strengthen you each time you go over one, then you're going to be a success."

Ben makes no secret of his belief that God has given him

his talent, even though he knows his religious faith makes him an anomaly in a hospital setting. "It's not fashionable by any stretch of the imagination," Carson admits, "but it's what I believe. I don't have any qualms about telling people."

Ben lives a simple life-style. He does not drink, smoke or eat meat. He married his college sweetheart and is the father of three children.

In many ways, Dr. Benjamin Carson's story epitomizes the message I would like to communicate throughout this book. Dr. Carson was blessed with a marvelous, encouraging mother who never gave up, who believed in him and loved him enough to stay with him during those turbulent years when he could have made the wrong choice.

Unfortunately, the next example reflects the result of a wrong choice. Stanley Wilson, formerly with the Cincinnati Bengals, is a tragic example of a young man who could have had it all, but he made a wrong choice.[2] All of his football life, Stanley, like most football players, dreamed of making it to the NFL and reaching the ultimate goal of playing in the Super Bowl. He came within twenty-four hours of reaching that objective, but along the way he experimented with drugs and became addicted to cocaine. His problem surfaced in 1983 after his first NFL season and the nightmare of addiction was relentlessly moving on. Two warnings and suspensions from the NFL came his way. He had freely chosen to "try" cocaine, but he traded his freedom for the slavery of addiction.

The day before 1989 Super Bowl Sunday, he missed the noon and evening meetings, and the die was cast. Later that night the coach and other players found him apparently under the influence of cocaine which had been given to him by some "friends." The next day he was barred for life from professional football.

A tragic irony is the fact that just a few days earlier Stanley had publicly stated that he had finally come to realize that cocaine was "slow suicide" and, though he knew it would be tough, he was through with drugs. Although he fought the addiction with all his might and had been assigned a constant companion, cocaine was not through with him.

Now pause for a moment and think about what you just read. Here's a gifted, intelligent professional with a deep love for the game and the highlight of his career directly in front of him. You know he desperately wanted to play in the Super Bowl. His parents were there. (They were "devastated" when he was suspended.) His teammates were counting on him, and an adoring public was awaiting the kickoff. Lurking in the wings, however, was that deceitful seductress, cocaine, waiting to claim another victim. The addictive power of cocaine toppled Stanley Wilson's dream of fame and fortune.

The message is clear. Tell your kids again and again not to even think about trying cocaine or crack, even once. They have everything to lose and nothing to gain by trying cocaine or any other drugs. Remember Stanley Wilson and remind them that when they choose a habit, they choose the end result of that habit, and sometimes they choose that habit the first time they try the drug. Curiosity not only kills cats, it also kills dreams and people.

As we shall see in the following pages, raising positive, drug-free kids in a negative world is a tough, demanding, sometimes discouraging, often disheartening task. The obstacles are substantial. The difficulties are great. At times it will appear nothing is going your way. There will even be occasions when you'll feel inclined to throw your hands up in despair and sigh, "What's the use?" I plead with you, don't give up. The rewards can be magnificent, and there are some things you can do to stack the odds in your favor.

Over the years every moment you invest and every proper choice you teach your child to make will return incredible dividends to both you and your child. The good news is that you can do it. In the next chapter we'll identify some of the obstacles, then we'll look at how we can overcome them and raise those positive, drug-free kids.

> *When you choose a habit,*
> *you choose the end result*
> *of that habit.*

Time for Personal Evaluation

1. What is the first major principle Zig talks about that helps parents in raising positive kids?

2. Think of a specific instance in your life which illustrates how your thinking has affected your performance.

3. State the second principle that is equally important in raising positive kids.

4. Do you protect your child from life's tough places?

5. List some ways you can change your discipline and instruction so that your child will be prepared to stick it out in life's tough places over the long haul.

6. Complete this quote by Steve Brown: "Anything worth doing is worth _____ until you learn to do it well."

7. Did your parents teach you to persevere? How did they do it?

Additional Reading

Home-Grown Kids; Dr. Raymond Moore, Dorothy Moore, Word, Inc.

CHAPTER 2

We've Got Problems

> *Be positive parents. For every page I devote to identifying the problem I invest twenty pages offering solutions.*

So What Does a Negative World Look Like?

Chances are excellent that people who open *Raising Positive Kids* to this chapter and read the next few pages will close the book convinced I've got to be the most negative man they've ever read—especially if they don't read the last few paragraphs in the chapter. However, I want to tell you in advance that, despite the fact that I'm going to provide a considerable amount of input as far as identifying what our negative world is really like, I positively and emphatically believe there is a solution to these problems.

I feel I would be remiss if I tried to gloss over these problems and make them appear simple. They're not. I believe the first, most logical and most sensible step to solving a problem is to carefully identify that problem and then positively work to solve it. Now, let's look at some specific problems.

The first problem is negative conversation and negative

self-talk. For example, a parent sends a child off to school with the instruction, "Don't get run over!" An overweight person sits down to eat and says, "Everything I eat turns to fat!" If anyone has a wreck, within a matter of minutes a "wrecker" will be called, which is ridiculous, because the "wreck" has already happened. A "tow" truck is needed.

Most people wake up with the aid of an electronic rooster they call an "alarm clock." This is about as negative as you can get. When someone's robbing a bank, an alarm is sounded. That scares people. When a building is on fire, an alarm is sounded. That, too, scares people. If you wake up to an alarm clock, that will scare you. Actually, it's an "opportunity" clock, because if you can hear it you have an opportunity to get up and go. If you can't hear it, that might mean you've gotten up and gone.

Even our terminology is negative. We take a loaf of bread and label the very first slice "the end," when in reality every loaf of bread has *two* beginnings.

Recently when coming into Dallas, the captain of the aircraft himself—the man in charge, the "head honcho," or, as we would say down home, "the daddy rabbit"—came over the intercom with these ominous words: "We are now making our *final* approach." It almost frightened me out of my seat! I said to the flight attendant, "Ma'am, would you please tell him to make it his *next* to final approach? I still have many things I'd like to do!"

As a golfer I have frequently played in foursomes and watched one team member hit a ball into the lake, then turn to the rest of us, and say, "I knew I was going to do that!" The question is obvious: If he knew he was going to do it, why in the world would he go ahead and hit the ball into the lake? That is not the object of the game! It does not improve the score. A positive individual would have backed away, reprogrammed his thinking, declared his intentions to hit it straight down the middle, stepped up to the ball, and done exactly that.

Traditionally, when the average person is up late and has to rise early the next morning, the last thing he says to himself is, "Boy, I'll bet I'm going to be tired tomorrow!" Too many times we look at a difficult task and say, "I *can't* do that." Or if a lot is involved, we say, "I'll *never* finish this." How negative can we get?

A father once introduced his three little girls to me as "this is the one who won't eat, this is the one who cries all the time, and this is the one who won't mind her mother." Talk about negative programming!

Many parents talk about the "terrible" two's when they're really the terrific two's, tremendous three's, etc. There are also super Sundays, marvelous Mondays, etc.

Things Have Changed Over the Last Forty Years

To accentuate the comparative difficulty of raising a positive child in the 1990s versus the 1940s, let's look at some more negative and frightening information which makes our approach and philosophy even more important.

In 1940 the top offenses in public schools were as follows: running in hallways, chewing gum, throwing spitballs, wearing improper clothing (which included leaving a shirttail out), making noise, and not putting paper in wastebaskets.

In 1980 the top offenses in public schools were as follows (not in order of occurrence): robbery, assault, personal theft, burglary, drug abuse, arson, bombings, alcohol abuse, carrying weapons, absenteeism, vandalism, murder, and extortion. Since twelve of these are felonies, not a great deal of comment is necessary, except to say that times and conditions have changed.[1] Anyone who says these changes are good is simply not thinking. With your child possibly facing these problems at school and in the rest of society, it's obvious that your job at home with your child is increasing in difficulty *and* importance.

> *The all-time bestseller clearly states:*
> *"As ye sow, so also shall ye reap."*
> *The computer people say, "Garbage in, garbage out."*
> *Positive people say, "Put the good stuff in*
> *and you'll get the good stuff out."*

Here is an interesting phenomenon of American life. If I were to stand in front of an audience of virtually any kind in America, whether it was a sales organization, educators, a patriotic group, or athletes, and advocate drunken orgies, getting high on cocaine, pot, or any of the other mind-bending drugs, they would look at me in stunned astonishment. If I gave them a sales talk on incest, adultery, homosexuality, necrophilia, bestiality, and even suicide, while generously sprinkling four-letter words throughout the presentation, not one group in a thousand would sit still and listen. I'm confident the parents in the audience who knew I was going to be making the same speech to their sons and daughters at the local school the next day would move heaven and earth to get my speaking engagement cancelled.

Music

An interesting fact is that these same parents often provide their children with money to buy records or cassette recordings that openly advocate those things I mentioned. Music, the lyrics and tunes, is another major problem for today's families. I challenge you to go to the local record shop, pick up a list of the top ten records in both rock and country and western, get a copy of the lyrics, and read what they say. You will be shocked at what is being advocated.

More significant is the fact that since these words are sung into the minds of your children with a beat, dozens, even hundreds of times, the impact is far greater than the same words would be if I used them in a speech and they were heard *one* time. As a matter of fact, parents, the odds are great that your children can sing the lyrics of many of these songs. When you understand that words paint pictures in the mind and then the mind goes to work to complete the picture, it gets easier and easier to understand why suicide, drug abuse, violence, promiscuity, etc. are *increasing*. The frightening thing about this is that you can be conditioned to believe anything, especially when you are young and impressionable. Voltaire was right when he said, "Those who can make you believe absurdities can make you commit atrocities."

Just How Much Impact Does Music Have?

In 1703 Andrew Fletcher, the great Scottish patriot, made this observation (and I paraphrase him): "You write the laws, let me write the music, and I will rule your country."

Just in case you can't get to the store to find out more about these lyrics, here are a few of the hundreds of examples. One rock group has a song about hell being the ultimate party place; you should go there because all your friends will be there. Other songs mock Christianity and, in places, blaspheme God. One band has a song that encourages the listener not to listen to his parents or to any authority, just "do your own thing" at anyone's expense. Another well-known hit says you've tried whiskey, and it doesn't help; drugs, and they didn't help. You've tried sex, and that doesn't help. Why not try suicide? Music by one group has been banned in twenty-two countries because those governments fear the impact of the lyrics on their people in terms of education, jobs, responsibilities, and families. Incidentally, much of the country and western lyrics are terribly negative, and medical research in Montana confirms the unhealthy connection between country music and heavy drinking.

A recent (October 25, 1988) NBC two-hour TV special observed that in 100 percent of the cases of Satan worship, heavy metal music was involved. Despite the overwhelming evidence of the destructiveness of some of the music, *millions* of parents pass it off as just a "phase," but do nothing about it because he's a "good kid," and "everybody's doing it." However, I believe that Al Menconi was right when he said, "If you don't deal with the issue of rock music, it will undermine your family. If you deal with it improperly, it will destroy your family."

Ross Campbell, M.D., says that the lyrics of much of the rock, hard rock, heavy metal and now speed metal, death metal and thrash openly advocate rebellion. A young acquaintance of mine candidly states that many of these songs are anger, rage and rebellion set to music. Unfortunately, it's set to music so loud that Forest Tennant, M.D., says that it is virtually impossible to endure the aural pain of music at a concert unless you are on drugs. This partially explains why, according to newscaster Paul Harvey, up to 60 percent of our college freshmen have suffered some loss of hearing.

Names Say a Lot

The names of many of the groups and some of their songs reek with evil, negativism, Satanism, immorality and violence. Consider these names: Suicidal Tendencies, the Dead Milkmen, Twisted Sister, Mötley Crüe, Mega Death, Judas Priest, Violence, Death Angel, Black Sabbath, Black and Blue, Malice, Slayer, L.A. Gun, etc.

Bruce Britt of the Los Angeles *Daily News* describes Metallica's new albums as loud, lusty and tragic.[3] Regarding the latest "in" music called thrash, he says, "Whatever one calls it, there is no disputing thrash's overall gloomy lyricism. Though sentiments vary from band to band, thrash seems to thrive on negativity. Slayer and Rigor Mortis favor horror-show lyricism, while Suicidal Tendencies sings about communication breakdown between youth and the establishment. An early Tendencies song, 'Institutionalized,' was a harrowing dialogue between a frustrated teen and his hounding mother, who wants to deal with his moodiness by institutionalizing him.''

Don't misunderstand. I'm not making a blanket indictment of rock music, but I am encouraging you to become acutely aware of what your kids are listening to and viewing. That's the only way you can intelligently and lovingly talk with and guide your kids through some of the childhood and teenage mazes they face daily. Understanding those sexually suggestive lyrics will also help you to understand how your child (''he's only a baby'') can have chewing gum in his mouth and sex on his mind.

Good Music Is Helpful

At this point I just can't resist slipping in something positive. To combat this negative, immoral input, parents should make available good music—and from early childhood days— not merely as a last-gasp unwanted option for the children after their music preferences have been established. Great music can lift a person to heights of accomplishment and inspire marvelous contributions to society. Research indicates that beautiful melodies played as background music enhance creativity and provide relaxation and considerable listening pleasure.

TV—The Destroyer of Values

To be realistic, I have to admit that TV is here to stay in America. The question is, is it good or evil? Does it help or hurt? Regardless of how we feel, it is a fact of life. Many families would love to eliminate the television set from their homes, but the fact they are hooked on it, combined with the fear of being publicly ridiculed and having their children embarrassed at not having a set, prevents most of them from taking that step.

If I were a young man just starting my family, I would

have no television set in our home. I say this with the full knowledge that occasionally there are some excellent programs on television, and I love to watch some athletic events, such as golf, football, and tennis. Overall, however, the fare is so negative that I would not expose my children to it.

The documented evidence about TV's negative impact is strong. A March 7, 1985, Associated Press release pointed out that *for the first time the American Psychological Association has taken a position on potential dangers in television violence, concluding that there is a link between the mayhem on children's programs and aggressive behavior in children.* In a resolution the association encouraged "parents to monitor and to control television viewing by children" and asked the TV industry to reduce "imitatable violence in 'real life' fictional children's programming." These findings are echoed and expanded in a report from the American Academy of Pediatrics' Task Force on Children and Television, released the same month and reported in *USA Today*. The pediatricians concluded, as did some prior researchers, that *TV violence can make children not only accepting of real-life violence, but more violent themselves.*

The behavior TV causes is bad, but the behavior it prevents is worse.

When your child is in front of a television set or a movie screen, you're permitting him to be educated (indoctrinated) by the most effective and persuasive educational tool in America today. Through TV we can be (have been) conditioned to believe incredible things. Many of the most widely viewed TV programs have conditioned us to believe that premarital, even extramarital, sexual relationships are perfectly all right provided they are "meaningful relationships." Eighty percent[4] of the 14,000 sexual references seen and heard annually on TV by the average American child are between unmarried people.[5] Less than 1 percent make any reference to birth control and as far as teaching any moral restraint is concerned, forget it. Extramarital or premarital sex is not only okay but is exciting and "beautiful." That's the message our kids get!

We've been conditioned to believe that drinking is the preferred way of life. For example, every seven and one-half minutes on television we see drinks being offered; fifteen times out of sixteen the drink is accepted. Interestingly enough, whether it's the bad guy or the good guy being offered the drink, the ratio is still the same. The thought is firmly planted that if we want to have any fun at all, we need to take a drink. If we've got a tough decision to make, we should take a drink. If we need to steady our nerves for a real challenge, we should take a drink. No wonder teenage alcoholism is a rampant problem in America and more than 14,000,000 adults have serious drinking problems.

TV Exacts a Heavy Toll

We'll probably never know the toll that TV addiction has taken on our nation's youth as far as potential and productivity are concerned. I'm speaking of the paralyzing addiction that stifles human creativity and cripples personal relationships. Not only that, but every hour of staring at TV is one less hour invested in personal motivation, mental creativity, and actual involvement in the lives of others.

Here are a few other peculiarities that concern the pros who study this field: (1) increased communication in nearly nonverbal speech (like "man, uh, you know, uh"); (2) much less spontaneity and fewer imaginative, innovative concepts coming from young adults; (3) an intense, almost irrational, dependence on music with a heavy beat as their only art form; (4) the ever-present drug scene; (5) greater interest in passive experiences than in those requiring mental interaction and active involvement; and (6) creative problem solving among the youth is limited and rare.

Turning on the television set can turn off the process that transforms children into whole, perceptive people and changes passive viewers into thinking, caring persons. Values become strangely twisted and confused. That's why one little nine-year-old child in San Francisco was overheard saying, "I'd a lot rather watch TV than play outside, 'cause it's boring outside. They always have the same rides, like swings and slides and things."

Mary Ellison, in a Knight-Ridder wire, wrote about the addictiveness of television. "I couldn't get away from it," eleven-year-old Monica Pencz confessed. "My homework wasn't getting done; I just forgot all about my friends." "Once I got hooked on it, I couldn't get off," David Kahn, eleven, said. "I just watched any show." David and Monica were television junkies. David was watching ten hours of television a day and Monica five hours.

Patty Rebek, director of the psychology program at De Paul University in Chicago, says children often watch TV as a form of escape from academic, family, or social problems. *Children who watch TV excessively tend to be withdrawn.* "They do not develop initiative because it's such a passive activity," she said. "The problem comes when they don't do anything else—when they start missing out on other things because of the TV."

One mother complained that kids don't have to think when they watch TV. "When they have to write a story of their own for school, they just take something off the TV." Ms. Rebek agreed. "Remember," she told parents and children, "children do not need to be entertained all the time. Some of their most constructive times are those quiet moments when they're left entirely to their own resources. For a child, the imagination is the best source of entertainment."

The ultimate tragedy: at least twenty-six people took their own lives imitating the Russian roulette scene in the movie

"The Deer Hunter" after it aired on TV.[6] Input *does* influence behavior. Directly and indirectly TV also influences illiteracy, which is a major problem in America today. Twenty-five million adults (one in seven) are functional illiterates and forty-seven million more are borderline illiterates. The cost alone for this national disgrace is an estimated two hundred twenty-five billion dollars each year.[7]

And Those Commercials

According to *U.S. News & World Report*, the average twenty-year-old American has viewed over 1,000,000 commercials, including 60,000 selling beer and wine, and far more than that selling toys and cereal.

Our kids from birth are being conditioned to believe that life's problems have thirty- to sixty-second solutions, that "fun" and the good life are to be found in the bottle, muscles for athletic performance are in a box of cereal, and these toys will guarantee you'll be the most popular kid on the block. Later our children are assured that this toothpaste, mouthwash or deodorant will make them irresistible to members of the opposite sex, and this beer or wine will help them relax and be "sophisticated" or go through life with fun and gusto. Then, if they are confused, nervous, or irritable, they can just relax and dream it all away with this brand of decaffeinated coffee or sleeping potion.

By age seven or eight, the kids begin to grasp the fact that life does have its demands, disappointments, and defeats. Without being able to understand the "whys" of life, they nevertheless feel that something is wrong. That's when they begin to listen to the promises of drugs and alcohol, especially if a friend, sibling or parent is already using them to escape from the reality of life. It is then just one more step into a permanent escape from life via the suicide route. When you add the drama and vividness of television with its full-length programs, it's easier to understand why.

Today, according to the Department of Health and Human Services, in a study involving 11,000 eighth and tenth graders, 42 percent of the girls and 25 percent of the boys have "seriously thought" about committing suicide.[8] Another study showed that 20 percent of the girls and 10 percent of the boys had actually attempted suicide. Another study involving 300 middle class students showed that 20 percent had attempted to kill themselves or "tried to hurt" themselves during a 12-month period.[9]

The bottom line is that unrealistic expectations are the seedbed of depression, and the "quick fix, something-for-nothing" approach to life is patently untrue and has created some incredible problems. For example, *Psychology Today* (October 1988) points out that today a thirty-year-old is ten times as likely to be depressed as his father and twenty times as likely to be depressed as his grandfather.[10] Sadly, those who buy the something-for-nothing philosophy and frantically chase happiness seldom find it.

> *We all want to be happy.*
> *Some pursue it, others create it.*
> *Guess who is the happiest.*
> *—Anonymous*

How Much TV Should Kids Watch?

How much television do you watch? Unquestionably there are some outstanding programs on television from time to time. Some of the specials have messages that are beneficial to all members of the family. We can learn about geography, history, other cultures and civilizations, and a host of other things. Some programs provide much-needed relaxation and entertainment. "The Cosby Show," for example, is hilarious and effectively presents a positive, "traditional" family, which depicts the parents as intelligent, "in-control" people who believe in and teach some solid values.

There are also *some* outstanding religious programs and church services that provide inspiration and encouragement for old and young alike. On the basis of what is generally shown on television, however, I am highly skeptical of the overall merits of the medium.

Admittedly, there is the possibility that our children could be considered "different" if they did not have a television set at home. After the first couple of weeks, they would be "different." They would be happier, more communicative, productive, affectionate, relaxed, morally responsible, and socially acceptable. So what is the solution?

Many suggestions have been made, but one of the better compromises (and that's all it is) is this: Parents should sit down with their children with the weekly TV schedule and go over a list of programs that would be appropriate for each child, based primarily on the age of that child. Next, write out a list of the programs, giving the time and date for each showing so it can be referred to each day. Then give each child a book of tickets or a card with ten numbers, which the child assumes the responsibility for maintaining. The parent punches a hole in the sheet or card, and when all ten programs have been viewed, the child has certainly had enough television time. This process teaches the child to be selective in what he views and teaches him responsibility as well as self-denial, because undoubtedly there will be some programs he would like to watch but not as much as he would others. This helps to establish judgment and value within the child. In addition, there probably should be other "bonus" programs, such as parades, Thanksgiving or Christmas specials, a Fourth of July celebration, or programs the entire family views together.

One really neat variation of this process is to use money to control television viewing. For example, if you're going to permit your children to watch eight hours of selected programs each week, give them eight quarters on Monday morning. For each hour they watch, take a quarter back. At the end of the week they can keep the remaining quarters to use as they please. This has the added benefit of teaching them that time is money and that by denying themselves some temporary pleasure, they will have extra money for personal shopping or recreation. One enthusiastic supporter of this idea is Bonnie Baker of Lynchburg, Virginia, who attended one of my seminars. She immediately went home and put it to work using six hours and six quarters as her standards.

On the first day her ten-year-old son David persuaded his dad to videotape David's favorite TV show and to watch it and tell him whether or not it was worth the quarter. Bonnie knew then that the idea was already working. The maximum number of quarters either David or his sister Tami ever invested in television was three each week. After six months, Tami told her mother that she was really glad she had tested the idea because it had helped her to study more and become a better student.

An even better approach is taken by a school in Pennsylvania that has drawn up guidelines setting strict limits for watching television in an effort to rid students of hyperactivity, nervousness, and anti-social behavior. "Elementary level students who watch a great deal of T.V. tend to be hyperactive and anti-social," says Henry Blanchard, head of the faculty at Kemberton Farms School in Phoenixville, Pennsylvania. Kemberton Farms, with 320 students from nursery school through twelfth grade, has written guidelines calling for *no TV for youngsters through the first grade*.

Children in the second grade and above are urged to stay away from the TV on school nights and to restrict weekend viewing to no more than three or four hours. "You could observe the effects with some youngsters almost immediately," said Blanchard in *Parents Magazine*. "Three days after they turn off the set you see marked improvement in their behavior. They concentrate better and are more able to follow directions and get along better with their neighbors. If they go back to the set you notice it right away.''

One further thought if you are a TV-viewing family. If it's financially feasible, by all means buy a video recorder. You can record the choice programs for showing at a convenient time for the family, and you can take advantage of the many video cassette programs that can effectively educate your child in the important things of life.

As parents we can choose to a large degree the input in our children's minds. One more time: When we have positive input, we have positive output, and when we have negative input, we have negative output.

Child Pornography

Another major problem facing parents today is child pornography. An article in the *Dallas Morning News*[11] by Melinda Henneberger tells a grim story. It also gives a graphic picture of why parents need to watch their little ones.

> Two Dallas boys were held for questioning in an alleged sexual assault Wednesday of a six-year-old girl, but were released because Texas law says investigators couldn't file charges.
>
> The parents of both the eight-year-old and the nine-year-old boys say they doubt it happened, but both children told police they assaulted the girl—first in the back yard and later under the table, police said.
>
> The 8-year-old reportedly began abusing boys and girls in the neighborhood after he saw some pornographic movies, said the witness and the victim's mother.

Norman Cousins in the *Saturday Review* has said it well:

> The trouble with this wide-open pornography . . . is not that it corrupts but that it desensitizes; not that it unleashes

the passions but that it cripples the emotions; not that it encourages a mature attitude but that it is a reversion to infantile obsessions; not that it removes the blinders but that it distorts the view. Prowess is proclaimed but love is denied. What we have is not liberation but dehumanization.*

A report in the January 1, 1982, issue of *Christianity Today*, involving 38,000 victims of rape between 1956 and 1979 revealed that 41 percent of the victims were sexually molested *immediately* after the rapist had read a pornographic magazine or had seen a pornographic video presentation.

This article by Richard T. Pienciak, in an Associated Press release, really grasps the heart of the matter:

This year, in a nationwide crackdown on child pornography, U.S. Customs Service agents have identified 300–400 people in the 19 states who receive mailings, including a college professor, an air force officer, a children's psychiatrist and a high school counselor. "One usually thinks of a person who is obsessed with child pornography as being some sort of 'sickie,' living in the shadows of society," says Allen Wilk, a Customs Service regional official. "This description may fit some, but we found others who would be considered pillars of the community."

"While not every case of sexual abuse involved pornography, pedophiles almost always collect child porn to show the child how normal it is," says Kenneth V. Lanning, the FBI's expert on child sexual abuse. They also use the pornography, he says, for personal sexual arousal. Molesters will seduce, trick, and if need be blackmail a child

*©*Saturday Review* magazine. Reprinted by permission.

into a sexual relationship, and that is where the pornography often becomes essential to their schemes. Rarely is violence used on the children. The last thing the pedophile wants is an unwilling victim.

. . . Molesters select a child who is least likely to say "no." *Almost always the molester will give up on the child who resists.*

About 80 percent of all molestation victims know their attackers. . . . Once in the pedophile's domain, the child is seduced with candy and toys, trips to parks or movie theaters. As the child becomes more comfortable, "Mr. Nice Guy" may try some tickling, some wrestling, followed perhaps by some "innocent" fondling. "The pornography is the next step in the seduction process. It serves as validation material to lower the youngsters' inhibitions," says Lanning of the FBI. . . .

"All kids are curious," he explains. "They'll ask, 'How come these kids are naked?' So there's this person whom the child trusts explaining, 'Would I do something wrong? These kids are having a good time. You're as beautiful as they are. Would you like me to take some pictures of you?' " The more children get involved, the harder it is for them to escape. Still some try. That's when blackmail is often used. When pictures are taken then the pedophile will threaten to show them to the victim's parents.

To protect your child from the molester, you should *know where your child is and what he is doing at all times*.

If you allow a friendly, compassionate neighbor to help out by baby-sitting, you should first know a great deal about that person. Additionally, you should be extremely sensitive to anything your child says about the games played or pictures taken. You should start educating your child at an early age about the parts of the body that no one is to touch without mommy's or daddy's permission. (Some authorities suggest buying "modest" bathing suits—not bikinis or those that expose the hips up to the waistline—and instructing children that anything covered is neither to be exposed nor touched by anyone without parental permission. This eliminates confusion when you take your child to a doctor.) Another excellent safety precaution is to periodically "pop in" on the adult who is keeping your child.

Are Drugs Number One?

Many people in America today consider drugs to be our number one problem. Certainly their dollar and "misery" cost is so astronomical that it is mind boggling. So awesome is it that many of these same people believe there is no solution to the problem. Naturally, I reject that thought completely and believe that much of the solution to the problem is found in the pages of this book. Drugs, violence, immorality, etc. are not the problems. They are the outward manifestations of those problems, and we must deal with the *cause* of the problem, which is the only way to solve the problem.

Dr. Forest Tennant of UCLA is a world-renowned expert on drugs, drug abuse, drug treatment, and drug prevention. He's the consultant for the NFL, the Justice Department, Texaco, and the L.A. Dodgers, to name just a few clients. He firmly believes that when we solve the smoking problem, we will have solved the major portion of the drug problem. His reasoning is simple, and the logic is irrefutable. Over 95 percent of the people who smoke pot started with tobacco as their first drug. (You need to know how to inhale to smoke pot, and smoking cigarettes teaches you how to do that.) Over 95 percent of those who are on heroin and/or cocaine smoked pot on the way. *He did not say* that everybody who smokes cigarettes will end up on heroin or cocaine. *He did say* that 95 percent of those on heroin or cocaine *started* with cigarettes.

Incidentally, Dr. Tennant also believes that soon an eighteen-year-old who enters the job market as a smoker will find it *almost* impossible to get a job (he already can't in over 15 percent of the job market) because it cost $5,502 (in 1988 dollars) *more* to hire a smoker than a nonsmoker. If the drug use stops with tobacco and never includes pot or coke, employment opportunity alone is a pretty good reason for not smoking.

Another good reason for not smoking is the fact that every cigarette you smoke means that you have *chosen* to die sixteen minutes earlier than you would have had you not chosen to smoke that cigarette. Today 17.4 percent of the deaths in America are a direct or indirect result of smoking cigarettes. That's 390,000 people (some authorities say 500,000) every year. (Thought: If 390,000 people died every year because of a flaw in an automobile, an unsafe drug, or contaminated drinking water, I'll bet our government would do something about it, don't you?)

The incredible damage done by marijuana and the appalling, almost total, ignorance of kids and their parents about the devastating, irreversible effects of smoking pot are shocking to me. I challenge you, even plead with you, to become informed on the subject. There is far more misinformation about pot than about any other drug in America. Dr. Tennant says pot is the most dangerous single substance freely available in America today.

Two books are *must* reading if you are a pot-smoking parent or if you have a pot-smoking child. Both are by Peggy Mann, who is a research writer with a unique ability to present scientific evidence in a fascinating manner that grabs and holds the reader's interest and then inspires the reader to take the practical action she suggests. The first book is *Marijuana Alert*, with a foreword by Nancy Reagan, written primarily for parents. Its significance is indicated by the fact that on February 26, 1985, an unprecedented United States Senate/

House reception was given to honor Ms. Mann as "our nation's foremost drug prevention author," on the publication of this tremendous book. The reception was hosted by Senator Paula Hawkins, chairman of the Senate Subcommittee on Alcoholism and Drug Abuse, who called the book, "A great step forward; it could be a turning point." It should be mandatory reading in all our schools, colleges, and universities. *Marijuana Alert* deals with the problems and dangers, as well as the solutions to the problems, of drug abuse. (*Marijuana Alert* is available from McGraw-Hill, Trade Book Division, 1221 Avenue of the Americas, New York, New York 10020. Paperback, $10.95.)

The second book is *Pot Safari*, written primarily to and for teenagers. (*Pot Safari* is available from Woodmere Press, Box 20190, Cathedral Finance Station, New York, New York 10025. Paperback, $8.85 [includes postage and handling].) I challenge almost anyone to read either or both of these books, which clearly reveal marijuana's short-term and long-term effects on brain cells, sex and reproduction, the lungs, etc. The exception would be those who have smoked so much pot they have lost their ability to think and reason.

Yes, we really do live in a negative world, and the obstacles we need to overcome will, on occasion, seem insurmountable. Let's look at what one man says about obstacles.

Gerhard Gschwandtner, editor of *Personal Selling Power*, points out that a wise philosopher once commented that an eagle's only obstacle to overcome for flying with greater speed and ease is the air; yet if the air were withdrawn and the proud bird were to fly in a vacuum, it would fall instantly to the ground, unable to fly at all. The very element that offers the resistance to flying is at the same time the condition of flight. The main obstacle that a power boat has to overcome is the water against the propeller; yet if it were not for this same resistance, the boat would not move at all. The same law that obstacles are conditions of success holds true in human life. A life freed from all obstacles and difficulties would reduce all possibilities and powers to zero. Obstacles wake us up and lead us to our abilities. Exertion gives us new power, so out of our difficulties new strength is born. Out of an obstacle comes strength; out of disappointment comes growth; out of deprivation comes desire.

To raise positive kids we must understand that there are some things we cannot do for our children. Even though we attempt to shelter them from harm, we can't remove them from the world's negative influences. We can't isolate them totally from evil. We can't hurt for them when they have sprained an ankle, broken a finger, cut a thumb, experienced an illness, or any one of a thousand things that happen to our kids. We can't sit down and take the test for them, nor can we make application for their jobs when they get ready to enter the employment world.

Instead of that being an unfortunate thing, it's absolutely marvelous that it works that way. If, in fact, we could "hurt" for our children, chances are good that most of us would assume those hurts and as a result our children would never grow and would remain children forever.

When our children do encounter difficulties and hurts, we need to let them know that we understand, that we're there, that we love and support them. We need to clearly understand the importance of empathy in situations like that. Parents who have sympathy, as a rule, will raise spoiled children because they will attempt to do everything for the children. More significantly, they will give in to everything the children want.

Empathy simply means that you feel what the other person feels. *Sympathy* means that you understand how the person feels, but you do not feel that way. Because you do not feel that way, you're able to back away from the problem and offer an objective solution. That is the role you as a parent need to play in raising positive kids. You need to be able to force yourself to back away from the problems and obstacles and look at the solutions you can offer to your children. My optimism tells me that *Raising Positive Kids* is going to be instrumental in helping you do exactly that.

I Apologize—Here's Why

This chapter has been terribly negative, but it had to be. To paraphrase James Baldwin, confronting a problem doesn't always bring a solution, but *until* you confront it there *will* be no solution. Later I'll elaborate on some of these problems, but I would like to make two things crystal clear. First, I am by nature an optimist, so I definitely, positively, emphatically and enthusiastically believe that there are solutions to the problems *and* that we will solve them. Second, I want to forcefully communicate to you that even though the world is definitely negative, *your* world can be enthusiastically positive. I believe that even though the world is violent, troubled, profane and selfish, *your* world can be filled with joy, excitement, love and peace of mind. I believe that even though the world is chaotic, *your* world can be orderly.

None of these qualities will come easily, but they will be tremendously exciting and rewarding. Now let's move on to the values and solutions in the next chapter.

Time for Personal Evaluation

1. Give some examples of negative conversations you may have with your kids. Now turn each one into a positive.

2. How about negative conversations you have with yourself on a regular basis?

3. In describing just how negative our world really is, Zig lists several major areas. Name some of them.

4. What are the areas of most concern to you? And your child? What changes can you make to turn these influences from negative to positives?

5. Do you have a family policy with regard to watching television or listening to various kinds of music? After reading this chapter, do you feel that your policy is adequate?

6. Zig says you can turn a negative family situation around. Do you believe him? If so, what steps will you take in your family situation?

Who's glued to the tube? One study revealed that the average blue-collar worker spends approximately 30 hours each week watching TV; his supervisor, 25; his foreman, 20; his plant manager, 15, his vice president, 12–15; his president, 8–12; and the C.E.O, 4–8, and 50 percent of that time is invested in watching training videos. I can't help but wonder what would happen to that blue-collar worker if he invested half of those TV-viewing hours in education and personal growth.

CHAPTER 3

Qualities of the Truly Successful

> You and your child were designed for accomplishment, engineered for success and endowed with the seeds of greatness.

Here's Where I'm Coming From

Now that we have identified some of the obstacles that exist in this negative world and consequently stand between you and raising a positive kid, let's get on with the solution. I have no idea where you are coming from as far as your definition of *success*, but when I speak of success, I'm speaking of *total* success.

From my perspective, if I were to acquire millions of dollars but destroy my health and sacrifice my integrity in the pursuit of those dollars, I would not consider myself successful. I would have bought those dollars at a grossly inflated price, as I've seen many of my colleagues do.

If I should go to the top in my profession, become the best in the whole world at what I do, and then have one or more of my four children come to me and say, ''You know, Dad, I sure wish you had saved a little time for me when I was growing up. Maybe if you had given me some of the advice you so freely give to others, my own life would not have been the disaster it turned out to be.'' I can assure you it would break my heart, because I deeply love my children, so I'm obviously pleased that I was able to dedicate this book to my four as being very positive kids.

The same dangers relating to achieving success also apply to you. Regardless of your age, sex, or occupation, if you have a loving, stable relationship with your family, you will be more effective and hence more productive and successful in your profession. That's one reason so much of this book is designed to give you an attitude lift, because you pass on to your family and, to a lesser degree, your co-workers the attitudes you possess. With your own attitude and future intact, you can more effectively work to develop *all* the qualities necessary for a child to be positive.

What It Takes for Success

What does it take to be what *everyone* wants to be but relatively few are? One of the things I do in my seminars around the world is to ask the audience to identify the qualities of the most successful person they know or an imaginary individual who would make an ideal employee, employer, mate, neighbor or friend. Interestingly enough, regardless of the geographical location and regardless of who is in the audience—whether dentists, salespeople, educators, ministers, the general public—the answers will be remarkably similar. The desirable qualities or characteristics are:

assertive	creative	good listener
caring	dependable	hard-working
character	energetic	honest
commitment	enthusiastic	humble
competent	faith	integrity
confident	friendly	intelligent
consistent	goal-directed	loving

loyal	prompt
motivated	self-image
optimistic	sense of humor
organized	sensitive
persistent	teachable
personable	thoughtful
positive mental attitude	understanding

Attitudes or Skills?

I next ask the audience to categorize the characteristics by identifying each one as an attitude or a skill. You should do the same thing. Write an "A" for attitude or an "S" for skill after each characteristic.

If your answers are consistent with the typical audience, you probably identified twenty-nine to thirty-one of the thirty-five qualities as straight attitudes, two or three as combinations of attitude and skill, and two or three as skills (such as "organized" and "good listener"). Qualities such as "creative" and "intelligent" can also be considered gifts.

Now, *do you think attitude is important in life regardless of what you are doing or plan to do?*

Question: Did you have even one course during your entire educational career that specifically taught you how to develop these qualities? My experience with audiences around the world has shown that only between 1 and 2 percent have ever had courses that taught how to develop these characteristics of successful people.

Who Is to Blame?

At this time I ask the audience, "Do you feel we are missing the boat in education?" With the exception of educators, all audiences respond with an enthusiastic yes to this one. They even feel a sense of relief because now they've got somebody to blame for their difficulties. "It's the educators. They're doing a lousy job. It's their fault. We've got to do something about them!" At that point everybody except the educators feels pretty good, so I caution the audience that the problem with pointing the index finger at others and blaming them for our problems is that it is seldom true, and additionally we will have three fingers pointing right back at ourselves!

Next I ask the audience how many hours each day and how many days each year the kids go to school. The answer in most cases is 6 hours each day and 180 days each year, so the kids are in school 1,080 hours and at home 7,680 hours. And the parents had those kids over 40,000 hours *before* they ever saw the teacher.

The next big question I ask is, "How many of you believe parents should accept a small portion of the responsibility for teaching these qualities?" Everybody enthusiastically, and a little sheepishly, admits that parents should accept part of the responsibility. I hope (and believe) you feel the same way.

The next question to the audience is, "How many of you believe that if these characteristics were taught at home and then reinforced in school, this would give us the best possible citizen with the best chance for being happy, successful, and well-adjusted?" Everybody agrees to that one.

Next question: "How many of you believe it would be helpful if the parents and teachers acquired these characteristics before teaching them to their children and students?" (If they don't acquire them before they *try* to teach them, they are hypocrites, and as you know, a hypocrite is a fellow who is just not himself on Sunday.) Again, everybody enthusiastically responds to the logic of that one. Then I say, "Well, let's see if these characteristics can be acquired." I'm going to encourage you to turn back to the list of characteristics and put a check mark by those you think can be learned.

Anyone who thinks he can go to the top and stay there who is not honest is dumb.

— Mortimer Feinberg, Ph.D.
(Conclusion reached by CEO's of 100 of the Fortune 500 companies)

Qualities of Success Can Be Learned

As you examine the list, you will discover that *all* of these characteristics can be taught and learned. *If they can be learned, they are skills.* Not only that, but you and your child(ren) already have every quality associated with the most successful person you know (possible exceptions would include serious birth defects!). Obviously, all of us are quite weak in some of these characteristics and qualities, but the *seeds* are all there. That means you can use what you already have to further develop those qualities and characteristics which are weak. I might also point out that many of those qualities are *values* which every legitimate employer your child will ever approach for a job will be favorably impressed with. Author, consultant and retired business executive Fred Smith says, "History records that invariably major failures are character failures." Over 2,400 years ago Plato wrote, "Education in virtue is the only education which deserves the name."

On To the Future

As parents with the objective of raising positive, drug-free kids, we need to understand that the purpose of each stage of life is to prepare us for the next stage. So every parent's goal is to prepare his children for their futures. In most cases that will include marriage and perhaps children. In all cases, it should include the objective of giving our children an honest chance of becoming self-sufficient, productive, happy and fulfilled.

Whether our child has athletic, artistic, musical, spiritual, administrative, business, or other abilities, you can count on one thing. Regardless of the direction our children choose to go, they are going to need a solid moral, practical, ethical, common-sense foundation from which they can launch their careers.

Dr. Robert Coles of Harvard, after a twenty-year study, concluded that parents who want to give their children the best chance for success in life will teach them strong moral values. A story in *USA Today* pointed out that 175 of the CEO's of Fortune 500 companies are former Marines. The motto of the Marine Corps is "Always Faithful," and the Marines are strong on discipline, commitment to excellence, loyalty, and accepting responsibility for whatever task they are assigned. Five of our last six presidents served in the U.S. Navy and twenty-six presidents served in the military, so apparently discipline, commitment, and loyalty are desirable qualities if we want to get to the top.

A major reason the Japanese are eating our lunch in today's marketplace is the values they teach in their schools and homes on a daily basis. I wouldn't swap America for a thousand Japans, but when you understand that this little nation with few natural resources, half the size of Texas, and 130,000,000 people is the largest creditor nation in the world, and that the top ten banks in the world are Japanese, and eight of the top ten publicly held corporations in the world are Japanese, then surely you'll buy into the idea that the Japanese must be doing *something* right. Maybe we should find out what it is.

What they are doing is simplicity itself. From kindergarten on through high school they teach a course one hour *each* day on the importance of honesty, character, integrity, hard work, positive mental attitude, enthusiasm, responsibility, thrift, free enterprise, patriotism and respect for authority.[1]

When their kids finish school they are trained and ready to go to work building their careers.

By contrast, the average American high school graduate has spent 10,500 hours listening to music and 15,000 hours watching TV. That means he has spent over three hours being *entertained* for every one hour he has invested in being informed. The Japanese student learns about free enterprise on a daily basis, but 66 percent of America's eighteen to twenty-four-year-olds cannot explain the term "profit." No wonder Japan is the number one creditor nation in the world and America is the number one debtor nation.

Think about this. America has four enormous advantages over Japan. We have more people, more land and infinitely more natural resources. Our imagination and creativity are the best in the world. Our higher educational system is light years ahead of Japan's, and our Judeo-Christian faith gives us the biggest advantage of all.

Now, combine these advantages with what the Japanese are teaching and what our country taught when we experienced our greatest period of growth, and you will see a dramatic surge of real prosperity in our nation. I believe with all my heart that in one generation our country can dramatically change and improve in *every* area of life.

Think About It

Suppose the "skills" identified on page 37–38 were taught in every home and school in America. Can you visualize what that would mean to our country? More to the point, can you imagine what it would mean to your child and your family if these skills were taught from birth to your child? He or she would be accepted enthusiastically by peers (no "need" for drugs or illicit sex); would be welcome in any home, school or social gathering; and could get a job almost regardless of economic conditions. In short, your child would be successful here—and hereafter.

The following story explains how a person can have *all* the qualities necessary for true success and yet accomplish little or nothing with his life.

Cashing in on Our Values

Around the turn of the century, just outside Beaumont, Texas, a farmer was having difficulty surviving. Although he owned a large amount of land, a recession and a drought were wreaking havoc. To provide for his family, he started selling parcels of his land. One day an oil company executive told him he thought there might be oil on his property and agreed to pay him royalties for drilling rights.

Since the farmer had nothing to lose and a great deal to gain, the agreement was made. In those days the oil derricks were made of wood, and when oil was discovered in any significant amount, the explosive force of the onrushing oil often destroyed the derrick. The greater the destruction, the greater the excitement. That was a sure indication of the size of the oil field.

On this particular occasion the derrick was obliterated. They had really hit a gusher. As a matter of fact, for the next eleven days over a hundred thousand barrels of oil flowed each day before they were able to cap and control it. They had brought in Spindletop, the most famous well in history.

That farmer became an instant millionaire. Or did he? Actually, the man had been a millionaire ever since he had acquired the property. But until they discovered the oil, brought it to the surface, and took it to the marketplace to cash it in, the oil had no real value.

People are that way, too. Until we recognize our own ability and worth, we're not going to take it to the marketplace to cash it in. Thought: If you had a million dollars in your checking account you would never write a check on it if you didn't know it was there. However, when you discovered its existence, there would be a substantial boost in the local economy. That's the way it is with our kids. Until and unless we recognize the ability and worth of our children, we're not going to be as excited about helping them develop and realize their potential.

Staking Your Claim in Life

Several years ago my son-in-law, Chad Witmeyer, and I flew into Sacramento to conduct a seminar. The host and hostess met us at the airport and drove us to Auburn, California. On the way they told us that Sutter's Mill was just thirty minutes from where I'd be speaking. Sutter's Mill is where James W. Marshall discovered gold in Sutter's Creek in 1848—the discovery that started the great Gold Rush of 1849. People came from all over America and much of the world to seek and find their fortunes in the gold fields of California.

What most people don't know is that in the late 1880s in an abandoned gold-mining shaft less than two hours from Auburn, the body of an itinerant gold miner was found. It was James Marshall—the same man who had discovered the gold that started the immigration into California which led to fortunes for many. He died a penniless derelict because he had never taken time to stake his own claim.

To raise positive kids, we as parents must identify the qualities necessary for success, convince our children that they have the potential for success, and show them how to stake their claims in life.

The Foundation for Success

It is a common belief that we start our careers when we graduate from school and acquire a job. This simply is not so. Our careers are started almost from the moment of conception and are well on the way before the first day of formal schooling. Many factors while we are still in the womb play a definite role in our future lives. It has been documented that we are receptive to outside influences as early as four months before birth. And from birth, our input and environment play a tremendously important part in our futures.

YOUR HOME IS BUGGED!

In every home there are two microphones per child—one in each ear. These highly sensitive instruments pick up the table prayers, the songs sung, ordinary conversation, and all types of language. These all-hearing microphones transmit all they hear to highly impressionable minds. These sounds then become the vocabulary of the child and his basis for action.

—Anonymous

Several years ago I had the privilege of going to Calgary, Canada, and having dinner on top of Calgary Tower, a structure six hundred twenty-six feet tall—taller than two football fields stacked end to end. That's high! As we rode the elevator to the top, a recording gave us the details of the height and other important data. The structure weighs twelve thousand tons, and seven thousand of those tons are beneath ground surface. With a foundation that deep and solid, there is little wonder we could go up so high.

A good engineer can look at the size of an excavation prepared for a structural foundation and calculate the limits of the finished building. The size of the foundation determines the size of the structure. The deeper and broader the foundation, the higher and larger the possibilities for the structure.

Do as I Do

A solid foundation for children involves a solid moral base. Parents who teach their children honesty but fail to practice it themselves create real problems.

For example, suppose parents repeatedly tell their children to be truthful, but when the telephone rings, they call out to the child who's answering it, "Tell them I'm not home." The message to the child is clear. If children are taught to lie *for* parents, they are taught to lie *to* parents.

As another example, suppose parents lecture their children on the importance of obeying the law, yet install a radar detector in the car to avoid being stopped for speeding. The message again is clear. If you're going to break the law, don't get caught. Be smart like your dad or mom.

And another, suppose parents instruct their children to be good citizens, yet they cheat on their income tax return. The message? It's okay to be dishonest when it comes to taxes because "the government is going to waste the money anyhow." Parents who do this are dishonest, and they're teaching their children to be dishonest.

There's a Market for Moral Values

The home is the place to lay the foundation for high moral values, but the process must be continued in our educational institutions. Franklin Delano Roosevelt said, "To train a man in mind and not in morals is to train a menace to society." Steven Muller, president of Johns Hopkins University, summarized this interplay of values, "The failure to rally around a set of values means that universities are turning out potentially highly-skilled barbarians."

Further, honesty is a marketable commodity. In 1982, the Forum Corporation of Boston, Massachusetts, studied 341 salespeople from eleven different companies in five different industries to determine what accounted for the difference between the top producers and the average producers. (Of these, 173 were top salespeople, and 168 were average salespeople.)

When the study was finished, it was clear that the difference between the two groups could not be attributed to skill, knowledge, or ability. The Forum Corporation found that the difference could be attributed to honesty! The persons who were rated top in sales were more productive *because their customers trusted them*. And because their customers believed these top producers, they bought from them.

Being effective parents hinges on trust, too. If kids know that their mom and dad believe what they're teaching, and if kids know that what their parents teach is consistent with the life they live, then kids will trust their parents and will respond positively to what their parents say. Hypocrisy—if it ever was "in"—is totally and completely "out" with kids today. We fail our children if we say, "Don't do as I do, but do as I say."

Accepting Responsibility

In any family where two or more people are involved, there will always be discussion and conflict about responsibility. One of the best opportunities for teaching moral values and responsibility lies in the daily functioning of the home. About four thousand things need doing every day (only a slight exaggeration). In many homes, unfortunately, arbitrary decisions decree that "that's not my job."

The following little story pretty well sums it up. There were four people named Everybody, Somebody, Anybody, and Nobody. An important job had to be done, and Everybody was sure that Somebody would do it. Anybody could have done it, but Nobody did it. Somebody got angry about that, because it was Everybody's job. Everybody thought Anybody could do it and that Somebody would do it. But Nobody realized that Everybody thought Somebody would do it. It ended up that Everybody blamed Somebody when Nobody did what Anybody could have done.

Anybody Can—and Everybody Should

The home environment is so important in the raising of kids. It is good when the home is neat and orderly. (Notice that I did not say "hospital sanitary.") Comfort and pride of ownership make us feel good. Because the home environment affects everyone who lives there, certain areas of responsibility may require definition.

For example, if a scrap of paper is on the floor, it is not anybody's job in particular to pick it up—it is everybody's responsibility. The first person who sees it should be the one to pick it up. Everybody benefits when anybody takes the simple step.

I offer this example because it seems that human nature doesn't change much, and the work habits, attitudes, responsibility, and team spirit we learn at home definitely carry into the marketplace where personal responsibility is reflected.

> *When we start with character as a base, our options are virtually limitless.*

Character Is Security and Money

The late J. P. Morgan was asked what he considered to be the best bank collateral. Without hesitation he replied, "Character." William Lake put it this way: "One of the most important lessons that experience teaches is that on the whole success depends more upon character than either intellect or fortune."

Nearly thirty years ago when the Dallas Cowboys were organized, the managers took an unusual approach. Instead of visiting successful football teams to find out how things were done, they went to the boardrooms of General Motors, IBM, Xerox, and other large corporations and asked the executives what they looked for in their leaders. Without exception the most outstanding and successful people in our country said that *they looked for character, for the integrity of the individual.*

When we start with character as a base, our options are virtually limitless. Doesn't it make sense to help our children develop this important quality?

A Good Name Is Worth Protecting

Every step we take has a definite bearing on the family name, which is extremely important. A couple of years ago we went home to Yazoo City, Mississippi, for a family reunion. The other members of the family generally bring some home-prepared goodies. But in our case, we generally fly into Jackson, rent a car, and drive to Yazoo City, so we're somewhat restricted as to what we can bring. For that reason, we stop and buy some things at a grocery store—a sliced ham or turkey, along with some other goodies.

On this particular occasion my wife wrote a check, handed it to the cashier, and was going through her wallet, saying, "I suppose you need my driver's license and a credit card." The clerk glanced at the check and said, "No, in Yazoo City this name is all the identification you need." I've got to tell you that my wife and I felt awfully good that our family, following the example set by my mother, had given us that legacy.

School credibility.

One of the most important things we can communicate to our children is the importance of protecting their name. Our names are synonymous with who we are, what we do, and what we stand for. We must teach our children that their word is their bond and that their name signed to a piece of paper is priceless.

In school, when our children put their names on their papers, they are either saying that they are cheats or that the work really does represent their own efforts. By teaching our children the value of a good name, we are teaching them that they're building a foundation for a productive, successful tomorrow with the building blocks of what they do today.

Social and business image.

Our kids must be taught the precious value of their name as it is associated with their social and business image. When we begin mingling with others, we either polish or tarnish our image. As an individual starts out in life, a name is like a book with many blank pages waiting to be filled in with the story of a life. That story will either build on one's total image or tear it down.

Protecting the heritage of a good name is one of the most important keys to a positive future. "A good name is rather to be chosen than great riches."

Looking for the Gold

At one time Andrew Carnegie was the wealthiest man in America. He came to America from his native Scotland when he was a small boy, did a variety of odd jobs, and eventually ended up as the largest steel manufacturer in the United States. At one time he had forty-three million-aires working for him. In those days a millionaire was a rare person; conservatively speaking, a million dollars in his day would be equivalent to at least twenty million dollars today.

A reporter asked Carnegie how he had hired forty-three millionaires. Carnegie responded that none of the men had been millionaires when they started working for him but had become millionaires as a result.

The reporter's next question was, "How did you develop these men to become so valuable to you that you have paid them this much money?" Carnegie replied that men are developed the same way gold is mined. When gold is mined, several tons of dirt must be moved to get an ounce of gold; but one doesn't go into the mine looking for dirt—one goes in looking for the gold.

That's exactly the way parents develop positive, successful kids. Don't look for the flaws, warts, and blemishes. Look for the gold, not for the dirt; the good, not the bad. Look for the positive aspects of life. Like everything else, the more good qualities we look for in our children, the more good qualities we are going to find.

Find the Good and Applaud

When you find something good (and it will be easy to do), *tell* your child specifically what you found that you like. Applaud your child. Do it often. Millions of parents love their kids, but, unfortunately, they never tell them. That's too bad, because applause is an effective confidence builder. Applause is so effective that in the world-renowned Suzuki method of teaching violin, one of the first things the children are taught when they are two, three, and four years old is how to take a bow. The instructors know that when the children bow, the audience invariably applauds. And "applause is the best motivator we've found to make children feel good about performing and about themselves."

Despite this fact, however, a study by the National Parent-Teachers Organization revealed that in the average American school, eighteen negatives are identified for every positive that is pointed out. The Wisconsin study revealed that when kids enter the first grade, 80 percent of them feel pretty good about themselves, but by the time they get to the sixth grade, only 10 percent of them have good self-images.

Applause is a great encourager, but real encouragement is more than being given a slap on the back or a position as a cheerleader. It is positive, affirming input from parents, which also affirms authority in the most positive way.

High school principal Dr. Frank Rainaldi says that our kids really need to hear a continual reminder of the things they do well. Any time we see our kids being good or doing good, we need to let them hear that approval. Our encouragement and praise should be specific. Not "You look really neat this morning," but "I like the way you matched your skirt and blouse. That really looks nice." And being good encouragers requires us to be good listeners. We need to hear what our children want us to hear.

Finding the good in every person and in every situation is

a learned skill that requires work, but because we love our kids, we must make the effort. As parents we must practice and be examples of "good-finding," a characteristic of the successful that is caught more than taught.

Reap the Benefits of Good-Finding

A study by Family Concern divided sixty school-children into three groups of twenty who were given arithmetic tests daily for five days.[2] One group was consistently praised for its previous performance; another group was criticized; the third was ignored. Those who were praised improved dramatically; those who were criticized improved also, but not so much; and those who were ignored hardly improved at all.

> *Quality of life,* including *a high standard of living, is an attainable goal.*

Charles Schwab said, "I have yet to find the man—however exalted his station—who did not do better work and put forth greater effort under a spirit of approval than under a spirit of criticism." By the same token, children who are raised in a spirit of praise and approval are going to be happier, more productive, and more obedient than the ones who are constantly criticized.

Attaining the Goal

Total success is an attainable goal for us and for our children. The quantity and the quality of that success in great measure depend on us. Identifying the key qualities of successful people is just the first step. Next comes the commitment to grow, to change, to apply, to nurture these qualities in our lives.

We do this primarily by changing the input into our minds, and the new, positive input will result in more successful performance.

Here's a special tip that I have found invaluable. The two most important times of day for this input are early in the morning and late at night. Some psychologists have estimated that the first encounter of a significant nature that you have each day has more impact than the next five encounters as far as your thinking and your attitude are concerned. With that in mind, it's extremely important that you start the day deliberately with very positive input. It can be an exciting book, a message from God's Word, a motivational recording, or motivational music. You can do this when you first get up, or you can listen to cassette recordings on your way to work.

The second most important time for input takes place late in the evening. For many years I've read something of a positive nature as I go to sleep. This permits my subconscious mind to work on it during the night and give my imagination real food for thought so it can develop in a positive way. I strongly encourage you to take this approach.

I close this chapter by relating some of what has happened in the lives of the Randy Flatt family of Memphis, Tennessee, since they have been listening to the positive input from our motivational tapes.

They told how one morning they were awakened by their eleven-year-old son, Jason, talking to himself. In Sandra's exact words here's what he was saying: "This is a great day. What a day for opportunity." I'm going to make straight A's today! I'm going to make straight A's every day! I feel great! I can do it! Yes, sir, this is a great day!"

"Randy and I cracked up laughing and are very proud Zig Ziglar has rubbed off on him. We laid in bed and listened while he continued to quote things you had said on tape. Jason began to bring A's home and also letters from his teacher saying how his attitude toward himself and others had improved. He set a goal for an electric guitar to be earned by averaging A's the entire school year. He also saved money from jobs outside our home. He reached his goal, and we gladly bought the new guitar.''

Jason was learning the qualities of success, and he was being motivated to put them into practice in his life. Now let's look at another important quality as we ask—and answer—a crucial question.

Whose Opinion Do You Accept?

One of the most important qualities the truly successful person must have is a healthy self-image. I devote chapter ten to the subject, but to tie this chapter down and to set the stage for that chapter, let's look at a truly profound thought which starts with a question. How can we harmonize Christian humility and good self-image, which some people identify as ego appreciation of one's self?

Our kids need to develop a good image of themselves, but their parents often have problems trying to correlate ego appreciation with Christian humility. Author, speaker, Christian businessman Fred Smith gives the best answer* I've ever heard: ''What we're really talking about is identification of worth. In ego we establish our own worth. In the Christian context we let God establish our worth? How does He establish our worth. First, He made us unique; then He died for us. This fact is incomprehensible. . . .

''If the President of the United States offered to die for me, I would expect to be interviewed by every member of the media and asked why and how it was to happen, and so forth. That would just be on his *offer* to die. If he actually was willing, his mentality would be checked out;

*From *You and Your Network*, Word Publishers. Used by permission.

there would be weeks of psychological studies on him and then there would be all kinds of studies on me. It would be one of the great events of history—that a President was willing to die for one of the citizens.

"Well, we're dealing with the same concept when we talk about God dying for man. It's too big to comprehend. Even if we had an inkling of it, it would give us self-worth. Egomania gives relative value; Christianity gives absolute value. It seems to me that I would be a total fool not to exchange my evaluation of myself for God's, if I really believed He existed. For if a person could see his worth by God's evaluation rather than by his own self-evaluation or somebody else's, it would give him absolute, eternal worth."

To this we can add that you *and* your children were created in God's own image, and in John 1:12 we read that we are given the power to become the children of God. For further scriptural evidence read Psalm 139:14, Romans 9:20, 21 and Isaiah 45:9,10.

Time for Personal Evaluation

1. How do you spell S-U-C-C-E-S-S? Check the qualities in Zig's list that you feel are most evident in a successful person.

2. In motivating our children, how important is the example we set for them?

3. In an imaginary conversation, list two things you could say to your child that illustrate how finding and applauding the good in him may change how he thinks about himself.

4. Do you agree with Zig that a positive attitude to life can be learned? What can you do specifically for your children to encourage them to have a positive outlook?

5. Name one prominent quality that your child has. How can you help nurture this for your child's good?

CHAPTER 4

Motivation and Positive Thinking

> *Positive thinking won't let you do anything, but it will let you do everything better than will negative thinking.*

This Young Man Was Motivated!

When I think of motivation, I think of an incident that took place out in west Texas. A super-rich Texan had a daughter of marriageable age, and he decided to give her a coming-out party. (Salespeople would describe this as "group prospecting.") At any rate, this Texan invited the young men from within a hundred miles to come to the big party on his spread. He had over two hundred thousand acres, and on that spread he had dozens of producing oil wells and tens of thousands of head of cattle. The old homestead itself was a mansion of indescribable proportions, which included an Olympic-sized swimming pool.

Toward the latter part of the evening, the host invited all the young men out to the pool which he had, with amazing foresight, stocked with water moccasins and alligators. He told the young men that the first one who jumped into the pool and swam the length of it would be given his choice of three things: $1 million in cash, ten thousand acres of his best land, or the hand of his beautiful daughter in marriage. He even pointed out that his daughter was their only heir and that when he and his wife passed on, all of this big spread would belong to her and to the man who would become her husband.

No sooner were these words spoken than there was a loud splash at one end of the pool, followed almost immediately by the emergence of a dripping young man from the other end of the pool. He had set a world's record that would never be approached, much less broken.

As the dripping young man emerged from the pool, the host excitedly ran to him and said, "Well, son, you've got your choice. Do you want the million in cash?" The young man responded, "No, sir." Then the host asked, "Do you want the ten thousand acres of my best land?" The young man responded, "No, sir." Finally the host said, "Then I assume you want the hand of my beautiful daughter in marriage?" To this the young man replied, "No, sir." Somewhat puzzled and even a little frustrated, the host demanded, "Well, son, what do you want?" The young man responded, "I want to know the name of that dude who pushed me into the swimming pool!"

Needless to say, this young man had been motivated to get out of that pool as quickly as possible. Motivation on a daily basis is necessary if you're going to do your best at whatever you do, but especially if you're going to raise positive drug-free kids.

Motivation is the Siamese twin of education and the constant companion of peak performers. Teaching how to do something does not ensure it will be done. Teach the why of doing, and students learn in spite of obstacles. Motivation is the fire that burns the log of knowledge students receive in education.[1]

Some People Are Especially Negative

There probably is more confusion about motivation and positive thinking than almost any other subject in our society. A study done several years ago at Harvard University revealed that 85 percent of the reason people get jobs and get ahead in those jobs is because of their attitudes. Evidence is overwhelming that parents who want to prepare their children for life will teach them how to develop a winning attitude as a way of life. Motivation and positive thinking are not things you turn on and off and use for special circumstances and events in your life. There are ways of thinking, doing, and being that bring incredible benefits to you and your family.

Of course not everyone—especially the media—feels that way. I recall my appearance on a national news program several years ago. The interviewer was what I call a "typical media man," meaning that he was so skeptical he demanded a bacteria count on the milk of human kindness! He was so cynical he actually believed that somebody *pushed* Humpty Dumpty. He was from a town that wanted to start a Pessimists Club but nobody thought it would work. They voted on a Procrastinators Club. It was 44-0 to wait.

At any rate, the interview was memorable. We visited pleasantly while the camera crew was getting set for the interview. Once the cameras were turned on, he put a microphone in my hand, and his opening statement was: "Mr. Ziglar, you go all over the world talking about positive thinking and getting to the top. You're a positive fellow, but do you think with positive thinking that you could whip Muhammad Ali?" (At that time he was the Heavyweight Champion of the World.) Obviously that's ridiculous, even though I fought in the ring for two years and it's on record that the worst I ever finished was second. As a matter of fact, the only reason I quit was because of my hands—the referee kept stepping on them!

Positive Thinking Won't Let You Do "Anything"

I replied, "No, I don't believe that with positive thinking I could whip Muhammad Ali or, for that matter, play quarterback for an NFL football team or make the starting lineup for an NBA basketball team. With all of my positive thinking I could not teach a class in chemistry or thermonuclear energy. With all the positive thinking in the world, a student who has not studied and acquired the information is not going to be able to answer questions concerning which he has no knowledge."

What Positive Thinking *and* Negative Thinking Do

No, positive thinking won't let you do *anything*; but it will let you do *everything* better than negative thinking will. Positive thinking enables you to more effectively use the ability you have. Here's what I mean. As a student, did you ever walk out of class after a test and have one of your buddies ask how you did, and you responded, "Man, I don't understand it. I really studied for the test. I knew that formula as well as I know my name. I wrote it out last night, went over it many times, but today I just couldn't remember it, and I don't know why!"?

Chances are excellent you've had that experience. What happened is very simple. Before you went in to take the test, you carefully instructed yourself to "forget" what you had learned. You did it by the self-talk you indulged in and the interchange with your classmates, statements such as, "Boy, I hope I remember all that stuff I've studied," or "Man, I hope I don't do the same thing on this one I did on the last one! I studied all night; studied for the entire quarter (or semester), but I *never* do well on tests. I just get tense and tight, and I forget the things I'm supposed to remember." You instructed your mind to forget, and your mind does follow instructions.

Daily motivation provides that daily check-up from the neck up and eliminates stinkin' thinkin', which ultimately results in hardening of the attitudes.

What positive thinking does is very simple. It allows you and encourages you—as well as teaches you—how to use your ability and how to remember what you have learned. With a positive mental attitude and thorough preparation, you can go into a class more relaxed. Your self-talk simply says, "Boy, I'm glad I studied for this one! I'm prepared, and I know that if the teacher asks the questions in the book, I'm going to do okay." It's amazing what positive thinking *and preparation* will do for you.

Just What Is Motivation?

The subject of motivation is intriguing and often misunderstood. The definition of *motivate* is "to stimulate to action, provide with an incentive or motive." The word *motivation* itself is a noun. My 1828 *American Dictionary of the English Language, Noah Webster Edition*, does not even have the words *motivate* or *motivation* in it, so it is a fairly new word but an extremely important one.

One of the things that I'm often challenged with in interviews concerns motivation and what it is and what it is not. The challenge often goes like this: "Mr. Ziglar, there are people who say that when they attend a motivational session they get all charged up, but a week later they're back where they were before they attended the session. In other words, motivation is not permanent. How do you respond to that?"

My answer is, "Of course motivation is not permanent. But then, neither is bathing; but it is something you should do on a regular basis." Eating is not permanent, but it is something you generally do on a daily basis. To think you could attend one motivational session, read one book, hear one speaker, and have immediate *and* permanent benefits for the rest of your life is, of course, absurd and farfetched because de-motivation takes place in one form or another every day of your life.

You can't make an overdraft on the bank of right mental attitude all your life and bring the account up to date with one deposit. What motivation does is stimulate you to action, give you a more optimistic viewpoint of life itself, raise the specters of both hope and accomplishment, and encourage you to accomplish objectives.

There are those who say that all motivation is self-motivation. That would be like saying one person cannot influence another, which won't stand up under any kind of serious thinking. My own experience tells me that I can hear inspiring music, a beautiful sermon, a patriotic speech, or a stimulating speaker and feel better about myself as well as my possibilities of accomplishing more of my objectives. Since the words we use can either motivate us or de-motivate us, let's take a good look at the importance of the right words.

Words Do Make a Difference

The words and tone of voice you use with your children are tremendously important. Whether the words are loving and constructive or hateful and destructive can have a substantial impact on your child's life. Words do paint pictures, and the mind completes the picture. Take, for example, Samuel Akwasi Sarpong from the Ashanti tribe in Ghana who attended our February 1989 BORN TO WIN seminar. His tribe names its children after the day of the week on which they are born. Those born on Wednesday are *Kwaku*, which means violent, mean. In Ghana, over 50 percent of all the crimes committed are committed by those born on Wednesday. Sociologists' only explanation is that apparently an expectancy is set up in the minds of the parents and of society. Incidentally,

Samuel's "day of the week" name is *Akwasi*, which means kind-hearted, loving, peaceful or godly. Interestingly enough, Samuel has a Christian ministry.

In China and Japan, according to an article in *Psychology Today*, there are "few, if any" learning disabled children. As you're aware, there are many learning disabled children in America. "Dis" means "un." When a child is told he is *dis*abled, he is being told he is *un*able to do something. In the Chinese and Japanese languages, there is no word or substitute word for disabled.

On America's Indian reservations, not a single full-blooded Indian stutters.[2] And in none of the Indian languages and dialects does the word "stutter" appear.

Now let's put these three vignettes together. Words paint pictures and then the mind goes to work to complete the picture. If I say the word "baby," nobody thinks b-a-b-y. Instead, you visualize a baby. If you call somebody stupid, that person does not think s-t-u-p-i-d, but instead thinks of someone who is really dense. Words are important. That's why it's always disappointing to hear anyone, especially parents, use filthy, barnyard, profane, put-down language. No nation or individual can rise above the pictures painted in the mind.

According to prison evangelist Bill Glass, over 90 percent of the men and women incarcerated today were repeatedly told by their parents, "One of these days you're going to end up in jail." I can't help but wonder what might have happened if they had been repeatedly told, "If you keep studying like that, one of these days you will end up with a scholarship at the university or you'll be president of your own company." Or "If you continue to be that thoughtful and courteous you'll have lots of friends." Input does influence output.

To the above thoughts add some positive "picture building" words which you can use regularly with your children, such as "You're a winner," "You can do it," "Excellent job!'' ''Keep up the good work,'' ''You're a bright young lady,'' ''I love you,'' ''Super great!'' ''Outstanding,'' ''Terrific,'' ''Nice going,'' ''Good for you,'' and many, many more. The point is simple, but important. Put negative garbage in and you'll get negative results. Put positive, loving words in your child's mind and you'll raise a positive, loving child.

Keep It Going, Folks

To raise positive kids, you must understand that to *provide* ongoing motivation for yourself and the kids you need to *receive* motivational input on a regular basis. With the positive input on a steady basis, you will automatically seek out and apply the positive approach to life's daily challenges. For example, when the kids come home from school, welcome them in a positive manner. Instead of asking, ''How was your day?'' or ''What happened at school?'' why not set the tone by asking them, ''What did you do today that was fun?''; ''What did you learn that you enjoyed learning?''; ''Who did you meet or play with that you really like?''; ''What did the teacher say that pleased you the most?''; ''Did you say or do something nice for anyone?'' (This approach also works wonders for the attitude and relationship of husbands and wives when they come in from work.)

This positive mind-set is especially important when the children first come home from school. If you can instill a positive association with the school experience, chances are enhanced that their experiences in school will be pleasant and positive. Then at a later time, when you're having some quiet time with your children, you can ask them to tell you all about what happened that day.

This makes certain you're not putting on rose-colored glasses and denying some of the problems that exist. However, it does enable you, and them, to keep events of the day in perspective. This procedure is important because children are inclined to let their imaginations run wild and blow simple little incidents completely out of proportion. Many times parents have been shocked to learn that the first thing the child told them when he got home from school was not exactly what happened. The child had simply described the event from his own perspective at that moment in time. Unfortunately, this information often comes after mom or dad has gone to the school "to protect their child's interests," only to learn that their child "didn't really mean it," it wasn't as bad as it seemed, or the incident had already been handled.

Working for a Raise

Attitude is an important facet of our lives at home, in school, and on the job. As a youngster in Yazoo City, Mississippi, while working in a grocery store, I knew the young boy who worked in the store across the street. In those depression years, most stores, of financial necessity, carried a very limited inventory and played it close to the chest. Once a basic inventory had been established, the store owners tried to anticipate exactly what was going to be sold the next week and ordered accordingly. Of course, this frequently led to shortages, and in these cases the merchants simply borrowed from one another.

The young man across the street who was their "runner," just as I was the "runner" for our store, was named Charlie Scott. I recall countless instances when Charlie would hit our front door at a dead run and sing out to the owner of our store, "Mr. Anderson, I need to borrow six cans of tomatoes!" Mr. Anderson always replied, "Well, go get 'em, Charlie. You know where they are." Charlie would dash back to the shelf, grab the items he was borrowing, quickly deposit them on the counter, scribble his name on the slip showing what he had gotten, and race off.

> *When we do more than*
> *we are paid to do,*
> *eventually*
> *we will be paid more*
> *for what we do.*

One day when things were slow, I asked Mr. Anderson why Charlie Scott always ran everywhere he went. He replied that Charlie Scott was working for a raise, and he was going to get one. I then asked him how he knew Charlie was going to get a raise, and Mr. Anderson replied that if the man he was working for didn't give him one, that *he* would!

In 1979 I spoke at Mississippi State University. I used the Charlie Scott example of why it was important that we all give the extra effort. When the seminar ended, a tall, red-headed gentleman came to me and asked me how long it had been since I had seen Charlie Scott. I replied that I believed Charlie had left Yazoo City during World War II in about 1942 or 1943, and I had not seen him since. He then commented, "You probably wouldn't recognize him if you saw him today, would you?" And I casually said, "No, I don't suppose so." With that the gentleman said, "I didn't think so. I'm Charlie Scott."

According to his friends, Charlie Scott had followed the same procedure he had learned as a young boy all his life. He worked hard, was enthusiastically courteous, and became enormously successful. As a matter of fact, he retired in his early fifties, a wealthy man.

This Way to Permanent Employment

I believe that if we teach our kids from the very beginning to give their best, and then some, they will never have to ask for more than one job—unless the company they're working for goes out of business. I'm convinced that when we show up early for work, stay late, do the very best we are capable of doing, and do it with an enthusiastic smile, we are making ourselves irreplaceable. I believe that when we learn new things to do and take on additional responsibilities, sooner or later it will come to management's attention.

It's a universal law—*when we do more than we are paid to do, eventually we will be paid more for what we do.* When we accept additional responsibilities, we become in essence like sailing vessels. On a sailing vessel, the more sail that is hoisted, the faster and farther it will go. In life, if we want to go farther and faster, we must hoist more sail or put more of ourselves into a project.

We need to teach our children that for eight hours a day, competition is extremely tough, but just twenty or thirty more minutes each day will make a difference in our effectiveness and future because competition will then decline dramatically. For example, the difference in showing up for work ten minutes early versus ten minutes late will positively affect management's view of us. Those twenty minutes will be more beneficial to our future than any full hour of the day. If we teach our children to work right up until quitting time instead of packing and clearing their desks ten minutes *before* quitting time, those few minutes will have more impact than an hour of regular work during the day because they reflect interest and excitement about what the children are doing. The old adage ''The only way to stretch your future is to stretch your present'' is true. We need to give our children the hope, direction and encouragement to go as far as their willingness to work, their belief in themselves, and their right mental and moral attitudes will permit them to go.

Another attitude which we parents also need to remember comes at the end of the day. If we return home every day griping about the people we work with and about how we have to do everything, and no one else can be depended upon, and our boss is not overly bright, etc., then our children will pick up the idea that work is not very pleasant. If we expect to sell them on the benefits of building an exciting career, we have to demonstrate some affection for our jobs. This is truly teaching by example, and who knows, maybe this will get you that raise!

> *Lectures often confuse our kids,*
> *but the example we set is crystal clear.*

I do know one thing for certain. Very few real opportunities are offered to negative soreheads who gripe and complain about their jobs. However, new opportunities are offered regularly to people who brag on their employers and their companies and who are genuinely excited about their work. Makes sense, doesn't it?

Time for Personal Evaluation

1. Motivation is necessary if you're going to raise positive kids. What are some things that motivate you?

2. Give an example of how negative thinking has caused you to fail.

3. The story about Charlie Scott highlights his enthusiasm. How did his enthusiasm make him a winner?

4. Does Zig teach that offering a reward is essential in motivating people? What do you think?

5. Why are the words you use so important?

Teach your kids and yourself that you can finish school—you can even make it easy. Not so with education. You never finish it, and it is seldom easy.

CHAPTER 5

Positive Steps to Developing Positive Kids

THINK ABOUT THIS

According to a study conducted in Missouri, 60–65 percent of a child's working vocabulary has been acquired by the age of three, and two-thirds of everything he will ever know will have been learned by the age of six.

By this stage of the game there is a chance you have come to the conclusion that to raise really positive kids you need the genius of Einstein, the insight of a psychologist, the stamina of a triathlete, the humor of Bob Hope, the faith of Daniel in the lions' den, and the courage of David as he faced Goliath.

If I've communicated that to you, I owe you an apology. One thing I have tried to communicate is the fact that raising positive kids is not easy, but a loving, dedicated parent following some relatively clear guidelines can handle the job and reap infinite joy as a result. This chapter has a considerable amount of information that will give you some clear-cut suggestions and a lot of encouragement, so hang in there.

The Education Starts Now

When do you start the education process with your child? When do you start taking those positive steps to develop those positive qualities? As you will see, the answer is quite clear. However, for those of you who have gotten a late start, let me assure you that it is never too late to do the right thing. Nor is it ever too late to do some good, so don't delay another day. Start *now*.

An article in the *Dallas Times Herald*[1] points out that Joseph and Jitsuko Susedik believe any parent can raise his child to be brilliant. The key elements, they say, are environment, phonics, and curiosity. Carole Taylor, Ph.D.—head of the Tolatr Academy in Pittsburgh—has two daughters, ages ten and fourteen, classified as gifted, who are enrolled in pre-med courses part-time in a community college. Dr. Taylor and the Susediks say the teaching of phonics is vital to a child's development. Once a child has mastered phonics, he or she can read anything, including college texts.

Joseph Susedik, who believes in talking to children while they're in the womb, stressed the need for a calm, serene atmosphere for an expectant mother in order for a child to be born with complete trust in the parent. "Only if the child has complete trust," he said, "can he or she be taught. You must teach your children with love, gentleness, and only at a time when they're willing to learn."

After their daughters were born, the Susediks devised a series of learning games including flash cards, phonics and vowel sounds, and vocabulary. "The first five to six years of the child's life are 'effortless learning,' " Mr. Susedik said, "and each girl responded positively to the learning games." In addition to the lessons, the Susediks, who described themselves as "child-oriented," emphasized the need for parents to spend as much time with their children as possible: "When they have a question, don't put them off."

Dr. Taylor agrees with the Susediks' approach to child

rearing and the necessity for developing verbalization skills at an early age. "Parents and teachers should be interacting with their children, not just talking to them," she said. "If they are busy, they should still not send a child away saying, 'Tell me later.' " Dr. Taylor and the Susediks both said training in phonics teaches the ability to verbalize and organize one's environment. By breaking down words into proper sounds, children eventually learn to analyze words and their definitions. "Once a child has mastered this skill, the ability to memorize facts and principles follows. After that, applying facts and principles to other areas of learning becomes possible," and enables a child to think analytically and logically, which translates into an increased capacity to absorb technical information.

Results Are Spectacular

Sounds pretty good—even great—and logical, but does it work? Read on. At age twelve, Susan Susedik was a junior at Muskingham College; Stacey, at age ten, was a freshman in high school; Stephanie, at age eight, an eighth grader; and Johanna, at age six, was a fourth grader. All of these girls have an I.Q. in excess of 150, with Susan's registering beyond the maximum 200 score on the Stanford-Binet Intelligence Scale. This puts them in the top one-half of 1 percent of the entire United States population.

Since the parents are of average intelligence, how did this come about? Considerable evidence indicates that their prenatal uterine conversations had a great deal to do with it. Mr. Susedik says this has been around "ever since God talked to Jeremiah and Job in the womb."

Mrs. Susedik points out that by age five months, the unborn baby's ears have been developed and it can hear and move its eyes. It already has more brain cells for memorization than it will use in its lifetime. She also maintains that by talking with the child before its birth, when the baby is born, it has instant recall.

Mrs. Susedik sang to each newborn; danced with her to soft, beautiful music; provided her with toys; and began explaining her small world. She did this during the day while Mr. Susedik was working. The Susediks taught their children to read with feeling, to express surprise, sadness, happiness, to fill the story into a rounded form. Hansel-and-Gretel-like stories were avoided, along with cartoons such as Popeye, "who's always fighting," and Bugs Bunny, "who's always getting shot at." Their TV fare included "Sesame Street" and "Electric Company," but programs on marriage problems, violence, sex, thrillers, and such were off limits.

In answer to the question, Is intelligence determined by heredity or environment or both? Mrs. Susedik responds that it's definitely more than heredity. She believes that her children are so remarkably bright because of their early education. She points to the abundance of love she has for her children as the most important element in their development. Mrs. Susedik warns parents, however, that physical and emotional problems are some of the biggest obstructions in teaching and learning. "I strongly suggest that you do not start teaching your child if your main purpose is to raise a genius rather than for the child's happiness." This information is tremendously exciting, but please don't overlook the last sentence. Additional information suggests that babies have amazing observation and learning capabilities.

The British medical journal *Lancet* describes a condition known as "fetal soap addiction." Newborn babies whose mothers regularly watched the same soap operas before their birth instantly recognized the theme songs after birth.[2]

Even though children do start to learn at a remarkably young age, the evidence is mounting that the education and learning in the early years should be taking place in the home rather than in the schoolroom. Developmental psychologist Raymond Moore in his book, *School Can Wait*, points out that it would be far better if our children started school when they are eight years old rather than six.

The education a child receives from his parents the first four years of life is more significant than four years of college.

He notes that boys especially benefit from starting school at a later age; he maintains that boys have three times the learning failure, and four times the hyperactivity, of girls at ages five to seven. "Unnecessary out of home care for the children under eight," he says, "may endanger the child emotionally, behaviorally, academically, and socially." He considers the greatest teacher to be the example of loving, caring parents. Dr. Moore is supported by most school teachers and administrators, with over 80 percent of them in favor of sending their children to school at a later age instead of an earlier age.

The educational process actually involves—or should involve—the parents, schools, churches, and "the University of Life," which includes our peers, trainers, bosses, associates, and others. Since the child, until he enters the sixth grade, is home with his parents approximately 90,000 hours and in school approximately 5,000 hours, it's easy to see why I've put so much emphasis on the role parents play, especially in the important areas of life.

The Age of Regulation

Now let's look at some of these important areas.

Author John Drescher points out that children actually go through three ages.[3] The first is the age of regulation, which is from the ages of one to seven. This is clearly illustrated when he writes, ''A first-grade girl shared the day's activities at school with her mother. 'We had a substitute teacher at school today,' she said. 'She let us do anything we wanted and we didn't like her.' ''

This comment carries both the response and need of a child during the early years, particularly from birth through age seven. During this time the child needs to know what is expected. The child without definite, clear rules becomes unruly. He is unhappy and insecure, and he develops feelings of not being loved. Further, he will kick out—sometimes in the most annoying ways—to feel where his boundaries and controls are.

The early years of childhood are the prime years in the child's moral development. He needs to know what he ought to do before he can think or put into practice what he should do. This learning begins at birth and will be taught primarily by those closest to him. There will never be a better time to teach obedience, which is the first element in the development of the conscience and moral sense.

During these early years the child lives in a world of feeling and discovery rather than reason. The physical touch, the emotional climate, the tone of voice, and the atmosphere of the family in general are felt very early. But the child is not helped by trying to reason with him. He is dependent upon parents for direction. He needs rules to follow. The small child becomes confused if made to reason and decide his own conduct.

Take Control Early or Lose Control Forever

Paul Tournier in his excellent small book, *To Resist or Surrender*, writes, ''There are many parents who do not want to argue with their children over every mistake. They reserve their authority for serious matters, but then it is too late. By forever giving in they lost all authority.'' Alexis Carrel has observed that most parents give in to their children's whims when they are small, the very age when they need a firm hand. The parents laugh at their antics then but later, in adolescence, try to lay down the law—the very time when children need more freedom in order to gain their own experience.

If parents exercise proper control in the early years, they can relax later because the child will have developed controls. If the limits and controls are lacking in the early years, the child will not only be at a loss in the later years but will also be more likely to react and rebel against any kind of control. Direct orders are best during the early years. Let the no's be few, but consistent and in love.

> *Obedience is the first element
> in the development of the
> conscience and moral sense.*
> —John Drescher

At no time is the mother more important in determining the direction in the child's life than during the early years. At no other time are the mother's own purpose, persuasion, personhood, and goals more significant. Her strong sense of direction, emotional stability, intellectual pursuits, along with such characteristics as strictness with love, persistence, consistency, clear expectations, and confidence, will have much to do with the child's moral development. Particularly the mother, because of her closeness, becomes the child's moral compass. Of course, the father is important during these years, especially as he stands strong beside his wife with love and warm emotional support to both mother and child.

The Age of Imitation

The second age of childhood is the age of imitation, which occurs between the ages of eight and twelve. This is the period of time when, as John Balguy says, "Whatever parent gives his child good instruction and sets them at the same time a bad example, may be considered as bringing them food in one hand and poison in the other." During these years, role models are most important to a child. Rules are important, but example is the great stimulus.

Larry Poland, director of the Agape Movement, and his wife, Donna Lynn, wrote,

> A child needs to learn by concrete example until the age of eleven, since his ability to think abstractly is not well developed until then. Our own character strengths and weaknesses are mirrored in our children's lives. Often the things we can't stand in our children are our worst faults. All of us have seen a hot-headed or profane father pass on these characteristics to his son or a sharp-tongued, immodest mother beget a sassy, immoral daughter. No amount of Scriptural training will counteract totally the example we parents set.*

It is "kiddie-see, kiddie-do," or as my mother said so many times as we began our own family, "Son, your children more attention pay to what you do than what you say."

> *Parents,*
> *if you will set the example,*
> *you won't have to set the rules.*

*Printed by permission from Worldwide Challenge. Copyright © Campus Crusade for Christ, Inc., 1981. All rights reserved.

God's Book gives a beautiful, clear, commanding, but frightening example in Luke 6:39–40: ''Can the blind lead the blind? Will they not both fall into the ditch? A disciple [a student] is not above his teacher, but everyone who is perfectly trained will be like his teacher.'' That is frightening if the parental example is bad, but it's tremendously exciting if the parental example is good. We're going to teach what we are, not just what we say or do. The old statement is true: What you are speaks so loudly I can't hear what you're saying.

An article in *Parents Magazine* indicated that during this stage of childhood, the child develops his basic disposition that he will bring to big decisions later on—what kind of people he will be attracted to, what kind of living he wants to make, what style of spending he feels comfortable with, how much reverence he pays to people in all the living world, how important integrity is to him. This is when he also establishes touchstones of belief and values, so he will have something to hang on to during the storms of temptation and uncertainty during adolescence. His attitudes about life and others are developed by how parents speak to salesclerks at the store, over the telephone to a neighbor, and to their friends at a social gathering. Attitudes toward people are reflected in family discussion about others and how the needs of the community and world are referred to.

Reading is at an all-time high during these years. The right books and magazines will help in determining values. Reading stories of good conduct, bravery in doing right, and honesty in different situations should be done during these years, when the child wants to imitate what seems to be heroic and challenging.

In a study several years ago it was learned that more than half of those who became Christian ministers had decided on this vocation by the age of eleven. *Now, more than ever before or after, the parent dare not be or do what he does not want his child to be or do.* Consistent living, which conforms to what is taught, is now at an all-time premium.

Therefore, it is important that the adults who teach and guide children during this period be the kind of persons worthy of imitation.

The Age of Inspiration

The next age is the age of inspiration—ages thirteen and up. During the teenage period the child is inspired by great ideas of one kind or another. He must have heroes. If he is not given heroes, he will find them; if he is not inspired by the right kind of heroes, he will be inspired by the wrong kind. During this period a great deal of stability and character is gained if the teenager has a certain goal in mind. He needs both short-range and long-range goals. Rules and limits are, of course, still important. By now, however, the adolescent needs to have inner controls to be effective because parents cannot possibly be present at all times. The teenager needs to bring all past experiences to bear.

It is true that by the time the child becomes an adolescent, he knows exactly what his parents believe. But he does not always comprehend the reasons behind the beliefs. And that's why it's important to take time to communicate to your kids why you believe what you believe. Standards and beliefs are reinforced by conversation; the youth needs to hear himself and his parents, as well as peers, talk about the important aspects of life. Informal discussions, particularly, can have a profound impact on the thinking of a youth. Above all, during the adolescent stage, the child needs to feel the love, confidence, and support of parents. *When acceptance and love come through, the teen will also be open to all kinds of change for the good.*

One of the most amazing articles I've ever read was in the January 1985 issue of *Reader's Digest*. It is so good, I reprint it, with permission, in its entirety.

How to Raise a Superstar*

An editorial review by Claire Safran

> From a new study comes
> heartening news for parents: given
> the right conditions, almost *any*
> child can rise higher, live better,
> shine more brightly

What makes an Einstein? A Van Cliburn? A Chris Evert Lloyd?

Great talent has always been a mystery. Where does it come from? How does it grow?

Recently, noted educational researcher Benjamin Bloom and a team of research assistants at the University of Chicago completed a five-year study of some 120 superstars—Olympic swimmers, tennis players, concert pianists, sculptors, world-class mathematicians and scientists—the best and the brightest, the tops in their fields. Surprisingly, the educational detectives found that such superstars aren't simply born—they are brought up that way. Their talents may differ, but their childhood experiences tend to be remarkably similar.

If Bloom is right—and many leading educators believe he is—then potential talent is more common than we think. Indeed, Bloom feels that the great majority of children, given the right conditions, can learn almost anything. "Human potential," he insists, "is much greater than we can measure in I.Q. or aptitude tests."

To find out more about "the right conditions," Bloom and his team looked at those who have climbed to the top in their fields. As they explain in their book, *Developing Talent in Young People*, they chose individuals who were still young, mostly under 35, whose childhood memories were still fresh and who often had parents and teachers still living and able to tell their parts of the story.

When the interviews were analyzed and compared, one startling finding was that similarities—the same patterns—appeared over and over again. The other big surprise: how strong the influence of home is on the superstar process.

Yet none of the parents in this study had a master plan. "If you set out to raise a great talent," warns Bloom, "you probably won't succeed, because you'll push too hard." Instead, at each step of the way, these parents simply did what they thought was good for the child at the time. Consider:

One mother tells of parking her baby's car bed next to the tennis courts, while she and her husband played. "The ping of the tennis balls may be the first sound my daughter remembers hearing," she laughs. Another mother recalls family trips to art museums. The son of the art lovers grew up to be a famous sculptor. In almost all of the cases, that's how the twig was bent. The child tried the activity his parents seemed to enjoy. As Bloom says, "If there's music in a home, that doesn't mean the child will become a musician. But if there's not music in the home, he probably won't."

Bloom had expected to see child prodigies, people whose talents were obvious at an early age. Instead, he found that most of the children in the study had not been identified as gifted until after several years of hard work. The pianists showed a natural feel for rhythm and a response to music, but less than half of them had perfect pitch. Several extraordinary mathematicians had learning difficulties. And while the Olympic swimmers were seen to have talent at an early age, they were not so unusual as to be considered prodigies.

What these children *did* have, beyond the basic physical and mental requirement, were alert and caring parents. Thus the earliest signs of potential talent were quickly noticed and encouraged. For example, a five-year-old girl banged playfully at the piano. "That's very nice," said her mother. She meant it; she loved music and thought it was good that her daughter did too.

In such small and ordinary ways, something extraordinary may begin. Parents praise one activity, ignore another, and children respond. A sculptor's mother saved every scrap of her daughter's artwork (though not a single English composition). A mathematician's parents praised their child for working out math problems alone in his room, something a sports-minded parent might have worried about.

A swimmer recalls that, as a little boy, he would watch his father do carpentry work. If a section wasn't done just right, his father would tear it up and start all over again.

The boy never forgot. Ten years later, in a room filled with silver trophy cups and Olympic medals, he told an interviewer, "My father taught me that if a thing is worth doing, it's worth doing well."

Almost all the superstars told a personal version of that story. Although for most of them success came early, it didn't happen overnight. None of them reached a talent peak in less than ten years of hard work. And all of them went through the same three stages:

Stage one is a time of playfulness and fun, of "falling in love" with your chosen pursuit. Next is the stage of precision, when techniques are worked on for their own sake, for the challenge and sense of competence. Then comes the stage of "making it your own," when a personal style is developed.

The parents in this study tried to give their children the experiences that seemed right for them at each stage. To encourage the first flash of talent, the children were given lessons, but their parents sought a teacher who was "good with children," not necessarily the best pianist or tennis player, but someone warm and friendly, quick to reward the child with praise.

After a while, the parent or teacher would decide the child needed something more to keep growing. The next teacher was more demanding, and kept the student working at a piece of music or a swimming stroke until it was right. The final teacher was both master and role model— an outstanding trainer of outstanding talents.

At every step of this process, the parents managed to find time, energy and money for needed lessons and equipment. For many, it meant scrimping. The father of a budding musician bought a grand piano instead of a badly needed new car. A tennis family spent its weekends taking the child to junior matches. Sacrifices were made, but one mother says, "We enjoyed it as much as the child did. It helped make us a family."

Like most children, these budding stars had to be reminded to practice. But a parent often sat with them. If the future star grew discouraged, the parents offered encouragement. When a young swimmer moved into a new age group and found himself losing every race, he wanted to quit. His father told him, "Just hang on until you win one more time. Don't quit simply because you're losing." By the time he won again, the boy wanted to go on.

The parents cheered them when they won and comforted them when they lost. If a child tried hard or did better than the last time, that too was a victory. Or a loss could be something to learn from, a way of seeing what you needed to work on.

After a while, though, it was up to the child. Some parents remember that another son or daughter was even more gifted, but not willing to work so hard. The superstars, by contrast, made a string of choices. It was time for practice versus time for school activities or just "hanging out." As they entered their teens, they were giving an average of 25 hours a week to their talent. That's more time than they spent on any other activity, including school, but no more time than the average child now spends watching television.

The parents enjoyed the talent and were there to help it along, but they weren't living through the child. They knew the talent was the child's.

There is a talent hiding in almost every child, according to Bloom, and parents can help nurture it into full flower. And even if superstardom is never reached, the accomplished amateur—the lifelong lover of sports, music or intellectual pursuits—will have a better life for it.

Is it worth the time and energy? Yes, for *the lessons of childhood become the instincts of adulthood.* Whatever they end up doing in life, children who have mastered a skill have learned to act like winners, doing and being their best.

You can't deny it, parent. Whether it's while the child is in the womb or as he or she goes through the stages of life to adulthood, the input is crucial to the child's success. Positive input in various forms will generally produce positive results.

Now let's look at some practical suggestions that will help you do a better job nurturing positive qualities in your children.

Develop Those Imaginations

Much can be accomplished by working with your child and helping him develop his creative imagination. How? By spending a lot of time reading to him. When you read a story such as "Snow White and the Seven Dwarfs" and your child becomes engrossed in the story, introduce the seven dwarfs and ask your child to talk as each one would talk.

> *The most difficult job our kids*
> *have today is learning good conduct*
> *without seeing any.*
> —H.G. Hutchinson

Chances are great that your child is going to want to go back to ''Snow White and the Seven Dwarfs'' time after time and go through the procedure of talking like Doc, Sleepy, Grumpy, and all the other characters. This does a number of things. First and foremost, it brings parent and child close together. Second, it stimulates the child's imagination and creativity, giving him some activities so he is not going to get bored. Third, it begins to teach him that he can do things with his voice other than keep it in the same tone with which he normally speaks. Who knows, maybe you will discover a budding Olivier in the process!

One of the greatest benefits of reading comes when you hold your toddler in your lap and read some wonderful stories, such as children's classics or *Taylor's Bible Stories*. These are educational, but more importantly, your child will come to identify learning with loving, so you are setting the stage for a child who's excited about learning. He will also identify his heavenly Father as loving, and that will help him identify with your spiritual values.

> *When your child clearly identifies*
> *learning with loving, he will love learning.*

There are other ways to develop creativity and to communicate with your child. Give him building blocks or modeling clay and ask him to use his imagination to build something different. A yard for the child to play in, a sandpile where he can build sand castles, or whatever his imagination permits him to do, will keep him busy by the hour. When you give your child things like erector sets as he gets a little older, his imagination can soar as he comes up with different structures.

One classic example of where children's real interests lie is in the fact that quite often at Christmas when the toys come out of the boxes, the kids end up playing with the boxes, not the toys. They design all kinds of things with them. And what little boy hasn't built his own fort and what little girl hasn't built her own dollhouse out of boxes, sticks, a pillow, an old towel or blanket, and anything else they can scrounge from their parents?

Humor Helps—Try It

To maintain our optimism and increase our chances for raising positive kids, we must have a sense of humor to overcome the problems, obstacles, and discouragement we all confront from time to time. To a degree, all of us are somewhat like the fellow who drove onto the used car lot and approached a salesman with a question: "Sir, are you the salesman who sold me this car?" The salesman looked the fellow over pretty carefully and said, "Yes, I believe I am." The owner of the used car said, "I wonder if you'd mind telling me about it again; sometimes I get so discouraged!" That's pretty much the way it is sometimes with parents. Things don't always go our way, and we need to be encouraged.

Humor can be a great encourager. Evidence is also mounting that humor is one of the truly great motivational teaching tools in our lives. A study from San Diego State showed that humor helped students do better on tests.[4] Four groups of undergraduates taking psychology were given the choice of attending either a serious lecture or a humorous one. The four groups scored equally well on a quiz immediately after the lectures; but on a retest six weeks later, students who had attended the humorous lecture demonstrated superior recall.

As I remarked earlier in discussing the positive qualities of successful people (covered in Chapter 3), humor was one of the qualities mentioned in every audience survey I've ever taken. In our world today there is too much grimness. Entirely too many people are walking around looking like the cruise director for the *Titanic* and acting like somebody licked *all* the red off their candy cane. Help your child develop a sense of humor.

Get 'Em Up—Lovingly

Another important step in developing positive qualities and raising positive, loving kids is to help them start and end the day in a loving, optimistic way. The way you awaken your little ones will make quite a difference. If it's with a gruff, "It's time to get up now! Don't let me have to tell you again!" approach, no child is going to look forward to the day.

Sometimes as parents we tend to make an issue out of everything, whether it's important or not. I believe there are instances when reasonable compromise might be in everyone's best interests.

In a sense, this might sound like a contradiction of some things I've been saying; but having watched three daughters and a son grow up, and knowing how completely different they are, I've concluded that some children are natural-born procrastinators—or else they acquire that characteristic at an early age.

Others have a streak of independence or resistance to authority, which seems to be brought out any time a parent asks them to make the bed, take out the trash, pick up their clothes, or get up in the morning. Still others are night people, and some are day people. The parents and the child, if they don't understand where they are coming from, can get involved in a never-ending series of conflicts, causing a wall to be raised between them.

Going to bed, for example, is something some youngsters hate to do with an absolute passion. Ironically, by the next morning the same ones have become so attached to that bed they don't want to get out of it! What's the solution? In our case we discovered that when we gave our children advance notice of bedtime, it made life more enjoyable and reduced conflict considerably. It eliminated the "Let-me-stay-up-just-fifteen-more-minutes-Dad" or "Can-I-make-one-more-phone-call?" or "Let-me-finish-doing-this" routines.

One of the most beautiful sights I am privileged to witness is watching my daughter Suzan awaken Elizabeth, our newest grandbaby. First she stands over Elizabeth's bed and looks at her for a few seconds. Then Suzanne gently strokes her forehead before she leans over and kisses her softly and gently awake. As Elizabeth starts to awaken, she invariably stretches, and as she is stretching, she opens her eyes. The delight of her introduction into the world of that day is certainly a pleasure to behold.

All the time, daughter Suzan is gently talking and lovingly welcoming Elizabeth back to the world of the waking. Thus, waking up becomes a pleasurable experience rather than a disagreeable one.

I believe most parents start with their babies like that, but I'm puzzled as to why they should ever change the procedure. I believe that regardless of the age of the child—infant, toddler, five-year-old, or fifteen-year-old—the child needs to pleasantly welcome the new day and bid the day farewell in the same way.

When the child gets older, considerate parents will make one alteration in the procedure, namely, they will gently knock on the door before they enter the room to awaken the child. If the child is already awake, he will not be caught in an embarrassing state of undress when mom or dad walks

in. This is especially important when mom is awakening a
son or dad is awakening a daughter.

Our Amazing, Changing Kids

I know you'll agree with me when I say that children are
absolutely amazing. Many times the child you had serious
trouble putting to bed the previous night will have suddenly
developed an incredible love affair with that same bed. He
or she clings to it with every ounce of strength and resistance.
Children love it so much they simply do not want to leave it.
During the day, however, they again develop a distaste for
that bed. Under no circumstances do they want even to approach it, much less get into it, so getting them back into the
bed is just as difficult for some parents as it was getting them
out of the bed in the morning. But if mornings and bedtimes
are both pleasant and planned, they can be a delight instead
of a nightmare.

About thirty minutes before the prescribed bedtime, tell
your child, "Now sweetheart, in thirty minutes you are going
to bed, so if you need to feed the cat, let the dog out, bring
your bicycle in, call Suzie about the assignment, get a drink
of water, go to the bathroom, brush your teeth, curl your
hair, or any one of the four thousand other 'gotta do's,' then
you need to do that right now." Say this in a gentle and
loving, but firm manner. Then at the prescribed time lead
your child to the bedroom regardless of any protests about
what she still needs to do. Share a story or experience as you
tuck your child in. Do not be in a hurry. Missing five minutes
of your favorite TV show will not affect your future or your
child's. However, those few minutes with your child reading,
talking, sharing and praying together will make a difference
in your child's life and your relationship with your child.

If mornings and evenings are pleasant for your child,
chances are greatly enhanced that the hours in between will
be much better for both you and your child.

For youngsters in the three-to-seven-year-old range, bedtime stories can be very effective. Bible stories are ideal, but in our home we frequently created our own stories as we tucked the children in. As a matter of fact, one of the best time investments and most effective ways of bringing the family closer together in a loving atmosphere is the sharing of original stories.

To this day our girls want me to tell their children—and everyone else—the stories of "Skeeter, Scatter and Scooter"—the three scared 'skeeters from Schenectady. When they were small, we often bowed to their pleas at bedtime to share a new episode of those three scared 'skeeters. Their delight never ceased to amaze me.

I might also point out that bedtime is a time when a child will "act out" any problems he might have. A loving, sensitive parent can nip many major problems in the bud by gentle, patient probing if the child appears upset, yet is not verbal about something. A few more unhurried moments just before lights out, or first thing in the morning, can be comforting and reassuring for your child.

A Child Needs to Know He Is Special

This idea is tremendously important. Richard Green, a dynamic Dallas businessman, has taken an effective and unique approach with his children. Both are adopted, and so the Greens celebrate two birthdays—one is the date of birth and the other is the date of adoption. This communicates to Creed and Brooke that they are very special and makes their adoption a plus with a resultant boost to their self-images.

Creed, who is six, and Brooke, who is three, are also given some other special treatments. When Creed was four years old, the Greens established a night each week especially for him. If he was "good" that week, he earned the right to do whatever he wanted, within reason, on his special night. One of the things he wanted to do one week was go to a discount department store and watch the fish. On that Friday night, the Greens went to the store, got Creed a little chair, and sat him down in the center of all those aquariums. For one solid hour he sat there in total delight, watching all the fish as they swam around.

Not only did Creed thoroughly enjoy every moment of it, but his mom and dad were communicating *his* uniqueness and their love for him. I'm convinced that, as he watched the different fish and other aquarium life and looked at the plants and rocks, he was absorbing some of the beauties and miracles of God through nature. The cost, of course, was zero with the exception of the gas and oil required to go to the local store.

From time to time, on super special occasions, Mr. Green takes Creed to his business with him. He dresses him up in a suit, making certain his shoes are shined and his hair is properly brushed. For a brief time he takes Creed around the business and introduces him to the employees. He has taught him how to shake hands and courteously respond to each person. This establishes an important relationship between father and son, and the process of dressing him up gives his self-image another boost. Going with his dad and observing his dad's managerial position plants in Creed's mind managerial objectives of his own that will someday be within his reach. The cost—still zero. Richard Green is building a "winner."

I close this chapter with an example told me by my friends Jerry and Jo Bacon who live in Charleston, South Carolina. Several years ago they encountered an interesting situation with their beautiful daughter, Beth, who truly is the little "Miss America" type of girl. She's enthusiastic, motivated, courteous, dependable, pleasant, loving, outgoing—all the good things! Her nature was cheerful from the time she got up until she went to bed.

Several years ago, Jerry and Jo gave Beth a clock radio for Christmas to awaken her in the morning. They did not realize it, but they set the radio dial on a rock music station. Each morning when she awakened, she heard five minutes of news that had taken place the day and night before. Then the station started playing rock music.

The change was slow and barely noticeable, but over a period of two or three months Beth became progressively more irritable and grumpy about a lot of different things. She didn't laugh as much, she complained a lot more, she was not nearly as loving and affectionate; in short, she became a different little girl.

Jo and Jerry noticed the changes and did some brainstorming. One thing led to another until they traced the change back to Christmas and the clock radio. The solution was simplicity itself. They took the clock radio out of Beth's room (yes, she fussed about that, too; but responsible, loving parents do what is *best* for the child *and* the family). Each morning one of them would go in and awaken her with hugs and kisses and a cheerful welcome to the new day. Obviously, you know the end of the story or you wouldn't be reading about it—and of course, you're right. In a matter of weeks she again became the happy, loving, enthusiastic girl she had always been. Change the input, and you change the output.

Children Live What They Learn
by Dorothy Law Nolte

If a child lives with criticism,
He learns to condemn.
If a child lives with hostility,
He learns violence.
If a child lives with ridicule,
He learns to be shy.
If a child lives with shame,
He learns to feel guilty.
If a child lives with encouragement,
He learns confidence.

If a child lives with praise,
He learns to appreciate.
If a child lives with fairness,
He learns justice.
If a child lives with security,
He learns faith.
If a child lives with approval,
He learns to like himself.
If a child lives with acceptance and friendship,
He learns to love the world.

Time for Personal Evaluation

1. How early is too early to begin the education process with your kids?

2. A young child needs rules to follow. Paint a picture in your mind of a child who lives free of rules.

3. What are some ways being consistent in setting boundaries for your child has benefited your family life?

4. Do you know anyone who has taught or is in the process of teaching their children at home? If so, have you asked them about the experience? Is this something you should look into?

5. Zig says the early days are critical. Can you finish the quote, "Take control _____ or _____"?

6. What are the "ages" children go through according to John Drescher? What is the major characteristic of each age?

CHAPTER 6

The Tridimensional Chi

Physically fit people are more intellectually inclined, emotinally stable, composed, self-confident, easygoing and relaxed.

—A.H. Ismail
Purdue University

No responsible parent would ever dream of denying his child the privilege of acquiring an education. If a child is reared in any environment where he is given absolutely no instructions of any kind on how to develop his mind, he will be seriously handicapped. Most parents, of course, agree with this and make at least casual efforts to see that their child is given the opportunity to learn and grow. As a matter of fact, every state in our nation has compulsory education laws.

Everyone will also agree that our physical needs must be taken care of. In the United States parents are punished for denying their children the basic needs of food, shelter, and clothing. Again, no responsible, loving parent would dream of starving his child or of giving his child a diet selected only to sustain life and not permit growth and healthy activity.

Freedom *of* or *from* Religion?

s not as evident on the surface, not as easy to measure as needs in the physical and mental arenas, but the case for teaching a child spiritual values is overwhelming. If parents really are serious about wanting to raise a positive child, they most emphatically will not neglect the spiritual needs of their tridimensional child.

Some parents piously adjust their halos and maintain that they do not want to impose their ''religious values'' on their child, so they will not take their child to church or give him any biblical training or instruction. They maintain that they will wait until the child is old enough to make his own choice. By any means of measurement that's a cop-out, and it's the worst kind.

> *Faith is*
> *your response to*
> *God's ability.*

Would these same parents trust the judgment of their six- or eight-year-old to choose his diet, his bedtime, the clothes he buys, or what he wears in freezing weather? I can't conceive of a parent leaving the moral and spiritual training of a small child to chance or leaving the choice to him ''when he's old enough.''

By the time the child reaches that age, he will already have made his choice and will have been influenced directly or indirectly *by the parent*. A parent who follows this line of reasoning has spoken loudly and clearly that since religion and faith in God are not a part of his own life, it must not be important.

We Teach—By Not Teaching

Constitutional lawyer William Ball says that when we took God out of our schools, we established a basic thought pattern. He says the most important reason for the presence of God in school is that a child spends a substantial part of his life within the school walls.

The child is told that is where he is getting his education. If religion is not present, if it is barred from the whole process, the child inevitably comes to consider it irrelevant. It isn't a part of his moral and intellectual learning environment. That teaches a very strong lesson. At the very least, the omission of religion teaches him that religion is nonessential.

That's one of the reasons I believe we need prayer in our schools. Of course, it already has returned to some schools. Not long ago I saw a neat little sign in a principal's office that stated, "In the event of nuclear attack, fire, or earthquake, the ban on prayer is temporarily lifted."

The ancient Chinese, Egyptian, Greek, and Roman civilizations all recognized that man is a tridimensional being. The spiritual aspect of man is the most important but the most neglected. I believe a child's spiritual condition is the controlling factor behind what he will become. Out of the soul of man flow his attitudes, and his attitudes, not his aptitude, will determine his altitude in life. In the final analysis, the depth of his spirit will determine the height of his success.

The Need for Balance

We need to have a reasonable balance in all of life. We can go overboard with just about anything, but the problem in our day isn't that we've gone overboard with our faith and religious involvement. We're far from that! As a recent study showed, only 40 percent of the members of all religious groups attend weekly services, which is down from 49 per-

cent recorded in 1958.¹ What's missing among us is a balance
of the spiritual in a society that is obviously seeking, but not
finding, satisfaction in only the mental-intellectual and
physical-sensual realms of life. There's something out of balance.

There is a way to be right—not perfect—but "right" in
the sense of being "in balance" mentally, physically, and
spiritually. Just as a person who wants to be mentally sharp
attends seminars and refresher courses and reads journals in
his field of endeavor, and just as a person who wants to be
physically fit exercises regularly, so a person who wants to
live his potential will daily seek spiritual refreshment.

In this chapter I'm going to concentrate on the physical
and spiritual aspects of raising a positive child, since I devote
so much of the rest of the book to the importance of positive
mental input. Now let's take a good look at the physical.

Physical Health for Mental and Social Growth

An article in the *Kansas City Times* by Dr. Gabe Mirkin
emphasizes the importance of our physical condition. He
used twelve-year-old Jamie as an example. Although a bright
child, Jamie did poorly in school last year. He was slightly
overweight, and his muscle tone was below what it should
have been. Jamie was restless and unable to sit still very long.
It seems that about all he did was watch TV or go to the
movies, and he was not involved in any kind of sports. During the summer Dr. Mirkin put Jamie on an exercise program
that Jamie himself had chosen.

Dr. Mirkin pointed out that many children are like Jamie
and do not get enough exercise, even though we usually think
of childhood as a time of great activity. *"Being out of shape
is associated with a greater chance of scholastic under-
achievement, so I recommended that Jamie get more exercise.* The results were good. Jamie's doing much better. He's

now playing on a youth football team and is doing well in school.''

According to Dr. Mirkin, several studies have shown that being unfit is a characteristic of many students who do poorly in class. Eighty-three percent of the students who flunked out of Syracuse University could not pass a minimal physical fitness test. Most of the students who failed to graduate from the United States Military Academy at West Point were at the bottom of their class in physical fitness.

Pioneering studies by A. H. Ismail, a professor of physical education at Purdue University, have shown that ''physically fit people are more intellectually inclined, emotionally stable, composed, self-confident, easygoing and relaxed.

''The very act of keeping in shape reinforces these personality attributes,'' says the Purdue researcher. ''Exercise not only makes you fitter, it can even sharpen a person's ability to process information, consequently enhancing one's learning capabilities,'' Ismail says. ''A subject who is rebellious, emotionally unstable, uptight and aggressive can change his personality through a long-term physical fitness program. Such a program, besides making one feel healthier, also causes one to calm down, be more composed, self-confident, easygoing and relaxed.''

Exercise and Diet for Mental Agility

''We know that physically fit people who exercise consistently and keep fit become more systematic and organized in their problem-solving abilities and improve their verbal and numerical skills.'' Ismail cites the results of research at many universities, including Purdue. In his own studies, sixty men—ranging in age from twenty-five to sixty-five—were psychologically tested before and after completing a four-month physical fitness program. ''Subjects who tested low in emotional stability before the exercise program showed marked improvement in final tests after the program,'' Ismail says.

The link between physical fitness and academic accomplishment may be the fact that young people who exercise feel better about themselves. The self-confidence, it is theorized, carries over into their study habits.

As an enthusiastic jogger, I can assure you from personal experience there are definite mental and possibly psychological benefits that go with physical exercise. Scientifically speaking, Dr. Kenneth Cooper says that when you exercise, you activate the pituitary gland that floods the system with endorphins, which are two hundred times more powerful than morphine. As a result, for the next one to three hours, your energy level is higher, and your creativity is at a peak. The increased energy level combined with the added mental alertness certainly should be helpful academically.

One of the most critical areas in a child's life is his personal appearance. Too often, this relates to what a child eats and drinks. Many things we cannot control, such as how tall or short we are, whether or not we have freckles or red hair. We can't control whether we're left-handed or right-handed, but there are many things we can control by diet, exercise, and common sense.

Ideally, the child should never be given candy, soft drinks, or most of the junk food so prevalent on the market today. Realistically, that would be a tough regimen to follow. The prevalence of so many sweets, the public acceptance, the advertising, the availability in our friends' homes, at parties, and virtually every other place would make abstinence extremely difficult. However, a great deal can be done about the amount consumed, and the parent really interested in raising positive kids will make an all-out effort to do exactly that. For example, the average American adolescent consumes 836 cans of soda pop each year.[2] That's over two every day. That borders on insanity and is absolutely ridiculous! Recent reports from the American Psychological Association show that cutting down on sugar intake sometimes results in as much as an 80 percent drop in misbehavior amongst severe delinquents in this country.

Cute, Chubby Baby Often Means Obese Child

At the first sign their baby is overweight, parents should ask the doctor specifically what they can do to control the weight, because the earlier it is addressed, the simpler it's going to be to control. I've seen parents put soft drinks in a baby's bottle, so the infant gurgles away on a high-sugar drink with totally empty calories that add up to a considerable amount of bulk. That's the easy way—temporarily—for the busy mother, but it makes no allowances for the devastating effects it can have on the child. Just think of the time and tears involved later with an overweight child.

The reduction of sugar can have a dramatic impact on the weight problem with which so many children are afflicted. One of the saddest sights in our society today is little guys and gals on the sidelines of life not being invited to participate in athletic events, kids' games or social activities because they are overweight and cannot perform as well as the other kids.

The habits the little ones acquire early determine whether or not they're going to become overweight. The amount of food, the circumstances under which the food is eaten, and the type of food will certainly play important roles.

There are probably four thousand rules that could be followed to keep your child's weight under control, but let's look at a few simple ones. Mealtimes, when humanly possible, should be the most casual, relaxing experiences of the day.

Family problems need to be discussed at other times. Watching a blaring television set and reading magazines, newspapers, or books during meals are absolute no-no's. The emphasis should be on the family and on the food. You can eat an entire meal accompanied by outside distractions and not really be aware of the fact you're eating. The result is that often you will eat more than you should.

One critical stage of life for the youngster arrives when he is old enough to select his own foods and concentrates on sweets and junk food. The time quickly comes when the parent must put a foot down and say no to this destructive habit. If the child rebels and doesn't eat anything, don't sweat it. By the next day or even the next meal, he will discover a real taste for enough of the foods with some nutritional value that he won't starve to death.

This reminds me of the humorous story my speaker-brother, Judge Ziglar, tells of the two ''old boys'' talking about feeding their dogs. One of them said he gave his dog the finest dog food money could buy. The second said he fed his dog turnip greens. The first one replied that his dog wouldn't eat turnip greens. The second came right back and said, ''Mine wouldn't either—the first three weeks.''

Your child might not eat anything (or so it appears) for a day or two, but it's important that neither mom nor dad gives in and lets the child have that soft drink, package of cookies, or bar of candy because he ''hasn't had a thing to eat all day.'' People who fast will emphatically tell you that a day, or even two or three days, without a single bite of food might not be a bad idea for all of us to follow.

Good Health Is Simple—Not Easy

For too many Americans, breakfast is a high-sugar-content cereal with little staying power. A choice of fruit, whole grain cereals, whole wheat or rye toast with a low-calorie spread, and a small glass of milk is excellent. Add a small portion from dinner the evening before, particularly if it is chicken or veal, and you have an ideal breakfast for a child. Since the speed at which your child eats makes a substantial difference in the amount he eats, be sure to allow plenty of time for breakfast by starting the day thirty minutes earlier.

Study after study reveals that children who start the day with a good breakfast do better in school. Additionally, children who skip breakfast often compensate later in the day by eating salty snacks, which can lead to weight gain and hypertension.

Eating a nutritious breakfast also gives the kids time with mom and/or dad before going to school, which is extremely important. This allows the parents to set the stage for the day and to provide encouragement.

> *If there is hope in the future*
> *there is power in the present.*
> —Dr. John Maxwell

Along these same lines, it is extremely important to be patient, noncritical, and loving. The kids need to leave home feeling secure and accepted, or they might seek acceptance from the wrong crowd at school. When they return home and the time frame is more leisurely, you can deal with appearance, unmade beds, or poor eating habits in a more effective manner.

The second most important meal is in the evening. In most homes that is the day's heaviest meal, but in reality, it should be the lightest one. A general rule is to eat breakfast like a millionaire, lunch like a man on a strict budget, and dinner like you had just lost your job. The evening meal should be eaten as early as possible, preferably by 6:00 P.M.

Common Sense Is the Answer

It is important for parents to realize that it is unwise to stuff the baby on a wide variety of foods, force it to overeat, and then take drastic action with the four-year-old youngster who is substantially overweight. It is wrong to suddenly make a dramatic change in the child's eating habits while mom and dad continue to eat breads, pastries, sweets, and other delicacies. When one member of the family is overweight and hurting, every member of the family needs to cooperate and work together to help the overweight one lose weight. Incidentally, nagging and criticizing are the wrong course to follow. Loving encouragement and firm discipline are the elements of the proper approach.

Most Americans will drive around a shopping center ten minutes looking for a parking spot closest to the entrance. Parents should park a reasonable distance from the front door and then walk to the shopping center unless the weather is severe. A brisk walk is certainly one of the nicest things that can happen to a family. Not only does it bring the family together, but it also has the added benefit of burning calories and getting everyone in better shape physically. Another simple exercise procedure for you and your children is to always walk up to second- and third-floor offices. It's good for you.

Handle with Pride—and Care

Above all things, here's an area where common sense should apply. If your child is substantially overweight because of eating too much and never doing anything physically, you're not going to effect a 180-degree turnaround instantly. As a matter of fact, you will create resentment and possibly have a rebellion on your hands if you attempt drastic action.

One simple and effective step is to deliberately run out of the villains in the kitchen—cakes, cookies, ice cream, potato chips, and high-fat foods. Another thing you can do is to cook more realistically and scientifically. Start eliminating sauces, gravies, and the extras that make such a difference in the number of calories.

Changing from white bread saturated in butter and topped with cheese to whole grain or oat bran bread with one of the low-calorie spreads on it can make a difference of a hundred calories or even more. The nutritional value, in addition to the dramatic reduction of cholesterol, can substantially affect your child for the better.

Parents, the example you set will be the greatest single influence on your child's weight and eating habits. Robert Dunham, who writes for the *Los Angeles Times* Syndicate, says,

> When parents eat excessively, it's only natural to assume that their children will also over-indulge. The clean-your-plate syndrome and the ideal of the chubby-cheeked, over weight baby seems to be deeply ingrained in our society. "It's just baby fat; he'll outgrow it," is a common expression. The problem with that is it's probably not true. The claim that the child has a glandular problem is actually the result of overeating or eating too many of the wrong foods.

It's a well-documented fact that overweight children are often rejected by their peers. Teasing "fatties" starts in kindergarten or first grade and intensifies through grade school, junior high, and high school. *Fat children are teased because they are overweight*. Because they are overweight, they are less active and can't play as long or as hard as other children. Subsequently, they develop fewer friends. Many of them go home alone, rejected by their playmates, and take out their frustrations by overeating.

A real plus is that children do not need a significant weight loss to slim down. If children maintain their weight over a two-

or three-year period, they're actually losing excess body fat since they're growing in height. One major villain in the weight battle is continual snacking, which is often a bigger problem than overeating at mealtime. If children really need snacks, make sure they eat them at the table and not in front of the TV. Also, serve snacks such as fresh fruit, whole grain bread, yogurt, carrot sticks, and fresh juices instead of jelly donuts, chocolate milk, and ice cream. At least a once-a-week weigh-in is a must for the overweight child.

Team Effort and Exercise

Weight loss is a team effort. The mother can partially control the amount the child eats by serving less on the plate, not offering seconds, and cutting out desserts except for a rare treat. Remember, if the child loses weight or even stays the same, that's progress. However, if the child loses two or three pounds per week over an extended period, normal growth could be adversely affected. *Moderation* is the key word. Experts say one pound per week for an obese child should be the maximum amount to lose.

Do not expect nine-year-olds to outgrow their weight problems. These problems need to be treated while they are still young. If children are still overweight by the time they reach seventeen, chances are that they will never return to normal weight for any extended period of time. Obese babies often become obese adolescents, and obese adolescents usually become obese adults who are prime candidates for heart disease, hypertension, and diabetes.

> *The only way to permanently lose weight*
> *is to combine sensible eating habits*
> *with a consistent exercise program.*
> —Dr. Kenneth Cooper

Repeated or prolonged dieting often makes it easier to gain weight on less food. Psychologist Martin Katahan, director of the Weight Management Program, says that the body interprets severe caloric restriction as a threat to its survival and lowers the metabolic rate to conserve energy. Whereas 2,000 calories a day may have maintained the pre-diet weight, consuming only 1,400 calories may now cause a weight gain. Katahan recommends expending 200 calories' worth of daily exercise, such as a 45-minute brisk walk. Burning just those extra 200 calories a day results in twenty or thirty fewer pounds of fat within a year.

Now let's take a look at the most important and often the most neglected aspect of your child's life, the spiritual.

Start Early on the Spiritual

Dr. James Dobson, psychologist and author, has remarked that kids begin to "buy in" to your spiritual guidance and direction in values at about five years of age. At that point in your child's life and experience, you are the role models—the most significant people to whom your child looks for direction in every aspect of life. What your child needs above all in a world that is spiritually out of balance is the example of a clear, consistent, disciplined approach to faith in God. It is most important that he sees this beginning in his earliest years.

The inner spiritual qualities of a man—the spiritual substance—make him and society great. Our nation was built on, and it will stand on, a spiritual foundation.

In the 1830s Alexis de Tocqueville toured America. When his tour had been completed, he made this observation (and I paraphrase):

I have toured America, and I have seen most of what you offer. I've seen the richness of the fields and the wealth of your mines. I've seen your industrial might, the beauties of the rivers, the streams, the lakes, and the grandeur of the mountains. I've noticed the abundance of the forests and the marvelous climate with which you are blessed.

In none of these things did I see the cause for the greatness of America. It wasn't until I went into your churches that I saw the reason for America's greatness. America is great because America is good; and as long as America is good, America will be great. If it ever ceases to be good, it will cease to be great.

In her book, *Pathfinders*, Gail Sheehy reports her study to determine what characterizes people who have a strong sense of satisfaction about themselves and about their lives. One thing she discovered was that *in every group she surveyed, the most satisfied people were also likely to be the most religious*. Another of her findings showed the strong role commitment plays in shaping lives. The results among high-satisfaction people were dramatic. The greater well-being a person reflected, the more likely he or she was to have an outside purpose. The distinction is so considerable as to make the current philosophy of ''looking out for number one'' sound like a national suicide pact.

Christian psychologist Henry Brandt says, ''Adequate parents must be adequate partners, and before a person can be an adequate partner, he must be an adequate person.'' Before you can have peace with others, you must have peace with yourself, and that happens only when you have peace with God.[3]

Your Future Is the Key to the Present

In a speech made in Indianapolis, Dr. Anthony Campolo, a noted professor of sociology at Eastern College in Pennsylvania, had a great deal to say about psychology's current preoccupation with the influences of one's personal past. His own conclusion was:

What you commit yourself to be will change what you are and make you into a completely different person. Let me repeat that. Not the past, but the future conditions you because what you commit yourself to become determines what you are—more than anything that ever happened to you yesterday or the day before.

Dr. Campolo is saying that your past is important, but it is not nearly as important as the way you see your future.

Now, tie this statement to that of Dr. John Maxwell of San Diego, California, who says if there's hope for the future, there's power in the present, and you have a winning formula. The reason is simple. *The way you see your future in every area of your life is the determining factor in your performance today.* Since today's performance determines tomorrow's destination, our daily objective should be to "make today worth remembering." You and your children must forget the mistakes of the past and concentrate on building a better future. I continually meet people who say, "The major problem with today's youth is that they have an identity crisis!" Why do they have an identity crisis? They often don't have a commitment to their physical or mental, much less their spiritual well-being.

I'm not suggesting that merely attending a house of worship will give you a relationship with the Creator of heaven and earth. I am saying that your life and spiritual walk, so necessary for reaching your potential while raising positive kids, will only be successfully nurtured and strengthened through your commitment to, and regular participation with, a body of believers. When I speak of faith, I speak of the most essential aspect of a man and his "potential." Our future—your future and the future of your kids—depends on the spiritual principles upon which this country was built and now stands.

This Is What Lasts

The basis of the spiritual life was described by the apostle Paul. He wrote down what is one of the greatest revelations of God, "Now abide faith, hope, love, these three; but the greatest of these is love" (1 Cor. 13:13). He said, "Now abide"; in other words, this is what lasts; this is what remains; this is what endures.

The pricelessness of precious gems is significantly due to the fact that they endure, that they have a lasting, abiding quality. The pricelessness of these gems of the spirit—faith, hope, and love—is the fact that they endure. And these three elements bring the enduring, abiding, strengthening qualities of character into a person's life that provide the foundation upon which real success can be built.

These three gems speak of attitudes. *Faith*—faithfulness is an attitude; it speaks of the qualities of trust, reliability, and loyalty. *Hope*—hopefulness is an attitude; it describes the qualities of sincere expectation, confidence, inspiration, and enthusiasm. *Love*—love describes the most lasting, the most precious and valuable spiritual attitude that bears the solid gold fruit of commitment, sacrifice, and honesty. Bundle all these things together and they describe integrity, the inner essence of a person with whom anyone would want to associate.

Faith: The Unifying Principle of Life

Faith is the unifying principle of life—it's what gives life meaning and definition and direction. Faith unifies a person and provides the spiritual "glue" that holds life together and keeps a focus on goals and the future. Faith is what makes life livable. Faith is the attitude of man that results in his ability to believe in the future and to work toward tomorrow.

I've seen enthusiastic, hard-working individuals who apparently had it all but inside they were still cornered, going virtually nowhere. They were as equipped for blast-off to success as an astronaut in a space shuttle, except that they still lacked the fuel of faith that would deliver the power to their ideas, dreams, and aspirations.

For your kids, your faith will be a living lesson they will learn from you. Your example will be the most influential factor, and your parental coaching through life will be the next most influential factor.

Tomorrow may bring difficulty, trial, and distress, but I know the God of heaven and earth will already be there and a solution will be available if I have the faith to find it. Faith is the first step and is a unifying principle that gives us a sense of confidence. Faith adds to life a sense of definition and purpose; it provides a belief in that which is possible. It is hope with believability. Fortunately, you already have a foundation of faith which is built into every person.

The chairman of the board of a major company in America, with branches in over two hundred cities, personally told me that because of the nature of their business, they give polygraph (lie detector) tests to every prospective employee. They ask many questions, and *always* ask each prospective employee "Do you believe there is a God?" In 100 percent of the cases, when the person replies "No," the polygraph needle literally jumps, indicating that person deep down does believe that there is a God.

As parents, we need to build on that foundation by taking—not sending—our children to church. When mom and dad take the kids to church, 72 percent will follow the faith of their parents into adulthood. If dad takes the kids, 55 percent will follow the faith. If mom alone takes the kids, only 15 percent will follow the faith. If neither parent takes the kids to church, only 6 percent will end up in the faith.

Hope: The Great Motivator

Hope is the fruit of faith. Unfortunately, when most people talk about hope, they're talking about something they don't really expect. When people talk about an idea, a challenge, or a goal, you'll often hear someone say, "I hope so," which really means, "Not a chance! However, I don't want to be entirely negative about it." But the hope that is discussed in the Bible is defined as "expectation with desire." Expectation gets us going and often determines the end result.

This kind of hope is more than just a refreshing aspect of life. It is a medically documented healing fact as well. Dr. Viktor Frankl studied the survivors of the Nazi concentration camps after World War Two. He found that there was among the survivors a strong will, desire, and hope that characterized their attitudes.

Hope—with believability—is one of the greatest gifts you can give your child. It's an essential tool in his success arsenal.

Hope is the power that gives a person confidence to step out and try! Hope, through a spiritual relationship with God, produces an attitude of enthusiasm (*enthusiasm* literally means "God within") and encouragement that adds the energy of aspiration to a person's every inspiration. Faith opens the door to inspiration, and hope powers the forward thrust of aspiration.

Believe—and Teach with Your Life

At the age of forty-five when faith became a fact of life for me, my life was changed and enriched. My health has improved substantially—physically, mentally, spiritually and financially. I'm happier, have more real security, and far more peace of mind than I ever dreamed possible. My relationship with my wife and children is better than ever, and it's always been good. I truly have the peace of mind that passes all understanding. Even as I write these words, I can't help thinking of the tragedy and basic unfairness if your child was never introduced to God and the Scriptures. That is not the way to raise positive, drug-free kids.

By the way, if you are affirming these essential values in your life, I believe you need to reinforce them by regular attendance in your house of worship. You need to go as a family, regularly, diligently, as a matter of commitment. Dr. Henry Brandt has an answer for the question, "Do you think we should make our kids go to church?" Dr. Brandt says that even if the kids don't want to go, you take them anyhow.

Parent: "Suppose the child really objects? Just flat doesn't want to go?"

Dr. Brandt: "You still take him. Let me ask you a question. If your child was sick and didn't want to go to the doctor, what would you do?"

Parent: "Obviously, I'd take my child to the doctor."

Dr. Brandt: "Why would you do that?"

Parent: "Because it's good for the child."

Dr. Brandt: "You use the same line of reasoning. It's good for your child to take him to church—so take him."

However, the age of the child is a critical factor. When the child reaches the age of twelve, you will be firmly planting seeds of rebellion and rejection of your spiritual values by forcing him to attend church with you if he hasn't already bought into your faith, value system and life-style. He *must* see in you the love, values, compassion and concern for him that your Heavenly Father has for you. If your life personifies those values, you won't have to force your child to attend worship services with you. If your life doesn't personify those values, the day will come when you *can't* force him to accompany you to worship services.

Psychiatrist Ross Campbell stresses that if you force a rebellious fourteen-year-old to go to church with you, the odds are great that when he leaves home at eighteen, he won't be back in church and will probably be anti-God. In short, you can't permanently force your value system on your child, but chances are excellent that you can by example and loving leadership "sell" your beliefs and values to him, particularly if you also teach him how to handle his anger.

If spirituality is not presented in the home, children will consider it only a peculiar aspect of the life of some people who are seen at church. They may even come to think of spirituality in terms of going to church, which is a gross misunderstanding if a person is sincerely seeking the way to a positive, powerful, productive way of life.

Yes, your kids can make it through life, have a job, have a family, and be respected without having a meaningful spiritual life. They can make it through life all right, but it takes a solid spiritual life to draw out and develop all of their abilities and potential—to give them the tridimensional foundation to be all that God intended them to be.

Time for Personal Evaluation

1. Because of your actions—or lack thereof—about religion, what view of God does your child have?

2. Physical fitness and academic accomplishments are linked. What are some ways you can insure your child stays in good physical health?

3. Zig says good health is simple, not easy. What does he mean by that?

4. Why is a team effort important in the area of a child's physical and spiritual development?

5. How different is the religious training you are giving your children from that which you received from your parents? Why?

CHAPTER 7

For a Child, Love Is Spelled T-I-M-E

Workaholic *or* Peak Performer

> *The workaholic works out of fear*
> *and/or greed and is basically lazy.*
> *Peak performers work out of love.*

Motivational speaker and leadership trainer Sheila Murray Bethel expresses a profound thought in this manner: "Never once have I heard an older person look back on life and say, 'Boy, oh boy! I wish I had spent more time with the corporation!' or, 'If I had it to do over, I would get up even earlier in the morning and go down to the company and really get after my job!' "

This little vignette says it well: a young man was to be sentenced to the penitentiary. The judge had known him from childhood and was well acquainted with his father, a famous legal scholar. "Do you remember your father?" asked the magistrate. "I remember him well, your honor," came the reply. Then, trying to probe the offender's conscience, the judge said, "As you are about to be sentenced and as you think of your wonderful dad, what do you remember most clearly about him?"

There was a pause. Then the judge received an unexpected answer. "I remember when I went to him for advice, he looked at me from the book he was writing and said, 'Run along, boy; I'm busy!' When I went to him for companionship, he turned me away, saying, 'Run along, son; this book must be finished!' Your honor, you remember him as a great lawyer. I remember him as a lost friend.'' The magistrate muttered to himself, ''Alas! Finished the book, but lost the boy!''

In our highly competitive world, the workaholic approach to life seems to be growing in popularity to the detriment of the workaholic's child and mate. Strange as it may sound, the workaholic is lazy. It requires very little effort to continue doing what you are already doing, enjoy doing and are rewarded for doing. On the other hand, it requires considerably more effort and risk to learn how to communicate effectively with your spouse. And it requires considerably more energy for the workaholic to learn to play with, deal with and communicate with a child on his emotional level.

A recent study conducted by Korn Ferry International, a New York-based executive search firm, in conjunction with the U.C.L.A. School of Management on 1,136 vice-presidents with an average income of $215,000 and a record of having changed jobs an average of only twice reveals that these men were peak performers, not workaholics.[1] There is a difference.

A workaholic works primarily out of fear and greed. Those are powerful, but negative emotions. (I hasten to add that there are two groups of peak performers who may appear to be workaholics. I refer to the single mothers who must work overtime or even take second jobs to make ends meet because their husbands abandoned them and provided no child support. They truly are the unsung heroes of our times. Ditto for the fathers who work overtime to take care of the *needs* of their families. The next paragraph explains their motives.)

The peak performer works out of love: love for his job, love for the service he's providing, and most importantly, love for the family he's providing for. Peak performers work slightly more than fifty hours a week, which is a long week, but not nearly as long as a workaholic's week. Seventy-two percent of these peak performers said that when they had extra time, they always spent it with their wives and children.

This brings us to an interesting "fringe" benefit. Evidence is solid that when relationships at home are good and loving, the performer does even better on the job. The personal life just can't be separated from the family life or from the business life. Since 89 percent of these men had two, three, four or more children, 87 percent of them were still married to their first wife, 92 percent were raised in two-parent families and their mothers did not work, it's pretty obvious that you don't "pay the price" to maintain good family relationships, but you "enjoy the benefits" of those relationships. The *total* success of these highly successful executives makes a strong case for the fact that those who make "quality of life" their first priority have a better chance of also enjoying a high standard of living.

The message is clear: The workaholic who is "doing it for the family" should carefully explore his motives to determine if those long hours are helping or hurting him and his family. Chances are good that if he asks his children and his spouse, they will tell him they would prefer dad to designer jeans, that they would rather have his time than an exotic trip every couple of years, that they would prefer his time, love and affection to his store-bought gifts.

Fellow citizens, why do you turn and scrape every stone to gather wealth and take so little care of your children, to whom one day you must relinquish it all?

—Socrates

Change "If Only" To "Next Time"

Looking back, I can tell you the thousands of hours my wife and I invested in our children were not wasted. Most of my other time and energy investments have gone by the board, but the investments of time and energy in my children are now paying dividends of love and enjoyment (and grand-children) beyond my wildest imagination. That's why you'll often hear me say, "You don't 'pay the price,' you enjoy the benefits."

Surely the saddest words in the English language are "if only." The only really bad thing about these words is that they take us back. In looking back, I can tell you the thousands of hours my wife invested in our children and the considerable time I invested in them were not wasted. Our children are worth every moment of it. Should you ask us what we would do differently if we had to start over, here's what I would say: "I would do *more* of the things I did, spend more time with them, have far more family outings and vacations. I'd be a little more firm, a little more demanding, and lots more loving and understanding."

The fortunate thing is that you're in a position to change *if only* to *next time*. Here's what I mean. Don't say, "If only I had known it was important to my son that I attend his basketball game"; or "If only I had known it was that important to see my daughter in the school play, I would have made a special effort to be there." As a positive parent raising positive, drug-free kids, you need to say, "Next time this opportunity presents itself, I'm going to be right there for the special event in my child's life."

It's Not Easy

One thing I have emphasized throughout is that the task of raising positive kids is not easy. It would be much easier to do only what you have to do to coast through life and just "let 'em grow," as millions of parents seem to be doing. However, I can tell you, after seeing the tears of countless heartbroken parents, that the price you pay for not investing the time and for not giving your best shot to raising positive kids is far, far too high. The time-and-energy-investment bargain of all time is that time and effort you give to your kids. Dividends will come your way all your life.

The story is told that Fritz Kreisler, the world-famous violinist, was once approached by an enthusiastic music fan who cried, "Mr. Kreisler, I'd give my life to play as you do!" "Madam," he quietly replied, "I did." I am not suggesting you have to give your life to raise a positive, drug-free child, but I am suggesting that you're going to have to invest many hours and expend lots of energy.

Please understand that there are exceptions to every rule. I have known some parents who did everything right. They are loving, caring, and concerned. They spent a great deal of time with their child. They taught good, sound, moral values and still lost, at least temporarily, the child to drugs, crime, or an immoral life style. By and large, however, the odds improve dramatically on your behalf and on your child's behalf if you will spend a quantity of quality time with your child early in his life.

As a matter of fact, it's fairly safe to say that you will spend time with your children, one way or the other. You will spend time with them when they are toddlers coming along, as you teach them your values and your beliefs, or later in life you will spend time attempting to get them out of the difficulties they got into because somebody else, namely, the world, taught them its values and beliefs.

A Quantity of Quality Time

I'm obviously talking about quality time here, but it is represented by a considerable amount of quantity time. There is no way you can sit down with your child and say, "Okay, now, let's have ten minutes of quality time.'' I vividly remember one Sunday evening after nine o'clock when Tom and I, along with his good friend Sam Wing, were out running. We finished the run, and as we walked past Sam's house and he made his departure, my son said, ''Dad, let's walk.'' He and I walked for an additional ten minutes.

Those ten minutes were among the most meaningful ten minutes I've ever spent with my son. To be honest, I've forgotten what we talked about, but I vividly remember that I've never felt any closer to him. However, those ten minutes would probably have not been so important had he and I not spent some time together before then. We'd been in Sunday school and church together; we'd been to lunch together; we'd been together the entire afternoon; we'd had dinner together; and we'd run together. We were totally relaxed, at ease, and were communicating—and that's what made those ten minutes possible and so beautiful.

The question of quality time is one that has been kicked around for several years. Initially it was, in my opinion, a term invented by the ''experts'' and used by many parents as well as husbands and wives as a cop-out. They justified their lack of time with their children or mate by using the phrase as a catchall, as an excuse for the limited time they spent with their loved ones.

Quality family time is tremendously important. For example, it could be a planned visit with close friends or relatives. It could mean a leisurely but informative afternoon at the zoo or the museum. It could mean a family picnic where all members of the family participate in preparing the food, choosing the location, and planning the activities for both before and after the meal. It could be a trip to a nearby historical site or a walk in the park or neighborhood.

Seldom, however, is quality time significant if it is time dutifully set aside so that you can spend an hour with your mate or your child with the attitude, ''Now let's have this quality time together—what do you want to talk about?'' On the other hand, if it is a time when you plan to be at home together, visiting, cooking out on the grill, or doing something else planned or spontaneous, it can be a meaningful event.

One of the quality-time events at our house for a number of years has been to have all our daughters and their husbands, along with the grandchildren, come to the house on Christmas Eve. All of us spend the night together and then celebrate Christmas morning together the next day. It is truly one of the highlights of the year.

The Early Years Are So Important

One of the most important decisions a couple ever makes is to bring a new life, through the grace of God, into this world. With all the problems we face in society—child abuse, violence, crime—and with all the difficulties of daily life, it is not a decision to be taken lightly.

Once the decision is made to have a child, then other issues must be considered. What are your plans for raising the child? Does the mother plan to go back to work if she is currently employed? Does she plan to stay at home for six weeks, six months, one year, two years? In many situations that decision is dictated by the financial necessities of life, but on this score, I would like to advance several thoughts. Think about what is best for the baby. Let's say you decide it would be best for the baby if the mother stays home. But this decision conflicts with your concern that one paycheck won't meet the family's needs. At this point you need to weigh several factors to make *certain* that it's in the family's best financial interests for the mother to work outside the home. An excellent place to start this evaluation is with other mothers, both those who work outside the home and those who don't.

Many families find that if only one member of the family works, they can eliminate one of the cars and save a phenomenal amount of money in the process. You must also consider parking fees, gasoline, car payments, depreciation, insurance, repairs, taxes, emergencies, toll fees, and other car-related expenses. Don't overlook the cost of additional clothing to weatherproof your baby, or of extra diapers, powders, and other items required in day care. Generally speaking, medical bills are higher because of the environment in which the baby is kept, the weather conditions under which he or she is transported from home to day care, the changes in temperature, etc.

> The saddest words
> in the
> English language
> are if only.

To these figures you must add a considerable amount of money for the clothes the mother has to buy and keep clean and repaired. Now, throw in the contributions for office parties, for birthday, wedding, retirement, Christmas, and shower gifts, along with the boss's pet community project, and you're talking about some real dollars. When you consider the fact that a second income puts your family in a higher income tax bracket and possibly necessitates another car, you need a pretty healthy income to reach the break-even point. So, is it worth it?

You need to evaluate the fact that the energy level of the working mother has its limits. She can't be a supermother, a superemployee, *and* a superwife. Somewhere along the line compromises will be made which will affect her relationship with the baby and with her spouse. Consequently the lifestyle of the baby will be affected.

There will be far more occasions when you'll end up stopping at a fast-food place on the way home because it's convenient not to have to cook after a hard day at work. The cost of that extra meal must be figured in your overall budget, and, remember, there will be a difference in the nutritional value of the meal prepared at home compared to that of the fast-food meal.

Obviously there are many factors to consider, but on average, if you can get moderately priced day care for your child, you must still earn approximately $5.60 per hour in order for working outside the home to reap financial benefits.[2] However, you may want to consider the fact that you and your child might be better off if you can only provide everything your child needs and not necessarily everything your child wants.

For example, it took 10,000 families in which the father was a skilled craftsman, 5,000 families in which the father was a lawyer, and 2,500 families in which the father was a dentist, but only seven Christian missionary families to produce a listee in *Who's Who*.[3] Of course these missionary families were short on material possessions, but long on love, faith, direction, discipline, sacrifice and togetherness. The kids got along without a lot of "things" because two of the "things" they did have were parents. Sadly, the kids who are given all kinds of "things" often end up with few "things" as adults. Of the 75,000,000 "baby boomers" (born between 1946 and 1964), the majority can barely pay their bills on time and 40 percent of them earn less than $10,000 annually.[4]

The financial advantages the family gains when the mother goes to work at anything less than an executive position are questionable at best, but in the vast majority of cases, the advantages of mom's staying home with the baby are beyond question.

The mother's impact is evidenced from the very beginning. For example, Marshall Klaus and John Kennell of Case Western Reserve School of Medicine in Cleveland have demonstrated that mothers who are allowed an hour with their infants immediately following birth, in addition to five hours in each of the next three days, behave differently from other mothers denied the same amount of time with their new-borns. Intrigued with Klaus and Kennell's findings, other researchers extended their studies and found that *increased contact between a mother and her healthy, full-term infant in the first few days and weeks after birth is associated with fewer instances of later child abuse*. Increased contact also correlates with less infant crying, more rapid infant growth, and increased affection and more self-confidence on the part of the mother.

By the same token, the mother who immediately goes back to work after the birth of her child experiences a considerable amount of separation and does not establish the same degree of bonding with her child.

Some Other Considerations

Author Marion Taylor approaches the issue by asking some probing questions:

1. Can the mother be certain the person (or persons) caring for her child is emotionally stable? In day-care centers the emphasis must of necessity be custodial and disciplined. Will the discipline coincide with yours? If you must work, leaving a child with one person is less harmful. Or, a part-time job for the mother would be preferable, of course.
2. What about the much-talked-about quality versus quantity time a mother gives her child? Does a child decide to need the mother only during that "quality" time on Saturdays and Sundays or in the evening hours (when multitudinous chores scream to be done and you're tired)? Will this be the time a first step will be taken, words and concepts learned, or can a child choose this time to be ill?
3. Can a mother decide what time of day "teachable situations" will occur? ("Mommy, who made me?" "Why does it get dark?" "Why did Grandmother die? Where did she go?") Would these questions be answered the

way you would? Will your child learn impatience, revenge, nonforgiveness, selfishness, frustrations from someone else? I recognize a child may certainly learn positive qualities from others, too; but how will you know? And, I don't mean to imply that stay-at-home mothers are never irritable or unfair to their children. I *do* believe a godly mother's responses will be far more beneficial as input to a child's *spongelike mind*. (Emphasis this author's.)

This is especially true in the teaching of moral values, which you can't transfer to a child in the same way you pass a glass of milk to him. You must teach them from birth, or the child will not have them. And they can't be taught in a few easy lessons. *It takes time—lots of time*—and no teacher in any school, no matter how talented, can fully compensate or make up for the several years of time neglect by the mother.

After School Time

As the children get older and begin school, they have a real need to relax in the protection of a grown-up who has always been their refuge, when they come home in the afternoon after six or seven hours of social combat. Conversation somehow flows more freely; both joys and disappointments are nearer to the surface. "You can't expect a child to go home by himself for several hours every day and not feel abandoned and frightened," says John Yunker, director of guidance services in a suburban school district outside St. Louis. "They suffer from a lack of adult contact and a lack of security."[5]

The hazards are not only internal—loneliness, boredom, and fear—but practical as well. One out of six calls to the New York Fire Department involves children alone at home. As the kids reach adolescence, surveys show that the backseat of a car is no longer the prime site for teen intimacy. It's the girl's home when parents are away. The dramatic increase in abortions, teenage pregnancies, illegitimate births, and venereal disease provides irrefutable proof that "opportunity creates the activity." The physical presence of mom at home could well prevent the incalculable tragedies that occur when teenagers *and* preteenagers become sexually active.

> No human being
> can be all things
> to all people.

For the mother who can and does stay home, one advantage is that she has a chance to keep the home in a neat, orderly way. An orderly house clearly establishes, in the child's mind, that he lives in an orderly world. A sloppy house leads to sloppy thinking on the child's part. At the same time, with mom at home, when dad needs to take care of household chores such as simple repairs or heavy yard work, he can handle those without any unreasonable demands on his time and still be able to spend time with the child. This gives the child a feeling of security, knowing that mom is keeping things neat and dad is keeping them in repair. The child can identify the ideal roles mom and dad have in the home.

Despite the many problems associated with working mothers, they are still joining the work force. One reason is there are more divorces that result in more households led by single parents. Second, the need in some homes for two incomes has risen in recent years as inflation has sucked up more family dollars and government has handed out less. Fifteen percent of all Americans are now officially classified as "poor." Third is desire. These mothers work outside the home not because they must, but because they wish to. *This*

group now runs as high as 67 percent of the total, says poll-
ster Daniel Yankelovich.[6]

"In the past it was mainly blue-collar women who worked
for pay," he continues. "Now it is the better-educated,
upper-middle-class women who increasingly work outside
the home." A corollary finding is that 66 percent of those
polled feel "parents should be free to live their own lives
even if it means spending less time with their children."[7]

Now for Some Good News

Though the trend is hardly noticed, the back-to-home movement among working mothers is definitely on the increase.
Houston Post columnist Kate Thomas points out that while
the employment trends of the past fifteen years haven't been
reversed, this emerging pattern does pose broad implications
for the future, whether you happen to be an employer, a
member of the two-paycheck family, or a youngster seeking
your first job.[8]

She notes that while it's true there are more working mothers with children under six than ever before, for the past five
years there has been a steady decline in the number of mothers with children this age who enter the work force each year.
Government figures indicate 55 percent of the women who
gave birth in 1982 did not re-enter the labor force, even after
a full year of mothering.

There are many possible reasons for this, but evidence is
increasing that *the ideal of the superwoman is seen strictly
on television and nowhere else*. The woman who has the
energy to arise early in the morning to care for her family's
needs, rush madly to the business community and work for
her employer for a full eight-hour day, dash home and prepare dinner, get the children ready for bed, and then entertain
her husband is purely a figment of some press agent's over-
active imagination. *No human being can be all things to all
people.*

A second possible reason is the realization on everyone's part that the job of mother and housewife is an extremely important one and that the very future of our country depends on how well that job is done. *Statistical data is overwhelmingly convincing as to the advantages of the mother being at home.* Among other things, according to the Department of Education, children are more likely to drop out of high school if their mothers work outside the home.[9]

Alan Ginsberg, director of planning and analysis for the Department of Education, discovered in a study that *children whose mothers work outside the home tend to do worse in school than do kids of stay-at-home mothers.* He cited a study showing that a working mother spends only about eleven minutes on a weekday in educational pursuits with her child and only twenty-three minutes per day over the weekend on such activities. Tragically, according to the study, the fathers in these dual-income families do nothing to take up the slack.

Yet another study involving 2,400 fifth graders revealed that the *one thing that upset the children the most was spending too little time with their parents.*

Dr. Armand Nicholi, psychiatrist at Harvard Medical School and Massachusetts General Hospital, says that even when parent-child separation occurs for valid reasons in a loving home, the child frequently interprets parental departure as evidence of rejection. And rejection almost inevitably produces a variety of harmful emotions, from deep-seated anger to feelings of worthlessness.

He says that *an overcommitted life-style that makes parents inaccessible to their children produces much the same effect as separation itself.* Herein lies our most serious failing as mothers and fathers. Cross-cultural studies make it clear that parents in the United States spend less time with their children than in almost any nation of the world, including the Soviet Union.

No wonder our kids are more and more turning to drugs, sex, rebellion and, tragically, suicide—particularly since spending too little time with their parents is their number one concern.

Kids Without Timely Direction Equal Problems

The benefit to the child of living in a two-parent family is well documented; but as a reminder, children of divorce are more likely to abuse alcohol and drugs, commit suicide or crimes, be depressed, and fail in school. Since crimes such as murder, rape, and robbery committed by children increased by 11,000 percent from 1950 to 1979 and half the burglars arrested in America are under eighteen, the need for full-time mothers becomes more obvious.[10] In the last fifteen years the arrest of youngsters for use of or trafficking in drugs rose 4,600 percent, and venereal disease among adolescents now accounts for one-fourth of all cases reported.

Getting to Know Your Kids

One of the real joys of my life has been spending time with my children. Admittedly, I have had more time with my son, since my work schedule was a little less hectic and our family situation a little less involved when he came along. I might explain that he followed our youngest daughter by ten years. Instead of having three relatively young ones in the house, we only had one, so things were not quite as rushed as they had previously been.

Even with our daughters, however, I had the privilege of spending considerable time with them. When they came along, I was in the cookware business; and as each daughter got to be about five or six years old, I occasionally took them on trips with me when I was working with some of the managers in my organization.

During those long road trips, we had a chance to do a lot of talking. The purpose of all of this was for them to get to

know the men and women with whom their daddy was working and to learn exactly what their daddy did to earn a living.
They also came to know their father as a person.

Obviously, my wife, "the Redhead," spent the vast majority of time with them, and I'm grateful that she was able
to be there throughout our children's infancy and adolescence. I believe the close ties she and I established during
those formative years with our children are the reason we're
so close as a family today. As a matter of fact, each of our
daughters, as well as their husbands, has a key to our home,
and they come and go as they wish.

In the case of our son who is also married and working
part-time while preparing for a shot at the P.G.A. golf tour,
I did have that additional time. When we first moved to Dallas, he was only three-and-a-half years old, and we had a
chance to be together often. There were some woods behind
the house, and from one to three times each week, he and I
would go exploring down the creek through those woods.
We always went to the same area, always saw virtually the
same thing, always ended up under the same old oak tree
where we would sit and talk, sometimes for five minutes and
sometimes for as much as an hour. He still fondly remembers
the day we were walking along the creek bed and saw a
mother raccoon and three baby raccoons. The prime message in much of this is to communicate the importance of
placing the family at the top of the priority list instead of
mixing it in with a thousand and one other things it would
be nice to do.

What Are Your Priorities?

Larry and Donna Lynn Poland, in an article in *Worldwide
Challenge*, pointed out an important fundamental for a successful family: make your family a priority. Unfortunately,
too many parents seem to communicate the idea that they

can build a family on a catch-as-catch-can basis in their spare time.

Priorities are extremely important. When you look at what your priorities are, it will be relatively easy to see what's important in your life by simply checking the amount of time you spend doing each thing. The parent who watches several hours of television a day but doesn't have time to take the child to the soccer match clearly communicates to the child that watching television is a much higher priority than spending time with him, watching him grow and develop.

The father who spends ten hours a week on the golf course but doesn't have time to take his family to dinner is clearly communicating what his priorities are and where his family ranks on the totem pole of importance. The father who buys expensive sports equipment and has time to go hunting and fishing but does not have time to take his children to Sunday school and church, because it's the "only day I have for myself," is clearly saying that the importance of teaching spiritual values and honoring God is a distant second to his own personal indulgences.

On the investment of our time in our children, Donna Lynn Poland observed that one week she counted thirty hours she spent helping with school projects. Would television have been a better use of time? Garden club? Volunteer work? Part-time employment? No. Her children were higher priorities. Making the family a top priority will invariably bring success. Making it a medium priority will bring a mixture of success and failure. Making it no priority will bring failure, disgrace, and God's judgment. The choice is ours.

The Polands identified another fundamental: "Plan your character-building and stick to the plan." Aiming at nothing will guarantee the direct hit. Take aim at the character weaknesses of your children. Drafting a plan to deal with them constructively, and sticking to the plan, is the only way to success.

Hurray For Stay-At-Home Mothers

For those mothers who are sometimes looked down upon because they have chosen to stay home and raise their babies, I love what Linda Burton, a mother of two, says when her working friends tell her that "her mind is too good to stay at home": "I decided my mind was too good *not* to stay home with my children. The best minds are required there." I'll second that and add that the most important, demanding, and rewarding career a mother can have is to raise positive, drug-free kids in a negative world.

Ruth Hampton clearly expressed the importance of the wife and mother's role when she said, "The most influential position in the nation today is held by a woman. She enforces law, practices medicine and teaches—without degree, certificate of competence or required training. She handles the nation's food, administers its drugs and practices emergency first aid. She cares for all the physical and mental ills of the family. A man literally places his life and the lives of his children in the hands of this woman— his wife."[11]

With tongue slightly in cheek the wife of one well-known Christian leader, when asked, "What do you do?" responded, "I am socializing two homo sapiens into the dominant values of the Judeo-Christian tradition in order that they might be instruments for the transformation of the social order into the kinds of eschatological utopia that God willed from the beginning of creation. What do you do?"

Realistically, while mom is raising those positive kids, she also needs to prepare for the day when the kids are grown or for the day when the family may be dissolved through death or divorce. As an insurance policy for your own future, you can take correspondence courses or enroll in one of the community colleges or universities for one or two evenings a week.

Spending your evenings in a stimulating environment

keeps your mind and personality tuned in to an adult world. It makes you a far more engaging conversationalist and companion for your husband and helps you maintain your excitement as a mother. (A significant fringe benefit is the opportunity your husband will have to get better acquainted with his children as he meets their needs and demands. Chances are excellent that he will stop asking what you've been doing all day after he looks after the kids in your absence on a steady basis!)

To further encourage you to take that additional educational step, let me point out that the overwhelming majority of people who go back to school do *considerably* better academically than they did in school the first time around. One hundred percent of the people I personally know do much better the second time around.

To accomplish this additional educational objective, you need to establish a disciplined course of study that requires some concentrated effort on a daily basis, but always with the knowledge that in the event of a family emergency you're not fighting a life-or-death time schedule to complete the course(s). If it takes you four years to finish a three-year program, your number one priority is still to be the best mother and wife possible. (But don't use this as an excuse to wait until "tomorrow" to get started!)

And Hurray For Mothers Who Must Work

For those mothers who must work because you are single or because your husband's income simply will not adequately provide for the family, I have the greatest admiration and respect for the effective way the vast majority of you are handling your responsibilities. In most cases it is far better to work and teach your kids from the beginning that "there ain't no free lunch" than it is to go on welfare and let your kids think that the world will provide a living for them.

In order to keep matters in proper perspective, I also need to stress that absentee or uninvolved fathers represent a far greater threat to the family than does the working mother who usually suffers from responsibility overload.

For those mothers who need a small income but who do not have to work every day, an increasingly popular job-sharing approach might be the ideal solution. *U.S. News & World Report* points out that 16 percent of American companies offer "formal" job-sharing opportunities and others are flexible to the arrangement when presented with a well thought-out plan.[12]

Author John Grossman points to some interesting data. For several years, the Rolscreen Company in Pella, Iowa has had such an arrangement. It was started at the request of Joan Waits, who had worked there for ten years and needed to continue work but not necessarily full-time. She approached the company about having someone else alternate days with her on a veneer-splicing machine. The company agreed, and she recruited her sister-in-law. For the past four years, the two have successfully alternated work days. The benefits to each employee are the opportunities to spend time with their families and to pick up additional income. The advantage to the company is they do not have to pay fringe benefits; and for the short period of time each woman works, the productivity is higher. Thus everyone benefits.

Rolscreen has forty-three such teams working together—thirty-eight in the plant and five in the office. A big plus has been the drop in absenteeism. Since the job-sharers have alternate days off, they can schedule doctor and dental visits, home repair calls, trips to the beauty shop, and any number of other things to handle on days off. Also, built into most job-sharing arrangements is the understanding that should the scheduled member of the team fall ill, the other will pinch-hit. At Rolscreen the absentee rate for full-time employees is about 6 to 7 percent. It is less than .5 percent for the job sharers.

Mel Petersma, the personnel director, points out that "although it's hard to measure, our supervisors report better productivity. On the days they report, job-sharers are full of fire and vigor. They give you full measure." (I might insert here that I'll bet they are also full of love and enthusiasm for their families on the days they are home.)

Similar results are reported at Walgreen's at the company's corporate headquarters outside Chicago.

Some companies engaged in job-sharing say the arrangement gives an edge to recruiting, especially with young career women looking ahead to when they will start families; but the most often cited advantage of job-sharing is that it enables the employers to hold onto experienced employees.

One parent who is particularly thankful for a job-sharing opening is Nancy Handa, a personnel policy and research specialist with Levi Strauss and Company in San Francisco. For her, returning to work full-time after a five-month maternity leave proved far from ideal. "I found that when I was at work my mind was at home, and when I was at home, my mind was at work," she says, "plus all the running around   I had to get up earlier, get Kurtis to the baby-sitter. I was always running late. When I finally did get to work, I had to take a deep breath just to calm down. After work, I would pick up the baby, feed him, put him to bed. Then my husband and I would have dinner and clean the house and get ready for the next day. When the weekend came, I was exhausted."[13] By working only half the week Handa relieved the time pressures and reaped other benefits.

The job that offers the most opportunity and flexibility lies in the world of sales. Many fine companies will permit you to work as many—or as few—hours as you wish. You can also choose the days of the week and the time of day or night that fits your family schedule best. *No*, you don't have to be a "natural-born" salesperson. Yes, the good companies have excellent training programs. No, it's not easy, but the overall rewards *can* be substantial. Caution: Be careful about inventory investments until after you have demonstrated that you can sell and that you like the business. Incidentally, if inventory investment is required, the dependable companies will give you a guaranteed repurchase plan.

I mention these various activities and possibilities, because in some areas, jobs might not be readily available. In cases like these, young mothers can jointly apply for a job. In a retail store, which generally is open six days, each one could work three days; or because of the difference in the husband's hours, one might work in the morning and the other in the afternoon. If the husband has a job in law enforcement, with the fire department, or as a truck driver, the wife's schedule of working three consecutive days with the other person working three days would work out well. A little imagination should enable the mother who must have a few extra dollars in income to get a job and still maintain far more hours with her family without becoming physically and emotionally exhausted.

Balancing The Scales

The question comes up for those women who just plain do not want to be stay-at-home mothers. There are those individuals who are unhappy outside the job market. Quite frankly, research indicates that if they hate staying at home with their babies, they're not going to be effective mothers. As a matter of fact, if after giving it an honest try, they find themselves growing increasingly restless, irritable, and less loving and attentive to their babies, they should probably go back to work.

There are also many cases in which the children are better off if they spend a portion of each day in the care of another loving, responsible adult, such as a family member, trusted neighbor, or carefully selected day-care center (yes, there are some good ones). In some cases the child has a chance to grow socially and scholastically under the right conditions under other adults.

But whether the mother stays at home with her child or goes to work, she is in the best position to know what is best for her child. In today's topsy-turvy world, she needs all the help, support and encouragement she can get.

Countless mothers, many of whom are single, work full-time and still do a beautiful job of raising positive, drug-free kids. The job many working mothers have done under the circumstances—which are often extremely difficult is amazing. They are proof positive that if a job is important enough (and raising positive kids certainly is), a loving, committed person will find or create a way to get the job done.

I make that last statement with considerable conviction because my mother and my wife's mother were both single parents. My dad died in the heart of the Depression with eight children at home; six were too young to work. Mother managed by having a large garden and five milk cows. We didn't have much cash, but we had milk and butter and plenty of fresh vegetables and peaches. By canning our vegetables and peaches in the summer and selling the surplus vegetables and dairy products we managed to survive the winter months.

My wife's dad also died during the Depression and left four small children. Mrs. Abernathy took the small insurance policy, converted the lump sum into a monthly endowment, and sold her car for living expenses. By careful budgeting she provided her children with everything they needed, including lots of time and love. Needless to say, I believe our mothers were successful in their prime roles of raising children. I also believe that many single mothers working today are amazingly successful in raising their kids under far more difficult circumstances than those which confronted my mother and my wife's mother.

Yes, time with our kids is crucial. This song, "Cat's in the Cradle,"* by Harry Chapin says it better than anything I've ever seen. I urge you to slow down, read it carefully, and then put this book down and think about the message.

Cat's in the Cradle
by Harry Chapin

My child arrived just the other day;
he came to the world in the usual way.
But there were planes to catch and bills to pay;
he learned to walk while I was away.
And he was talkin' 'fore I knew it,
and as he grew he'd say,
I'm gonna be like you, Dad,
you know I'm gonna be like you.

And the cat's in the cradle and the silver spoon,
    little boy blue and the man in the moon.
"When you comin' home Dad?" "I don't know when,
    but we'll get together then;
you know we'll have a good time then."

My son turned ten just the other day;
he said, "Thanks for the ball, Dad,
come on let's play.
Can you teach me to throw?"
I said, "Not today,
I got a lot to do."
He said, "That's okay."
And he walked away,
but his smile never dimmed,

*Copyright © 1974 Story Songs Ltd.

it said, "I'm gonna be like him, yeah,
you know I'm gonna be like him."

And the cat's in the cradle and the silver spoon,
   little boy blue and the man in the moon.
"When you comin' home Dad?" "I don't know when,
   but we'll get together then;
you know we'll have a good time then."

Well, he came from college just the other day;
so much like a man I just had to say,
"Son, I'm proud of you, can you sit for awhile?"
He shook his head and he said with a smile,
"What I'd really like, Dad, is to borrow the car keys;
see you later, can I have them please?"

And the cat's in the cradle and the silver spoon,
   little boy blue and the man in the moon.
"When you comin' home Son?" "I don't know when,
   but we'll get together then;
you know we'll have a good time then."

I've long since retired, my son's moved away;
I called him up just the other day.
I said, "I'd like to see you if you don't mind."
He said, "I'd love to, Dad, if I can find the time.
You see, my new job's a hassle and the kids have the flu,
but it's sure nice talkin' to you, Dad,
it's been sure nice talkin' to you."
And as I hung up the phone, it occurred to me,
he'd grown up just like me;
my boy was just like me.

And the cat's in the cradle and the silver spoon,
   little boy blue and the man in the moon.
"When you comin' home Dad?" "I don't know when,
   but we'll get together then, Dad,
we're gonna have a good time then."

Time for Personal Evaluation

1. In changing ''if only'' to ''next time,'' fill in the blanks with what you will do. If only I hadn't _____, next time I will _____.

2. In your estimation, how important is it for a young child to have a stay-at-home mother? Summarize what Zig has to say.

3. If making your family a priority is what you desire, and if this means that some things have to change, what are they?

4. What advantages do career mothers have? Are there any disadvantages?

5. Do you understand what a job-sharing approach is? Can it help you? How?

6. Dad, Harry Chapin's song is potent. What response do you have to it?

CHAPTER 8

Raising Positive Kids
Is a Team Effort

> *The most important thing a father can do for his children is to love their mother, and the most important thing a mother can do for her children is to love their father.*

Parental Authority

Much of the music our kids listen to deals with their right "to be free" and "to do their own thing." In response to this, parents should remember that you can take the train off the tracks and it's "free," but it can't go anywhere. Take the steering wheel out of the car and it's under the direction and control of no one, but it can't go anywhere. As individuals we're not going anywhere, either, unless we maintain control and direction.

Though kids might say they want to be free, evidence is solid that what they really want and need is security. An ever-increasing number of depressed children have been given a tremendous amount of freedom.[1] Clinical psychologist Dr. Martin Cohen says this security is provided by parental authority and that it's scary for kids when they're not experiencing it. He says that a kid may press his parents harder and harder until they finally have to stop him.

What he's really doing is asking his parents to behave as parents. The child is checking to see if that strength he's always depended on is still there. He's just taking a peek to be sure he wasn't mistaken about his source of security. And parents, you can't disappoint him—you have to remain firm in your place as parents.

Authority, according to the dictionary, is "the power or right to give commands, enforce obedience, take action or make final decisions." One thing kids need—and even demand—is the right to experience the disciplining pressure of parental authority, which keeps them headed in the right direction.

When we deal with our children, we must remember that they *are* children. An old African proverb goes like this: Everybody's been young before, but not everybody has been old before. One of a child's most critical needs is having parents who understand their authoritative place in the dynamic plan for the family. It is to be an example, to lead, guide, direct, correct, and encourage.

Sometimes when our kids give us trouble and reject our authority, we often wonder just what's going on. Remember that though kids will often try us, deep down they want us to win and maintain our place of authority so their security will be complete.

Kids want to know that someone's in charge—they want to know who to follow, who's going to lead, and to whom they must answer. It's a basic fact of life. It's something that's a part of every social unit, including the family. And it's something that parents are going to have to grasp if their parenting is going to be a success and, as a result, their kids successful.

Mothers and Daddies Are Special

Recently I saw a thought-provoking bumper sticker: "Anybody can be a father, but it takes someone special to be a daddy." That's right, and anyone can have a baby, but it takes someone special to be a mother.

When you study some of the great, positive, history-making figures, you will often find they speak of the influence of a parent. Abraham Lincoln is quoted as saying, "All that I am I owe to my angel mother." General Douglas MacArthur said, "My sainted mother taught me devotion to God and a love of country which have ever sustained me. To her I yield anew a son's reverent thanks." The great preacher G. Campbell Morgan had four sons. They all became ministers. At a family reunion a friend asked one of the sons, "Which Morgan is the greatest preacher?" His eyes beaming with delight, the son looked over to his father and said, "Why, it's Mother!"

Likewise, there is an old saying that goes like this: One father is worth a hundred schoolmasters. It's true that in the hands of parents are the destinies of their children. In that sense, being a parent is really a sacred thing. Committed into the hands of parents is the future of entire nations in that our future resides with our kids and the world they will build. The humbling thing is that the model for the world our kids will build, their vision for tomorrow, largely depends on how they see us as parents and how we raise them today. What an awesome responsibility!

You are a parent only when you provide for and prepare your child to be ready for life.[2]

—Jay Strack

The very fact of who parents are in the structure of the family gives them authoritative power. That power can be used in a positive way to convince kids to make the effort, to win, to succeed, to respect their fellow man, and to be people of honesty and integrity. Parents can choose that route, or they can choose to leave their kids to themselves and the influences of a negative world.

It Takes Teamwork and Team Leadership

Raising positive kids is best done as a team effort, and since the family is truly a unit, it functions more effectively as a team. Families working together can accomplish more than they can as individuals. When you have a family project and family goals that everyone has chosen (whether it's scheduling a family vacation, conducting study courses, planning a picnic, or building a swimming pool), the results will be better. And working together on projects brings the family closer together. Fortunately, working together as a family helps the kids develop communicative and cooperative skills that can be taken directly into the school and business community.

Most people agree that any team must have a captain, a leader, a commander in chief. A football team without a quarterback would not be a team—it would be a disaster. A business without a board chairman or an army without an officer in charge would be inept and would quickly disintegrate. The same situation exists in the family. The family needs a leader, because while it is far *more* than a business, it *is* a business.

With the expected rate of inflation, if husband and wife raise two children and stay together until they're sixty-five years old, they will have invested well over $1 million in raising the kids and providing for their own needs. That's pretty big business.

In the regular business community, the corporate structure has, in most cases, a board chairman, president, vice president, treasurer, and secretary; but as President Harry Truman said, "The buck has to stop somewhere." In the corporate world, that's easy—it's the person in charge. In the family, it's not quite as easy, but it's just as clear *and* just as important. Using the Scriptures and several thousand years of history as the authority, I believe the individual who should be the chairman of the board of the family is the man, the husband, the father.

There are several reasons I say this, but one significant reason is that our society is organized that way. That's not to say that the wife (the corporate vice president) has little to say about decisions affecting the family. She's the second in command (*not* second in importance), and very important in the effective working of the family as a unit. Any chief executive officer worth his salt is going to hold conferences regularly with the second in command concerning significant decisions. Additionally, it is critically important that the second in command have full authority when the board chairman is gone.

Leadership Needed

Even a two-car parade gets fouled up if you don't decide ahead of time who's going to lead. With this in mind, you'll understand what I mean when I say kids need to understand that if they are going to be led, they need to know who will be leading and what it means to follow.

Author Helen Andelin brings another significant factor into focus when she points out that male leadership also conforms to psychological law. The male has within his makeup the necessary qualities to lead, in that he is more aggressive, decisive, and dominating than the normal female. In the normal male the desire to lead is strong—he will cringe when his position is threatened. When robbed of it altogether, he will feel emasculated.

She elaborates by saying that "Male leadership does not

suggest a dominating, high-handed action, based on selfish motives. To be successful in the family the father must have the welfare of each family member at heart and his decisions and plans must be based upon what is best for them. He carefully considers their viewpoint and feelings, especially those of his wife. They try to work things out together. When there are those unresolved differences and the wife cannot support her husband's plans, she can at least support his right of leadership.''[3]

Chain of Command Clearly Defined

Yes, a clearly established chain of command in our homes, as we have in *all* other *successful* businesses and institutions, is important. On occasion I've had people ask the question, ''Suppose the wife is smarter than the husband?'' That still doesn't alter the chain of command. In my own family I'm extremely fortunate in that I have a wife who in many ways has insights and wisdom I do not have. Her I.Q. is at least as high as mine, and her grades were certainly better in school. However, when important decisions are to be made in our family, and the Redhead and I, after a thorough discussion, disagree (a truly *rare* event) as to which route to take, she has the complete assurance that she is never going to be burdened with making the decision.

Naturally, I prayerfully ask for guidance before making any decision of any significance.

That Makes Sense

I remember an occasion in Rochester, New York, when I spoke at a large high school. After addressing the assembly, I was invited to talk with the student leaders. About twenty of the top students were present for the question-and-answer session. It was interesting, lively, and informative.

I'll never forget one young man who said to me, ''You

seem to put a lot of reliance on God in your life, in your family, and in your business. I don't believe in God, and I'm puzzled as to why you put so much emphasis on it.''

I responded that one of the reasons I did was because I wanted to have my children be as responsible as possible, and I understood the importance of authority.

He quite naturally asked, ''Well, what does God have to do with that?''

I said, ''It's simple. When my children see me bow in obedience to a Higher Authority, they instantly recognize my respect for authority. And that's not only the authority of God, but the authority of government, law enforcement officials, my employer, judges, the courts. When my children see that I respect authority, they know I am not being hypocritical when I insist that they respect my authority over them. The net result is I have better disciplined, more loving, and obedient children.''

The young man was taken aback for a moment, but then he said, ''Well, I still don't believe in God, but what you're saying certainly makes sense.''

> When a parent belittles or attacks any authority such as ''the government,'' his employer, his mate, a minister, policeman, etc., he is undermining his own authority with his children.

As a practical matter, from a numerical point of view, the family is a small unit, so it's vital that every member of the team—including the chief executive officer—forget about his ''title'' when work needs to be done. In a family unit made up of a husband, a wife, and two small children, if the husband acts *only* in the capacity of major decision maker, he will soon lose the love and respect of his wife *and* his children. Realistically, if *four* people *create* work in the home and only a part-time mom *does* the work, an impossible situation exists that is headed for trouble.

The Winning Team—Mom and Dad

The solution to the problem is simple, but far from easy. If the family is going to function as a unit, *both* dad and mom must make contributions that go far beyond bringing in a paycheck. For example, dad can look after the children if mom's skills are greater in the kitchen. He can help them with their homework and talk with them, instead of reading the paper and "relaxing" while an already tired mom prepares dinner. After dinner, mom and dad can work together to clean the kitchen. If the kids go to bed immediately after dinner, then mom and dad can alternate between cleaning the kitchen and getting the kids tucked into bed. When bedtime comes, if the kids are still up, dad can participate in the ritual of getting them ready for bed and tucking them in.

The main point I'm making is that to raise positive kids, if both a dad and a mom are in the home, they should both be involved in *all* aspects of raising the children. That's the *only* way mom, dad, and the kids are *all* going to win.

The One-Parent Family

In a one-parent family, the need for discipline and routine is even more important. The mother (or father) who has to get up early, prepare her children's breakfast, get ready for work, get the children ready to take by the nursery or the baby-sitter, then put in a demanding work day has already had a hectic, ten-hour day. At that point she has to shift gears and pick up the kids on the way home. Then she has to prepare dinner and look after the children, including preparing them for bed, reading bedtime stories, and entertaining them while maintaining a positive mental attitude. The demands are enormous on her physical and emotional resources. The only way for such a parent to survive on a long-term basis is to adopt an organized family life-style where discipline and routine are emphasized.

It is the only way the "must do" things will get done and we'll have time left for the "fun" things which are critical in building permanent, loving relationships between parent and child. This more demanding, organized approach helps assure the survival of the single parent while teaching responsibility, organization, teamwork and a balanced approach to work and play to the child.

When the Team Doesn't Function

In families where mom and dad don't function as a team, it's easy to understand why there is so much difficulty. It's also easier to understand why we see ever-increasing evidences of child neglect and abuse. Further, when dad often takes a spectator's seat in the home, it's also evident why we have more mothers than fathers abandoning their families. They are simply throwing in the towel and walking out on their husbands, their children, and their responsibilities. How tragic and how unfair! How those parents will regret those actions for the rest of their lives. Many a broken family relationship begins with a lack of team effort. I believe thousands of women have left their family responsibilities out of a growing sense of despair at their inability to cope in a situation in which the husband is not pulling his weight at home. Some parents will try to bury the memories of an abandoned family in a passionate romance and a temporarily carefree life-style, but they never quite succeed in doing so. The comfort of those little hands and arms around their necks, those calls of "Mommy" or "Daddy," those expressions of infant, toddler, and childhood delights will have been burned indelibly into their minds and will be part of them forever.

At this point I'd like to interject that as a result of the feminist movement, more and more women, in their demand for their rights, are losing a degree of perspective and balance. In some tragic instances reason, judgment, and love drop out of the picture.

To avoid the temptation of even thinking about dissolving the family through divorce or desertion, dad needs to climb down out of his ivory tower, roll up his sleeves, and do his part. Mom and dad, as a team, need to instruct and encourage the children to pitch in and make their contributions for their own good (preparing them for their own possible future roles as husbands and wives), and for the good of the family.

Every member of the family can and must be taught and required to do a part. Even a four-year-old can pick up toys, clothes, or papers that are lying around on the floor so that mom is relieved of these responsibilities and save an incredible drain on her energy. The beautiful thing is that the parent is giving excellent instructions in discipline and obedience. These are two superb characteristics that can help children build winning lives in their own futures.

This approach will help the child who needs to grow rich in every aspect of life learn that before he can "cash in" on life, he has to "chip in" a little, too. As he chips in as a family member and sees positive results, he'll understand why he has to chip in at school and then chip in in the business world. This approach greatly reduces the possibility of raising negative, overindulged, spoiled kids who have only a cash-in mentality and basically believe they should get all they can, while they can, without effort on their part and regardless of what it may do to other persons.

Another beautiful thing about having family projects and responsibilities with every member of the family involved is that most of us want—and need—to belong to some type of unit. It's natural that kids want to belong—and know they belong.

The wonderful thing about a solid family unit is that it teaches cooperation, mutual respect, and love. The acceptance of your child in your family unit with definite responsibilities makes him feel like an important member of the team. This will substantially reduce his likelihood of joining some other close-knit group, perhaps a neighborhood gang, just so he can "be accepted" and "belong." He doesn't "need" that, since his needs are being met at home.

Kids who are taught to "chip in" at home will "chip in" in the marketplace, which means they will be able to "cash in" on what life has to offer.

Build Respect—It's a Must

To build a relationship of love and respect, you must remember that your children respond to you according to the way they feel about you. If those feelings are ones of love and respect, you will receive obedient, loving responses from the children. However, if there is no respect, you can rest assured the responses will be rebellious and disrespectful. That's why parents should conduct themselves in a manner that creates respect and builds love. There's no real unity without respect.

One thing that destroys respect and the family unit is the incredible habit some husbands and wives have of belittling each other. To call your mate lazy, irresponsible, immoral, dumb, uncaring, etc. makes the child feel terribly insecure because he fears the family might split and somehow he is partially to blame. Name-calling makes the child doubt both parents and wonder just how secure he is with the parent who is drunk, a dope head, stupid, etc., and the other is a critic who foolishly thinks he can build himself up in the child's eyes by tearing his mate down.

The parents who break promises to their kids, scream

and shout at each other in private or in public, come home stumbling drunk, and treat each other with contempt and disrespect will destroy any sense of honor and respect the child might have for them. When that happens, obedience and discipline go out the door. In addition, there will be considerable confusion in the child's mind. He undoubtedly loves you as his parents; but without respect, he can't really like you, so he truly is in an emotional dilemma.

What's the solution? Answer: If the preceding paragraphs describe you in a reasonably accurate manner, the chances are pretty good you need help. Get it. If your emotions are shot, you can often get help through a local mental health association, or in many cities the pastors and ministers in the churches are excellent sources of help. If you have a drinking or drug problem, you need to demonstrate your maturity and your love for your kids by getting help before your behavior moves into serious addiction, alcoholism, or child abuse that ultimately will destroy both you and the kids.

Actually, one of the best sources of help, especially if your problem is not too severe, is in your hands. I encourage you to read, reread, and apply the principles emphasized in this book. I've shared them with thousands of people in seminars and recordings, and I can tell you that in hundreds and hundreds of cases they are working. You've got nothing to lose by giving them an honest shot, and to paraphrase an old commercial, "The family you save will be your own."

Father's and Mother's Work

Raising positive kids is definitely a team effort. It's neither "woman's work" nor "man's work." It's father's and mother's work combined. Many times, however, when husbands and wives both work, far too many men have been conditioned to believe that preparing dinner, cleaning the kitchen, helping the kids with homework, and tucking them into bed are things the wife and mother is supposed to do.

The real problem is brought clearly into focus by Sey Chassler in a January 13, 1985, *Parade* magazine article from which I quote, with permission:

About 20 years ago, my wife and I were having one of those arguments that grows into fury—the kind that leaves a dreadful pain that lasts for years. Suddenly, unable to stand my complaints any longer, my wife threw something at me and said: *"From now on, you do the shopping, plan the meals, take care of the house, everything. I'm through!"*

I was standing in the kitchen looking at the shelves, the sink, the refrigerator, the cleaning utensils. At my wife.

I was terrified. Tears trickled down my face. No matter what, I knew I could not handle the burden she had flung at me. I could not do my job and be responsible for the entire household as well. I had important things to do. Besides, how could I get through a day dealing with personnel, budgets, manuscripts, management, profit-and-loss figures, and, *at the same time*, plan dinner for that night and the next night and breakfasts and lunches and a dinner party on the weekend and shop for it all and make sure the house was in good shape and that the woman who cleaned for us was there and on time and the laundry done and the children taken care of?

How could *any*one do all that and stay sane? Natalie watched me for a while. Finally she said, "O.K. Don't worry. I'll keep on doing it." She put on her coat and went to her hospital office—to manage dozens of people and more than 100 patients.

Despite her simple statement that she would go on taking care of our home and family, I stood a while telling myself that *no one* could do all of that. Slowly I saw that *she* was doing it.

In the days and weeks that followed, I began to realize that most women carry a double burden: an inside job taking care of their homes and families, and an outside job, working for wages. Most men, on the other hand, can come home and do little more about their families than help with household chores and with the children. *Helping is useful, but it is not the same as doing;* it leaves the basic responsibility to someone else. In most homes, it leaves the basic responsibility to women: *All the worries, all the headaches, all the planning, all the management, all the DOING is theirs.* How many men understand this without being shocked into it as I was—or by the loss of a wife? How many of us appreciate how invisible to us women are? How many of us really see women or hear them? How often do we go to bed at night feeling the comfort and love of our wives but knowing them so little that we do not recognize the burden they bear?

Mom and Dad in Agreement

If you remember, I warned you earlier that there were no really easy steps or methods of raising positive kids, but there are many essential ones. And the most critical of all has to be the relationship between mom and dad. If the child grows up seeing mom and dad showing little respect and kindness toward each other and often engaging in verbal—if not physical—conflict, the child slowly but surely sees that marriage is a battleground and that the family is not something to enjoy but something to tolerate—and leave as soon as possible.

This can be compounded, of course, when one of the parents sides with the child against the other parent. As the child grows older, he becomes an expert at manipulating the parents. Each parent then has a tendency to want to win the child's approval; it will be two against one, with both parents making unwise concessions and overtures to the child; and the stage is set for conflict and disaster.

Blueprint for Disaster

When a child goes to one parent with a request that is denied, only to have the other parent grant the request, the results are disastrous. Whether the second parent knew or did not know that parent number one had turned down the request, the results are still bad. When a child approaches one parent and asks for permission to do something, the first question should be, "Have you asked your mom (or dad) about it?" If the answer is no and there's a question or doubt in your mind about the advisability of it, you can say, "We'll talk about it and let you know." If the child has talked to the other parent and the personal safety or the reputation of the child is at stake, both parents should definitely be involved in the decision.

> A strong, unified parental team
> has the best shot at raising
> positive, drug-free
> kids.

I remember one occasion when our son was a junior in high school. He had asked his mom about going with one of his classmates to a Friday night basketball game in a town roughly a hundred miles from Dallas. She told him, "I don't think so, but ask your dad." When he came to me for permission, I said no, and he naturally wanted to know why. I explained that on Friday and Saturday nights one driver out of ten on the road is legally drunk, that the hour at which he would return would be very late, and that I feared they might fall asleep while driving. I further explained that neither he nor his friend had been driving very long and that all of these factors combined indicated to me the dangers were simply too great. My son accepted without argument my explanation of why I did not want him to go.

To this day I believe I saw a half-smile on his face as we terminated the conversation and he gave it that last try, which really wasn't a try, as he said, "So you won't let me go, huh?" And I said, "No, not this time, son. Your day is coming, but not now."

Had circumstances been different, the answer could well have been yes. For example, had his friend's dad been going along to drive, that would have presented an entirely different picture. Had it been a shorter distance and on a night other than Friday, that too, would have made a difference. On that occasion in the Ziglar household, the team concept functioned well.

What can ordinary parents do to have a better chance at raising positive, drug-free kids? There is one sure thing that you can go to the bank on—a strong, unified parental team, which practices loving, mutual respect, has the best shot at positively influencing children.

Time for Personal Evaluation

1. Reflect a moment on at least one time when you, as a child, appreciated your parents. What did they do that was so significant?

2. What are some ways you've earned respect from your children?

3. If you agree that a unified parental team is the best approach to the successful running of a family, how do you

rate you and your spouse in that area? What could you do better?

4. Zig talks about a blueprint for disaster. Can you summarize what he means? Does this happen in your home?

5. When was the last time your family did something as a team? How did it go?

CHAPTER 9

Communicating with Family Members

> *If you start your day lovingly and gently with your child (mate, too) and end the day the same way, you'll eliminate a lot of trouble between the two events.*

Let's Talk about It

In many, many cases marital problems can be solved and serious family breakups averted with kindness and conversation. One member of the family, whether intentionally or not, closes out the other member by not engaging in simple conversation or, probably more often, not listening to what the other person has to say. To raise positive kids, parents must learn to communicate with their children and with each other.

On the surface, this appears to be reasonably simple, but in the rush of things we seem to have time for just about everything except good old-fashioned conversation. I became aware of this problem early in my career because for sixteen years I was in direct sales, which meant that I sold products directly to people in their homes. I have been in thousands of homes, and I have seen children treated in every imaginable way. I've seen families where five-year-olds were in complete control, and I have been in homes where teen-agers were so browbeaten and dominated that they would not even speak or, when addressed, could not or would not even look at you.

Surely one of the saddest and frequent sights was the desperate effort many children made to get attention, only to be completely ignored. I've seen children literally hang onto their mom's or dad's arms two, three, and four minutes at a time, saying, "Mommy, Mommy!" or "Daddy, Daddy!" desperately trying to get just a hint of recognition for a simple need or request.

I've often wondered what happened to those children later in life. I wonder, now that they're grown and possibly have families of their own, if they are now ignoring their own children.

Talking Takes Time

One thing that has become obvious over the years is that the input into a baby's mind, even before birth, is the greatest single influence in the baby's behavior. Tied to this is the knowledge that *conversation* can have a dramatic impact on the success rate of raising happy, well-adjusted children.

In our society today we are in an ever-diminishing conversational environment. Because of the involvement with our own active pursuits, because of radio, stereo, TV, and compact disc players, we find too many people spending too much time inputting mechanical messages into their minds and not nearly enough time exchanging messages with living, loving, caring human beings, notably other family members. When mom and dad are addicted to the television set with an average tuned-in time of over seven hours per day and to that are added hours for sleeping, working, and eating, almost no time is left for talking.

IT'S TRUE

Two-bathroom homes eliminated cooperation, television eliminated conversation and the second car eliminated association.

There is no way I can oversell the importance of husbands and wives talking to each other. The number one complaint the average housewife has is that her husband deals only in facts and figures and communicates only the barest amount of information. There are many opportunities, even when both husbands and wives work, for them to engage in small talk, which is so important to the health of the relationship and extremely important to the growth and stability of the child.

The evening paper, the nightly news, the daily or nightly soap opera—you name it. None of them holds a candle to the importance of the husband and wife communicating with each other, especially in the presence of the child. When that child hears the happy, informed, loving chatter of husband and wife, he has a sense of security. He feels he is part of a caring family.

From the moment of birth, the baby needs to be talked to. As a matter of fact, evidence is overwhelming that the more the newborn baby is held, sung to, talked to, hummed to, the more emotionally stable and intelligent the baby is going to be.

If you have babies in your home, remember to avoid the major problem many parents fall into—continuing the baby talk too long. Actually, the most appropriate time for baby talk is when you are holding, hugging, or kissing the baby or toddler. When the child is at arm's length or across the room and you are chatting with him, you need to chat with him in pretty much the same way you visit with older children. Talk a little more slowly, distinctly, and lovingly, but use more than just one-syllable words. The baby or toddler can understand infinitely more than he communicates to you.

In my own family, we are fascinated by our grandchildren's growth. One of the reasons for their vocabulary development is that their parents and grandparents talked to the kids in an adult manner. The children's vocabularies, even at ages six and nine, are amazing.

Handling Persistent Four Year Olds

Another problem in the "talking arena" is what to do when a persistent four-year-old keeps pulling on your arms and saying "Mommy, Mommy!" Psychologist James Dobson says you permit your child to interrupt you for brief, thirty-second episodes, during which personal consultation, comfort, information, and enthusiasm are exchanged. In most cases, the child is happy, at least for a few minutes.

You must remember that a child is not a miniature adult. A child has childish interests and a very short attention span. What is a very short time for an adult seems like an eternity for a child. I am not talking about inviting the child to join the conversation. I am suggesting that when the child comes in to interrupt the conversation, you will do yourself and your guest a favor and build your child's confidence, if you will respond quickly and then move back to your adult conversation.

If the interruptions come thick and fast, you need to use a little more creative imagination and give the child an assigned task or some activity. His attention will be diverted, and you can return to your conversation.

Children should certainly be included in the family conversations; and if it's only the family, they should frequently be included from the very beginning. That's the way they learn to deal with the adult world, improve their alertness, and build their vocabulary, which develop their social and conversational skills. This also makes them feel like part of the team.

In a social situation, it is relatively easy to determine how parents really feel about their children, particularly as they get a little older and enter the teenage years. Many times a ten-, twelve-, or fourteen-year-old will enter a conversation, and the parents will simply say yes or no, but will make no effort to pick up on the conversation and expand any area of interest. I believe this is one of the surest ways to drive a child into a neighbor's home or into an unhealthy gang or peer-group situation.

> Parents, if you don't listen
> to your children's problems,
> they won't listen to your solutions.

Get the Kids Involved

One common denominator we all have is the need to be loved and to be understood. In our family discussions when our children are made to feel like important members of the family from a communications point of view, we are building and establishing ties we can enjoy for a lifetime.

This doesn't mean that you call family conferences to decide every family matter, and certainly not the business matters. However, if you are discussing a critical issue, for example, a move to another city (especially if teenagers are involved), they should be—even must be—brought into the discussions. This way you can understand their feelings, and they will know from the beginning the reasons for the move. This procedure makes it a great deal easier on everyone, and the kids become part of the planning process. Anytime people, regardless of age, feel a project or idea is at least partially theirs, they are far more likely to be enthusiastic about it and support it. That's one way to communicate your love, concern, and respect for your child.

Another must for effective family communications is to let the kids participate in planning family activities, such as a picnic or a vacation. For example, if you plan a two-week trip, what better way to begin than to get a large atlas from the library and start looking at maps to figure out where you want to go? If time and money are limited, you take the map and say, "We can go anywhere within a certain radius." Together you list the places that sound interesting and write the chambers of commerce in those towns. They'll be delighted to send you information.

At that point you go through the information, noting points of interest and things to do. This procedure gives the family a solid basis for making the decision about where they want to go and what they want to do. With everybody participating in the planning, excitement about the trip will grow because people, even our children, invariably support things they help create.

A tremendous fringe benefit is the fact that you can literally invest hours in this planning. What better way to really keep those lines of communication open between you and the kids than with solid activity planning, which is far more beneficial for them than watching TV or roaming the streets? Of equal importance, they learn much about the geography of the country, as well as the history of many of the areas you consider. This contributes significantly to the overall education of your children and builds close relationships.

Saying No Effectively

Dr. Charles Swindoll believes that parents, if at all possible, should give the kids a yes and say no only when it's absolutely necessary. He believes yes answers build confidence and communicate to the children they are trusted. "When I say 'no,' " he says, "I'm communicating the idea that I'm not sure I can trust the child involved or that this thing is really good for that child." Dr. Swindoll does say no in his family, "but we talk more about our 'no's' because our kids have an opportunity to grow and understand when they have an explanation." (That makes the "no" a growth experience, doesn't it?)

There are many times when the need to say no is obvious. It's necessary, but sometimes difficult. There are many instances when kids, lacking maturity and insight, fail to see the dangers of a particular step, and their judgment permits no concern for their safety and health and, for that matter, the safety of the rest of the family.

Young children—the little guys and gals three, four, and five and, for that matter, the toddlers as they begin walking and exploring—will often do something or start to do something when a firm no is very much in order. With the toddler, as he reaches for something that is either dangerous for him or fragile and hence in danger of being broken, the proper step is to take his hands, pull him away, and say, "No. No. No." If the child persists, then a firmer no is in order. If he continues to persist, a slight slapping on the hands is appropriate.

For the young ones, all that is necessary is the word no, but as they get on up to four or five, you should add things like, "This is something that Mommy doesn't want anything to happen to," or "It is not safe for you to play with this," or "When you are seven, you can play with this."

Watch That Tone of Voice

Many times our children test us. They're checking our authority and attempting to see if we will give in or let them get by with something. However, once the rules and limits have been firmly established, the children are comfortable with them and grateful for those limits.

The tone of voice you use in giving instructions and issuing denials is extremely important. The primary thing is that your voice, which is your most effective communication tool, should by its tone and inflection communicate authority but also, at the same time, love and concern for the child. It will require work, sensitivity, and discipline on your part, but that's one more reason why we need our best minds and most loving people at home.

When you have to say no, you should say it in most cases after some reflection. The more often you change from a no to a yes, the more likely your child will be to test you on all your no's. This leads to an ongoing conflict and battle of wits, which is time-consuming, energy-destructive, and confidence-destroying. The child's ability and willingness to accept the fact that the parent really is an authority figure who is in control.

In most cases when you say no, it should be a firm one and you should stick with it. Obviously there are exceptions. When circumstances change or you get additional information that indicates that the no should properly be changed to a yes, then you should make the change. When you change, be certain you carefully explain *why* you made the change. Most often it will not be because you *changed* your mind, but because you made a *new* decision based on new information.

Say No Carefully—But Firmly

Here are some general guidelines for times when you say no. First of all, a snap no will too often bring a protest. The exception to that is when an older child wants to do something that is illegal, immoral, or definitely not in his or her best interest. Incidentally, on the illegal, immoral issues, husband-wife team unity will often make the difference in the route your child will go. (Get it together on this one.)

> *Firm direction
> with the proper voice control
> is powerful, convincing,
> and encouraging.*

A swift rejection of a request to go to a beer party, for example, simply reaffirms your position and makes it clear that is not within the limits of what your child can do. Obviously this brings on difficulty if you, the parent, drink beer and go to cocktail parties. A double standard is set up—one for parents and one for children. Even under those circumstances, however, you've got the laws of the state to abide by, and in many states the legal drinking age is twenty-one. I know of no state where it is under eighteen. Remember, a person can get just as drunk and be killed just as dead from drinking beer and wine as he can from drinking 90-proof alcohol.

Sometimes when you say no but are willing to discuss it later, you can say, "Well, son, at the moment the answer is no because I haven't had time to think about it. Why don't we talk about it after dinner or when I come home from work this evening? This is not a promise to say yes, but since I don't know all the facts, we need to talk about it more thoroughly." It's an absolute *must* that you keep this promise, because your credibility and your child's trust in you are at stake.

When your child understands that you really do want to say yes when possible and if it is in his best interests, he will be far more understanding and more likely to accept the decision without rebelling when the answer has to be no.

Have a Purpose for Your No's

When you say no, you should not direct the denial at your child's lack of judgment and maturity. That would be destructive to his self-image. Base the reason for saying no clearly on your own judgment and authority, giving good reasons when you do.

Sometimes when you say no and your child asks the inevitable why, you might softly ask, "What do you think the reasons are? Can you think of any reason why we would not want you to do this or go to this particular place?" Chances are, he's going to be able to supply you with some pretty good reasons; maybe some you haven't even thought about. (This is true *if* you've been fair and have kept those communication lines open.)

By all means, when you do have to say no, you don't want to give the impression that you took delight in saying it. That way you come across as a killjoy and as someone who is on the "other" side. You are, or should be, on your child's side. There should be some reason for having to say no, but don't make it look like an earth-shattering problem.

Incidentally, I'm convinced that too much has been made of the fact that we owe our children—especially the small ones—an explanation for everything. If time permits and the explanation is reasonably simple so the child can understand it, I believe you are wise to carefully explain your reasoning. However, there are some occasions when you do not really have a logical explanation, but as a parent, you have a strong feeling, based on experience, about why you should say no. In those cases you can say, "Son, I just feel that no is the best answer for you. I don't really have a good explanation, but someday you'll understand why it's this way." The words need to be gentle, but they also need to be firm; and there should certainly be no guilt feelings on your part. I need to point out, however, that most children, including all four of our own, feel a sense of frustration if you consistently fall back on the "just because" answer. Children view the indiscriminate use of "because I said so" as a cop-out, and parental credibility is damaged.

A Loud Voice Can Cause Problems

In communicating with children, perhaps the most serious mistake parents make is the volume they use. Some research done at Wayne State University involving a group of young children three and four years of age and another group five and six years of age revealed some interesting facts.

The children were given a number of commands. Some were positive, such as, "Clap your hands"; others were negative, such as, "Don't touch your toes." When the researchers spoke softly, both groups of kids did what they were told; but when they raised their voices, the three- and four-year-old group especially did exactly the opposite of what they were told *not* to do. In a nutshell, kids, especially the young ones, are more likely to do things that might harm them because the intensity of their parent's voice calls their attention to the subject at hand. For instance, a parent's screaming, "Stay out of the street!" can startle a little one, causing him to run into the street.

> *Obedience is the gateway through which knowledge—yes, and love, too—enter the mind of a child.*
> —Anne Sullivan

Mamie McCullough, our "I CAN" Lady, told me a story that supports this. Ten-year-old Brian McCullough lost his patience with Jennifer, his eight-year-old sister, and shouted, "I'm telling you—" And that's as far as he got before Jennifer cut in and said, "You're not telling me, you're *yelling* me!" (Out of the mouths of babes.)

Calm, confident, and firm—that's what authority is all about; and that's what kids understand, respect, and respond to. Saint Francis de Sales said, "Nothing is so strong as gentleness; nothing as gentle as real strength." Real authority is tempered and gentle, but firm. When you're out of control, you've lost your kids and their respect, because they know they've gotten to you. Firm direction with the proper voice control is powerful, convincing, and encouraging. When the kids see that you have control of yourself and the situation, they will respond to that soft, authoritative, self-assured voice.

Say Please for Best Results

Courteous communication is infectious in a family setting. When children have requests of you, require them to precede the request with the word *please*: "Mommy, would you please give me some more milk?" or "Dad, would you please help me take off my boots?" By the same token, you teach by word *and* deed, so you should follow the same courteous procedure: "Please make up your bed," or "Please be quiet." After the child follows through, you should say, "Thank you." That's being courteous without compromising your authority, and it teaches your child to say thank you when anyone does something for him.

This effectively teaches obedience as well as courtesy, and as Anne Sullivan said of Helen Keller: "I've thought about it a great deal and the more I think the more certain I am that obedience is the gateway through which knowledge—yes, and love, too—enter the mind of a child."

> Most *families do not*
> *communicate—they*
> *simply take turns talking.*

Everything Is Communications

We communicate with our kids in many different ways. Our body language indirectly says a lot, and we communicate directly with the spoken word and the amount of time we spend with them. The most positive or negative communications, as far as results are concerned, take place when parents talk about their children. How the parent really feels about the child is often revealed in the discussions either in the child's presence or ostensibly when the child is not listening. The kids *believe* this overheard conversation and respond accordingly.

I've heard parents call their kids monsters or dummies. I've heard parents say such cruel and thoughtless things as, "When he failed the third-grade reading test, I knew we were going to have trouble with him and that he never would be a good student. He does such dumb things in school, but that's to be expected; he does dumb things around the house."

You can be certain that what your child hears you say *about* him will be taken at face value, while the words you say *to* him are often taken with a grain of salt. That's why your true feelings and attitudes about your child are so important. That's why it's so important for you to become a "good-finder." If your kids overhear you saying positive, complimentary things about them, they will believe that is how you really feel and respond accordingly. That's why so much of this book is devoted to *you*, the parent. You can fool your kids on occasion, but there is no way you're going to fake them out for a lifetime. Your true feelings and attitudes will be communicated to the kids, and that's good, because by now you have developed a winning attitude about your kids, haven't you? (And, fortunately, it's getting better, isn't it?) All of this requires work and dedication on your part, but who said raising positive kids in a negative world was an easy chore?

I'm going to end this chapter with a thought on the one

key ingredient in family communication that is assumed as a given by most people but is most difficult to practice. That key is listening—*really* listening. When children or parents feel they are being listened to, they are able to respect the listeners and respect themselves—since their comments have value. This leads us to the next chapter where we discuss the importance of feeling good about oneself. That's right—how to have, and help your children have, a positive self-image.

Time for Personal Evaluation

1. When you were growing up, how was the art of conversation practiced in your home?

2. What deliberate steps are you taking to communicate with your kids?

3. Zig says the tone of voice is critical. It's hard to listen to ourselves. What would your spouse say if you asked him/her about your tone of voice with the children?

4. If the answer to your child's request has to be no, but you'd like to soften it, what do you say? Would Swindoll's advice help you here?

5. When was the last time you really listened to your children? What were they saying?

CHAPTER 10

Building a Healthy Self-Image

> *Your child can stand a lot if he can stand himself.*
> —Anonymous

Here we are at Chapter 10, and we're still spending a considerable amount of time and space on the parents. Here's why. The parents' self-images, attitudes, and moral values have a direct, powerful influence on their children. If the parents' self-images are sound, their approach to teaching, loving and disciplining their children will be dramatically different from what it would be if they suffer from low self-esteem.

Virtually everyone agrees that self-image is important. Thousands of editorials, books, pamphlets, and articles have been published to tell us how to improve our self-image. Dr. Joyce Brothers says that you cannot consistently perform in a manner which is inconsistent with the way you see yourself. Despite this fact, poor self-image or low self-esteem seems to be a national dilemma. Why? There are many reasons, many of them tied to the negative character of our society as stated in Chapter 2, so I won't elaborate further except to note that factors such as ridicule, abuse, abandonment, and low moral standards can be highly destructive. Let's look briefly at a couple of these.

Ridicule and Abuse

One thing that negatively affects a child's self-image is ridicule. Often this is associated with the child whose family suffers alcoholism, drug addictions, divorce, abandonment, a prison term, or other problems related to having only one parent. Further reasons for ridicule may include having profane, immoral parents or intolerable living conditions, which make it impossible to invite friends home to play.

One of the worst causes of poor self-image is child abuse. Since I deal with this problem in Chapter 14, I won't elaborate at this point other than to say that with the dramatic increase in addictive pornographic materials, drug and alcohol abuse, the immoral nature of so much of the fare in movies, TV, and music, and the ever-present breakup of families, the problem is getting increasingly severe.

Unconditional Love and Acceptance

Yes, ridicule, abuse, fault finding, etc. are destructive forces. From one perspective they all stem from a critical, harmful, negative spirit. As such, they are all tied together, but personally I have come to the conclusion that the number one cause of a poor self-image in adults and children is the absence of unconditional parental love. This unconditional love from the parent almost always precedes self-acceptance. I have come to this conclusion as a result of considerable research done personally and by various members of our staff through thousands of contacts made in our school "I CAN" program and our BORN TO WIN seminars.

What is unconditional love? It's just what the phrase implies—loving a person without any prior conditions, because of *who* the person is and not because of *what* the person does. Unfortunately too many parents love a child *if* he cleans up his room, makes good grades, is home by eleven, is a "good" boy or girl. In short, the love is conditional. This means that often a child doesn't feel he deserves love, even from his parents. The love is tied to performance, and if the performance isn't good, the indication is that there is no love. If the child feels the parents love only the good actions or good performance and not him, a Pandora's box of potential trouble is opened up.

If the child doesn't feel he *deserves* love from his own parents, he assumes that he is unworthy of love; therefore, he should not love himself. Logically, then, if he can't love himself and feel good about himself, who will love him? Indeed, it is a very short step to feeling of no value—a nobody. Such a blow to the self-image—namely, feeling "I'm a nobody"—is devastating.

Author J. Allan Petersen echoes these sentiments and points out three A's which will make your child *know* he is loved and do wonders for his self-image. To those three I will add two. The first A is for Acceptance, which is part and parcel of unconditional love. We accept our child not because of any physical or behavioral characteristics but because he is ours. The moment we put conditions on acceptance is the moment our children begin to wonder whether or not they can live up to our expectations. Insecurity results, and no insecure child is going to have a healthy self-image.

> *As parents we must remember*
> *that failure is an event,*
> *not a person.*

Tell 'Em You Love 'Em

The second A is for Affection, which is a manifestation of love. Today more than ever before our children are starved for affection and intimacy, and they may turn to drugs or sex as substitutes. In July of 1987, while I was speaking in Melbourne, Australia, a lady came to me during the break and told me she was thirty-two years old and had two little girls ages eight and ten who suffered all kinds of psychological problems. She had heard me repeat on my tapes that we must tell our children we love them, explaining that if we don't tell our kids we love them, they will grow up and refrain from telling *their* children that they are loved. She pointed out that in her thirty-two years of life no one had ever told her she was loved. Now, however, she knew what she must do. ·

One evening while seated in the den with her daughters, she blurted out, "Girls, I just want you to know that I love you." At that instant, the eight-year-old jumped up with a startled expression on her face, threw her arms around her mother, kissed her and started crying. The ten-year-old immediately followed suit, and by then the lady was also crying. She had no idea whether they cried two minutes or ten, but those tears washed away a tremendous amount of hurt, pain and bitterness.

After that, it was much easier to hug her girls and communicate verbally that she loved them. Within sixty days, 98 percent of her daughters' psychological problems, which included a reversion to infantile behavior, disappeared. Two thousand years ago a Jewish scholar wrote his relatives in Corinth, "Love never fails." He was right.

Now, if you think I'm getting "mushy" about this love and affection bit, I hope you will carefully weigh what Lionel Whiston has to say: "A retreat leader met with groups of high school-age youth and their parents and asked them if they were in the habit of expressing love for each other. Invariably, less than 10 percent declared that they had ever openly told their families of their affection for them. Sometimes within a given group there was not a single parent who had told his children of his love, nor had the son or daughter openly admitted that they loved their parents.''[1]

Love and affection can be expressed often, naturally and easily by stroking our child's hair, holding hands, embracing, and hugging when we part company and when we greet our child again. Infants and toddlers can't get too much hugging and kissing from mom and dad. For that matter, kids of all ages need affection, hugging and attention. You're just not as likely to be in a position to hug and kiss that sixteen-year-old as often as you are the six-week-old.

Little Boys (And Big Boys) Need Loving, Too

All kids need affection, but parents, especially fathers, should be aware that little boys often come up short in getting their share. According to psychiatrist Ross Campbell, six-year-old boys have only received one-sixth as much hugging and kissing as six-year-old girls.[2] Interestingly enough, little boys get into six times as much trouble in the first grade as do little girls, are nine times as likely to have a speech difficulty, and by age ten are ten times as likely to need psychiatric or psychological counseling. This is easy to understand when we realize that love gives birth to courage and security.

The third A is for Approval. Our children desperately seek and need our approval. If they don't get it at home, they will seek it from their friends and do whatever is necessary, which may include sexual activity, doing drugs, wearing "different" clothing and acting in a "bizarre" manner. Obviously, I'm not promoting approval of immoral or illegal behavior; I'm promoting the approval of our child as a person. We can approve of our children without approving of what they have done.

Please, Thank You, and I'm Sorry

The fourth A is for Appreciation. Too many parents require their children to do things which would be more acceptable if they were asked in a kindly way. Our requests should include that magic little word "please," which will train them to use the word when they ask something of us. And when the deed is done, we should smile and say to our children, "Thank you." Not only does this make them feel important and appreciated and promote a good self-image, but it is a great teaching experience. It helps prepare our children for the business community, where they will quickly learn that common courtesy is not only acceptable, but highly desirable.

The fifth A is for Apologize. For some reason, many parents believe that apologizing for mistakes weakens their position of authority. Actually, when we acknowledge the error of our ways, we're admitting we know more now than when we made the mistake. Apologizing will give your child a sense of worth, a feeling of importance, and will be tremendously helpful in the communication process because the child will realize that mom and dad do not consider themselves either perfect or infallible. By removing the impossible standard of perfection, it also makes it easier for the child to admit and apologize when he makes mistakes.

The profession you choose, the habits you acquire, the way you dress, your moral conduct, the person you marry will be determined by the image you have of yourself.
                                              —Dr. Joyce Brothers

Playing the *I Love Me* Game

For the little ones between the ages of about eighteen months and four years, the "who do you love" game can be a delightful, almost never-ending image-building experience. It goes like this:

Parent: "Who do you love?"

Child (laughing and pointing at you): "You!"

Parent: "Who else do you love?"

Child: "God." (Obviously you will have "educated" him.)

Parent: "And who else?"

The child, without prodding, names close friends, relatives, pets, but not necessarily in that order!

Parent: "And who else?"

The child, without prodding from parent, laughs, points finger at self: "Me!"

Parent: "Why do you love yourself?"

Child (without prodding): " 'Cause God loves me."

Parent: "That's right. And who else loves you?"

(The parent then goes through a long list of everybody the child knows and concludes by assuring the child that all of these people really do love him.)

This little game not only builds the child's self-image but draws parent and child even closer and is a great confidence builder.

Now let's explore the symptoms of a poor self-image so that we may recognize them in our children.

Manifestations of a Poor Self-Image

I identify some of these characteristics to enable you to recognize potential trouble spots in your child and improve your effectiveness in dealing with him. For example, a child with a poor self-image will reveal his true colors in various ways. Tell a youngster like this to stay away from drugs because they are bad news and he will often think, "Man, don't tell me that! My friends tell me drugs are fun; that they will make me feel big and will make me one of the gang. Besides, I've got nothing to lose because I'm nothing.'' Remember, parents, if there is a slight chance to be ''someone'' in a gang or to be accepted by doing something, however weird or wrong, some ''nobodies'' will leap at the chance—anything for acceptance, for an opportunity to be somebody.

Tell him to study his lessons, straighten up, and obey the law, and his thoughts invariably are, ''Why should I? The deck is stacked against me. Everyone else gets the breaks. You can't win against the bureaucracy. Besides, since I'm a nobody, I don't deserve anything good; so why shouldn't I have some fun, raise a little sand, gorge myself with food, get high on drugs or alcohol, engage in sex, and do the things my peer group tells me I must do to be part of the gang? I don't like me as I am, so what have I got to lose?''

Teenage depression is another common manifestation of a poor self-image. This one is particularly significant, because the ultimate in depression and self-hate is suicide. Suicide is the number two killer of our children in the United States.[3] When a person thinks very little of himself, he has a tendency to think very little of his chance in life. Then depression enters the picture and is tragically often the forerunner of suicide.

Those who have a negative self-image often have difficulty understanding how others could think highly of them. This creates an inner turmoil that hurts personal relationships, thus creating an almost self-destructive demand for rejection by friends, which further contributes to the depression.

Dr. James Dobson says some youngsters reveal their image problem ''by being very shy and quiet, by being extremely angry and mean, by being silly, by being afraid to participate in a game or contest, by blushing frequently, or by acting proud and stuck-up.''[4]

Another common occurrence is represented by the girl with a poor self-image who feels she is ''nothing'' and therefore can offer nothing but her body. She is easy prey for any guy who shows an interest in her. This possibility is compounded, of course, as more sexually explicit programs bombard our homes in living color on a daily basis with teenage role models serving as the principal characters.

If the youngster with a poor self-image doesn't find a "steady" and everyone else has someone, he or she will often dress in a provocative manner to catch someone or anyone. Any relationship primarily built on physical attractiveness is destined to be short-lived. This is one reason parents need to be especially attentive and discerning when their sons and daughters first start taking a real interest in members of the opposite sex. Wise parents will take serious note of sudden, provocative dress codes adopted by their sons and daughters.

It is safe to say that every area of life and every occupation is affected by a poor self-image. If you fit, or think you fit, into the group with a poor self-image, or if you have a child who fits, let me enthusiastically tell you that there is help available. In the next few pages I'll give you some step-by-step procedures to correct that poor image.

Vive la Différence

People are different. Yes, that's right—adults, children, teenagers—each of us is unique. In the same family one individual might be all thumbs and be unable to screw in a light bulb while a sibling might be quite dexterous and be able to repair sophisticated computers. One youngster might be a straight "A" student with a sparkling personality and a model's good looks while a sibling might struggle to make "C's" and to overcome shyness and feelings of being physically unattractive.

> *Unconditional love is*
> *loving a person*
> *without any prior conditions.*

Needless to say, you should not treat each youngster alike or with the same expectations. Nevertheless, each one can be reared as a positive child to make contributions to our society. It is vitally important to remember that regardless of what a child has in the way of mental alertness, brawn, and beauty, his self-image is to a large degree dependent on how he *thinks* you, the parent, *really* feel about him.

Remember, parents, generally speaking it is quite easy for the multitalented child to feel okay about himself and to be accepted by his peers. Often it's the less talented or unattractive child who becomes a victim of self-deprecation for one reason or another. With this child, parents need to be "good-finders" and encouragers, giving and using special love, compassion and wisdom.

Self-Image "Do's" and "Don'ts"

Now I'm going to give you some practical do's and don'ts mixed in with some examples, which will positively affect your self-image and that of your children. You will notice that some of these tips are covered more thoroughly in other sections of this book. No matter; the topic of self-image is so fundamental that it pervades the whole process involved in raising positive kids and influences many, if not all, of the other issues dealt with in this book.

Let's start our image-building process with a paraphrase of what St. Augustine said in 399 A.D. People travel for miles to gaze at the broad expanse of the ocean. They stare in wonderment at the heavens above. They look with awe on the mountains and streams. Then, without a thought, they pass themselves by, God's most amazing creation. We, and our children, *are* amazing creations and we should look at ourselves *and* our children in that light.

Next, parents must forego the temptation to constantly repeat to their children what they accomplished when they were in school. Somebody laughingly has said that time dramatically improves the parents' performance. In reality what most parents want from their children is something they themselves never had as students, namely, "A's" on their report cards, perfect reports on deportment, and 100 percent attendance. Nor should parents ever compare their children to each other. One child might appear to have it all over a sibling in looks, intelligence, athletic ability, etc., but I can assure you that every child has seeds of greatness and the spark that lights the fuse in that child is love and even-handed treatment by the parent.

Then we need to teach our children, and remind them often, that nobody can *make* them feel inferior without their permission, and they need to be taught not to give that permission to anyone.

Since your personality is judged by the way others perceive you, the way you teach your child to communicate and "come across" is extremely important for every phase of his life. For that reason I strongly urge you to help your child develop an enthusiastic outlook on life. You can do this in many different ways.

For example, when your children are introduced to someone, teach them to say courteously and enthusiastically, "It's nice to meet you," and call that individual by name. If you teach your children from an early age to repeat a person's name, you will convey to them that a person's name is important. This makes them more socially acceptable and helps them gain friends, which they often perceive as a measure of their own self-worth and importance. When the conversation is terminated, teach your children to say, "I'm glad to have met you,'' or ''Nice to meet you,'' and again repeat that person's name.

Also, teach him how to shake hands—not like a dead fish or a test of strength, but simply a good, firm handshake while looking the other person in the eye.

Be Proud of Your Child

Show him that he is valuable by the way you introduce him to others, especially after your child reaches the age of six or seven. During introductions, say, ''This is *my* son,'' or ''This is *my* daughter.'' Your voice inflection can either communicate to your child that you love him and are proud to claim parenthood or that he is not important to you.

Note: Never, never introduce your child in a negative way, such as ''This is my son Bill. He's a good kid, but he's very shy.'' Or, ''This is Sally. She's twelve, but she's still short.'' Such introductions devastate a child's self-image.[5]

Fifth, the completion of any task tends to improve the self-image. As often as possible, select for children jobs or chores around the house that have definite starting and stopping points. You can help ensure the finished job by giving them workable plans with reasonable time schedules. For example, a little guy cutting a big yard should be taught to break the assignment into two parts. The whole yard could look impossible to a youngster, but little goals or steps taken in sequence will get the big job done. You've heard it said a thousand times, ''By the mile it's a trial, but by the inch it's a cinch.''

Sixth, encourage your children to choose carefully their friends and to associate with other kids of high moral character who look on the bright side of life while studying for good grades, and the benefits will be enormous.

Several years ago at Belleville Township High School West in Belleville, Illinois, four of the nine students selected for the Hy News Citizenship Award were all part of a group of eleven close friends and, with one exception, had been together since junior high. Significantly, all eleven had made it to the final selection process. When kids associate with the right people who have a positive, moral outlook on life, they greatly enhance their chances of winning.

Seventh, it's true that everyone can't excel in *all* areas, such as brains, brawn, or good looks, but you can assure your child that he can be just as honest, courteous, cheerful, loyal, faithful, enthusiastic, and any one of a hundred other positive things as others are. Those are qualities he can take to the marriage or business marketplace and find ready buyers. When your child understands what he can have, can be, and can do by acquiring those qualities, you're on your way to raising a positive, drug-free child. So one of the most effective steps you can take with your child is to help him with a self-inventory of his positive qualities. Remember that many times a child gets down on himself because he does not think much about his positive attributes. You need to serve as a "cheerleader" for him.

Of all the things we can teach our children, surely learning how to read is one of the most important. According to Dr. Alice Blair, superintendent of Chicago's District 13, who has had phenomenal success with her disciplined, no-nonsense but loving approach to dealing with "impossible" educational situations, 90 percent of all male teenage delinquents read at below the third-grade level. She says that delinquency is a cry for self-esteem, which no one can have today if he doesn't read. Reading is the key to education in virtually every area of life.

In the case of your child's vocabulary, you have an especially attractive option with several bonuses. The library or a bookstore can provide numerous books for building vocabulary that are specifically for your child's grade level. Each evening spend a few minutes teaching one new word, and encourage your child to learn one word out of the book provided for him. Share with your child any new words you may have learned. This is a marvelous way for him to start learning the adult language, which can be so meaningful and significant in his life. It will also help you.

Don't just teach your child to read—teach him to *love* reading. A wise man said, "Language is the currency of all human knowledge and a solid grasp of it opens up new realms of learning." You teach a love of reading at an early age by holding your child in your lap and enthusiastically reading to him. Later, when he's old enough to have homework, let him see you reading while he's studying his lessons. The kitchen table is ideal. You should also display good books and magazines in every room in the house. The Harvard Preschool Project proved that infants and toddlers with the best grasp of language almost always scored highest in achievement tests.

Question: Wouldn't *you* prefer to teach your child the *right* language instead of permitting "the tube" to teach the language of the street?

To build your child's self-image, teach him manners. Our society over the past two decades has put everyone in such an incredible hurry that many parents have been "too busy" to teach discipline, common courtesy, and simple table manners. For a parent to neglect this area of a child's education is one of the really big sins of omission.

We've learned to dress for success, to speak for success. Now we need to learn how to behave for success.
—Marjabelle Young Stewart

An amazing number of parents do not know the simple rudiments of table manners. They talk with their mouths crammed with food and grab a fork like a baseball bat. They cut an entire piece of meat at one time, do not know which utensil to use for which food, leave the spoon in the tea or coffee after stirring in the sweetener, reach across the table, leave the house or restaurant with a toothpick in their mouths, etc. In the event you do not have the knowledge or the patience to teach your children good table manners, I suggest you encourage the children to take classes in home economics to acquire those skills and social graces.

Tenth, emphasize the development of a creative imagination; teach your child to "see." The word *imagination* is described in the dictionary as "the act or power of forming a mental image of something not present to the senses or never before wholly perceived in reality; a creation of the mind; resourcefulness."

Years ago when I lost the weight I needed to lose, one of the methods I used was to put a picture of a man in jockey shorts on the bathroom mirror and then I visualized myself looking like him. This is constructive use of the imagination. I saw myself as a slender person until the day arrived when I looked that way (well, almost).

Successful people in every field of endeavor follow this procedure. Golfing immortal Jack Nicklaus "sees" the ball dropping into the cup *before* he putts the ball. Basketball great Magic Johnson of the Los Angeles Lakers "sees" the ball dropping through the hoop before it ever leaves his hand. Great composers and playwrights "see" the completed work long before it is committed to paper. Successful parents raising positive kids need to "see" their kids as finished, competent, positive adults while they are still kids; and they need to help their kids "see" themselves as successful adults in the future. Whether you want to move into management, function as a sports star, be a successful mate or parent, or get into ownership of your own business, you need to "see yourself" in that position.

Eleventh, one of the most important principles in building a healthy self-image is to establish a positive, loving environment. Telephone etiquette is an important element. In this day of "cool" kids, a lot of them are so laid-back they're

laid out! The way we answer the phone can make a difference
in attitudes at home. In our own home, we have always answered it with enthusiasm and, as a result, our children
quickly learned that enthusiasm was not only acceptable, but
desirable. Equally significant is the fact that many of our
children's friends elected to visit our children in our home
because of the environment. Though this sometimes created
space problems, we always preferred to have a dozen youngsters in our den as opposed to having our children in someone
else's home without our knowing what was taking place.

Excitement and Love

Realistically, kids go where there's excitement and stay where
there's love. Admittedly, I have a built-in advantage because
my wife, the Redhead, is affectionately known as "The
Happy Hugger." If it's moving, she'll stop and hug it, and
if it's not, she'll dust if off and sell it! The bottom line is that
when the kids come to visit, the Redhead gives them a welcoming hug, which frequently is the only one they've gotten
since the last time they were home.

You're probably wondering what the magical words are
for answering the phone. I pick up the receiver with a cheerful "Howdy, howdy, howdy!" or my favorite, "Good morning, this is Jean's happy husband!" As an aside, I do that
because it's true and secondly because you fellows cannot
believe how many points I score with the Redhead!

Today, when one of my grandchildren is around, I pick up
the receiver with an enthusiastic "Good morning, this is Sunshine's proud granddaddy!" or "Good morning, this is
Keeper's proud granddaddy!" or "Good morning, this
is Little Lover's proud granddaddy!" You should see those
little eyes light up! These greetings do wonders for their
self-images.

I challenge you, next time the phone rings and one of your
children is near, to answer it with an enthusiastic, "Good

morning, this is Molly's proud mom!" or "Good morning, this is Paul's proud poppa!" You'll be amazed at what will happen the first few times you do it. Your fourteen-year-old may shrug his shoulders and say, "Aw, Dad!" But I can guarantee you, the next time the phone rings, he will wait for you to answer it in the hopes you'll answer it in the same way. The reason is simple: You are stroking him by verbalizing your love for him and his importance to you. At the same time you're visibly demonstrating that enthusiasm is important. As an added bonus, you'll feel better because it's true that we feel the way we act.

Needless to say, a child living in this kind of environment will be pleased to invite his friends over for a visit—and having friends improves your child's self-image.

Another effective way of creating a positive environment is judiciously playing good music. As the family arises, soft instrumental music provides a pleasant welcome to the new day. In the evening, when things slow down just before bedtime, some quiet, classical music provides the perfect backdrop for a transition from family activities to peaceful sleep. Music used this way not only creates an excellent environment for raising positive, drug-free kids, but teaches your kids an honest appreciation for good music, which is the best way to help them reject the really bad music.

Kids Love Posters

Yet another step for creating a positive environment is taken by corporate America, educational institutions, factories, the sales world, etc. I'm referring to positive posters and slogans which the whole family can produce together. Following are a few examples, but I encourage you to change them regularly and involve the entire family in choosing the slogans and printing the posters.

You've got to *be* before you can *do* and you've got to do before you can have.

You are not well-dressed until you put on a smile.

This is the day which the Lord has made—I will rejoice and be glad in it.

You (*your child's name*) were BORN TO WIN!

Winning is not the most important thing, but the effort to win is.

Failure is an event, not a person.

Get enthusiastic about tomorrow—today.

Words are powerful.

People who say "I can" and "I can't" are both right.

What you say is what you get.

People don't care how much you know until they know how much you care.

The best way to friends is to be a friend.

It's not where you start, but where you finish, that counts.

The only way to coast is downhill.

It's the part of the blanket that hangs over the bed that keeps you warm.

We can't tailor-make the situations of life, but we can tailor-make the attitudes to fit them—before they arise.

We do not sing because we are happy, we are happy because we sing.

Life can be tremendously rewarding, but it demands before it rewards. The *choices* you make in life play a major role in the chances you have in life.

Note: Posters are even more effective when the kids find their own slogans and make their own posters.

Twelfth, one of the easiest, fastest, and surest ways of building a healthy self-image in your child is to help him develop pride in being an important part of something worthy and noble that is bigger than any one individual. The family is the logical place to start. The church, school, and community can be real sources of pride. Obviously, pride and gratitude in being an American can have a significant impact on a child's self-image.

As an aside, but important enough for me to mention it here, to really help build a healthy self-confidence in your child, *and* to feel good about yourself and your country, I encourage you to get a copy of *The Light and the Glory* by Peter Marshall and David Manuel. *The Light and the Glory*, with the exception of the Bible, is the most meaningful, moving, important, and inspiring book I have ever read in ten years. It is the true, *documented* story of America that you and I were not taught when we were in school. It tells precisely how Columbus was really led to the discovery of America, who the Pilgrims and the Puritans really were, and the importance of their role in America. You'll learn how we won our independence and about the true greatness of George Washington. You'll be unbelievably inspired; you'll shed tears of joy and gratitude for America and for the men and women, inspired by God, who made it free—and great.

> *Successful parents*
> *raising positive, drug-free kids*
> *need to "see" their kids as*
> *finished, competent,*
> *positive adults.*

Teach your child the messages in *The Light and the Glory*, and you will have a child with renewed faith and confidence. His optimism for life and his zeal for serving God, his family, and country will be greater.

Sometimes a child has a physical problem that contributes to a negative self-image. These problems can occasionally be altered without a great deal of time, trouble, and expense. If so, I certainly encourage a parent to do that.

There are also occasions when plastic surgery can be quite

helpful in rebuilding or renewing the self-image. This is especially true when a child has an unusually large or long nose, protruding ears, or a harelip. This area, however, often involves psychological considerations that have to be dealt with on an in-depth and personal basis. *Caution* and *counsel* are the watchwords, but I have seen some dramatic personality changes occur following plastic surgery.

In retrospect, it seems incredible that we did not notice it, but when our youngest daughter, Julie, was seventeen, she talked with us about her ears. I had looked at my little girl tens of thousands of times, and all I had ever seen was a vivacious, bright-eyed, highly motivated, beautiful young girl. However, she asked me a question: "Haven't you ever noticed, Daddy, that I always wear my hair so that it covers my ears?" To tell you the truth, I had never noticed it. Then she showed me how her ears stuck out.

Frankly, I still couldn't see how they "stuck out"; but in her mind it was a serious problem, and if it's in her mind, then it is a serious problem! So her mother and I readily agreed that plastic surgery would be in order. Today if you see our youngest daughter, chances are ten to one you will see her wearing her hair in such a way that her ears are showing; and, yes, it did make a difference in her confidence and in her self-image.

As you review these suggested do's and don'ts to building a healthier self-image for your child, let me remind you that each step is designed to help your child accept himself. Ironically, once he does that, it will no longer be a matter of life or death for others to accept him. At that point he will not only be accepted by them, but his company will be sought by them. That's a good image-builder itself!

A Final Word on Self-Image Building

I can say with reasonable certainty that when your child is between the ages of nine and fifteen, you will have a better chance of losing him to drugs and immorality than at any other stage of his life. During these critical years children are going through many physiological and psychological changes. At the same time they're being bombarded with the moral values of the media, their peer group, family, church, and school. Many of these are often in direct conflict and create considerable confusion within the children's minds as to which values are real and which are artificial.

This is a period of time when kids desperately need you to put your arms around them, hug them and kiss them, tell them how much you love them, and how much you need them. Those are the needs, and they are real. Interestingly enough, although kids need you the most at this stage, they will probably seem to be the least comfortable with you. That's one of the reasons many of them seem to pull away. That pulling away, parents, is your signal to lovingly reach out with understanding and without too much pressure.

During these years your children probably will change schools twice. These "new" times and relationships make your children vulnerable to new pressures, friends (?), and influences. A child might well have been quite popular and accepted in the old school, but the move to the new one brings on a whole new set of circumstances. At this particular point, kids involved in drugs and promiscuity often try to reach out to those kids who are just coming in. In our case, when we first moved to Dallas, one of our daughters was offered drugs the first day in her new school. During this time I encourage you to be especially attentive to, and supportive of, your child, because these years are crucial for the well-being and happy development of your children. Spend extra time with him, notice his friends, be alert, and listen carefully when he talks about incidents and people at school.

One reason the lines of communication need to be established early is because when kids change to a new school, they're not likely to start telling you "everything" if they have not been telling you "anything" to that point.

Easily the single most important thing you can do to help ensure the ongoing healthy self-image of your child is to regularly—and often—look your child in the eye and tell him you love him. This is easy to do with a toddler, but more difficult, especially for fathers, with teenagers. But that eye contact and those words will make a difference. Do it.

Time for Personal Evaluation

1. Mention some of the ways kids manifest a negative self-image. Do your children have any of these characteristics?

2. How many of the self-image do's are you practicing regularly?

3. Summarize why Zig feels that a critical time in self-image building occurs between the ages of nine and fifteen.

4. What does Zig recommend specifically for parents in their relationships with children during this critical age?

5. Would you agree to banish ridicule and abuse from your ongoing relationships with your children? How can you do this? What do you think will be the benefit to your family if you do this?

6. Give your own definition of what it means to practice unconditional love.

CHAPTER 11

The Drug War Is Serious

> *Parent(s), if you are a non-smoking, nondrinking, church-going, consistent, family-oriented, loving disciplinarian, the odds are overwhelmingly in your favor that you will raise a positive, drug-free child.*
>
> —Forest Tennent, M.D.

Note: If you are *none* of the above, start saving money to put your child in a drug or alcohol rehab center.

It's a fact that we are in a war and at this moment we are losing it. One of the reasons for the loss is the lack of awareness of millions of parents that we're in a war. Still other millions have decided their kids are not in danger, so there's no need for them to get involved. Millions have decided they can do nothing, and even more millions have joined the wrong side of the war.

Taking it one step at a time, let's start with our illegal drug problem. It's serious. Our alcohol problem (yes, I know it's a drug) is even more serious, and the tobacco problem is the most serious of all.

We can "blame" TV for the problem. We can "blame" athletes, movies and musical recording artists, and we'd score a direct hit. We can "blame" family problems, society, greed, the times, our educational system, business and the government, and no informed person could disagree. All of the above share the "blame."

BUT: The bottom line is the simple fact that the drug war will be won or lost *with your* child(ren) *almost* entirely based on what happens in your home between you and your child. I did say *almost*. Some parents do everything right and still lose their kids to drugs, but generally the parents who establish the right environment, set the right example by living and teaching the right value system while showing plenty of love and using some common sense are the ones most likely to win the war and raise positive, drug-free kids.

How do you start to solve the problem of keeping your child off drugs? The answer is back on page one. Directly or indirectly everything in *Raising Positive Kids* is designed to keep your kids off drugs and on the right path. I really hope that the moment you finish this book you will take a pen and start over with the express purpose of making this a textbook and not a "nice book" with some "neat ideas" which you "really enjoyed." Pick up a small bound notepad and start compiling a list of "great ideas" and things to do which are triggered in your mind.

You will be amazed at the new things you will see upon the second reading that you missed the first time through. By using the notepad you'll be more likely to follow through on some ideas and projects which will make a difference.

Question: Is the drug problem really that serious? Is my child, to whom I've given "everything," vulnerable? Let's look at the facts and then I'll let you answer the questions.

Americans consume more illegal drugs than the other 5,000,000,000 people on earth. Over 9,000,000 Americans have tried cocaine, and 25,000,000 are involved in illegal drugs of some kind.[2] Ten percent of the babies born today have been exposed to drugs or high levels of alcohol in the womb.[2] A pregnant woman's use of cocaine—even once—

can have devastating effects on the baby and incur astronomical medical costs.[3] One American in twelve regularly smokes pot, while 52 million smoke an average of 31 cigarettes a day. Over 100,000,000 million Americans drink on a regular basis, and 18,500,000 have serious drinking problems.

What Are the Costs?

Nobody knows for certain, but a variety of sources, educated estimates and conservative common sense mathematical formulas give us some staggering figures. Let's start with tobacco, the "entrance drug." Purchase price, medical costs and productivity loss are well over 150 billion dollars. This cost doesn't include the human misery that smoking causes. The irony of the smoking scenario is that the extremely high percentage of people who devote their lives to growing tobacco often struggle for financial survival.

The purchase price, medical cost and productivity loss of alcohol total well over 250 billion dollars, not including the cost of the destroyed lives and families.

The purchase price, medical and rehab bills, productivity loss and direct crime bill for illegal drugs come to well over 200 billion dollars, not including the incalculable cost of human misery.

Add those three figures and you have over 600 billion dollars. Eliminate those three cancers on our society and all their related problems, and in ten years we could put a dent in poverty, pay off the national debt and move from the world's largest debtor nation to the world's largest creditor nation.

Now—Those "Related" Problems

Some other costs are infinitely higher. Three hundred ninety thousand people (many authorities estimate 500,000) die each year as a direct result of smoking.[4] That's 17.4 percent of all deaths in our country. Last year, fewer than 14,000 people died of AIDS. In the next *two weeks*, over 14,000 people will die as a direct result of smoking. And yet we spend billions fighting AIDS (we should), but even more billions subsidizing and advertising tobacco. Amazingly enough, one-third of our college students do not think that smoking is harmful.[5] Incredible, but then a $3,000,000,000 advertising budget by the tobacco industry combined with the powerful tobacco lobby can buy a lot of support and confuse gullible people.

> *We spend billions of dollars each year to smooth the wrinkles on our face and to flatten our stomachs. Smoking causes our stomachs to swell and our faces to wrinkle prematurely.*

And then there's booze, which 89 percent of our college students do not consider harmful,[6] yet: Alcohol is a contributing factor in 90 percent of all divorces. Alcohol is a contributing factor in 70 percent of all wife and child abuse cases. Alcohol causes 50 percent of all highway deaths. Alcohol is related to 70 percent of all boating accidents and 69 percent of all drownings.[7] Fifty percent of all people under professional care for depresesion are victims of alcohol. Surprisingly, only 3 percent of those with serious drinking problems are on Skid Row. The other 97 percent are in our homes, schools, factories and businesses.[8] Tragically, over 90 percent of these people deny having a problem.

Casual social drinkers have one chance in seven of developing a serious drinking problem. Exception: Casual social drinkers who are children of alcoholics have one chance in two of developing serious drinking problems.

Approximately 100,000 ten- and eleven-year-olds get drunk at least once every week.[9] America presently has 28.6 million children of alcoholics, and since children of alcoholics have a four times greater risk of developing alcoholism than children of non-alcoholics, it's easy to understand why the liquor industry targets those seductive TV commercials to ten-year-olds. It also helps explain why in 1985 an estimated 4.6 million adolescents had negative consequences of alcohol consumption: arrests, involvement in accidents, or impairment of health or job performance.[10]

It Gets Worse

More than 100,000 people die each year from the effects of alcohol and 5,000 babies are born every year with fetal alcohol syndrome. Although many of the ads are aimed at an adolescent market, we still permit them to be aired on TV. (If you doubt the validity of that statement, please explain why the average eight-to-twelve-year-old can name three times as many alcoholic beverages as he can presidents of the United States.)[11] When Sweden stopped TV ads of alcohol, sales dropped 20 percent.[12]

Incredibly enough, half of everyone between the ages of eleven and nineteen who uses or sells illegal drugs will be dead or incarcerated by 1995. Equally alarming is the fact that if your child is smoking cigarettes and is between ages eleven and nineteen, the odds are almost 50 percent that he or she is also involved in illegal drugs. Nicotine is the entrance drug; virtually every pothead, cocaine and heroin addict started with tobacco. One more time. When we solve the smoking problem we will have largely solved the drug problem.

I provide all this data because the more involved you are with your child in positive activities, the less likely he or she is to get involved in the destructive drug and alcohol world. If we don't solve the problem (it is already the number one cause of illiteracy, poverty, crime, violence and family break-ups), America will be destroyed. *All* reason and logic tell us that when enough of a nation's individuals are crippled or destroyed, the nation itself is in jeopardy.

We've confronted the problem, now let's see how we can solve the problem for America and more specifically, for *your* child.

Here Are the Steps

Start today by committing anew to raise your child as a positive, drug-free individual. Remember when you first held that bundle of joy and helplessness and you promised yourself that you were going to be a ''good'' (maybe the best) parent and give your child the best shot at succeeding in life? Now is the time to renew that commitment.

Be the role model you want and expect your child to follow. Lectures can confuse a child, but the example you set will be crystal clear. Show *and* tell your child by your life-style and words that drugs are a no-no..

Let's start in reverse and look at the factors at home which lead to alcohol and drug abuse: a negative parent; a live-in or stepparent who drinks and/or smokes; lots of freedom and very little discipline; little or minimal affection and display of genuine love; harsh, brutal, or inconsistent treatment; little or no religious commitment; lots of TV time; little or no community involvement; limited moral training and lots of listening to rock music.

Please notice that you can immediately do something about

all of these factors. You can (a) stop drinking or smoking, (b) restrict TV viewing and train your child to appreciate good music, (c) discipline your child, love your child and be gentle and affectionate with your child, (d) live your religious commitment and take your child to worship services; (e) develop and teach a positive mental attitude; (f) get involved in at least one community activity; (g) if you're married, work even harder at keeping that marriage together. If you're single, do not permit your dates to sleep over or move in. Exercise constraints and time control over your child so that he is held accountable.

Peer Pressure—Fact or Fiction

Follow up your commitment and personal example by encouraging your child to choose his friends carefully. However, don't use your child's friends as a cop-out if he gets involved in drugs.

One of the great misconceptions parents have about adolescent drug abuse is that peer pressure and a desire to escape reality got their kids involved in drugs. But in his book *How To Really Know Your Child*, Dr. Ross Campbell quotes Sergeant Bud Hulsey, the youth officer with the Kingsport, Tennessee, police department who said, "Of the 4,000 to 5,000 kids I've asked, not one of them said they take drugs due to peer pressure or for escape. Almost everyone said it was because they were bored, and that they liked the feeling, they liked the 'buzz.' "[13] (Forest Tennant, M.D., arguably America's number one drug authority, agreed completely with Sgt. Hulsey's observation.)

With this in mind, much of this book, especially the next two chapters, was written with many specific suggestions as to how you can get your child involved in so many fun, wholesome and inspiring activities that he won't even think about being "bored." He will get his "buzz" out of the love he feels from being secure in that love and from his belief that his fture is too bright to destroy with drugs. You betcha I'm optimistically confident that *you* can raise a positive, drug-free child. Read on.

Sergeant Hulsey told teens they're not just physical beings, but ''You are spiritual beings . . . and if you satisfy only your physical being, you're going to be retarded spiritually, emotionally and intellectually.''

Again, Dr. Campbell said, ''These kids do not realize that every illicit, external chemical known to produce changes in the nervous system also damages that system. There are no exceptions. There are no consequence-free drugs.''[14]

Teach Your Kids How to Say No

That last sentence clearly explains why our kids need to be *told* to say no and then taught *how* to say no. When your child reaches the age of seven, collect twenty or more cigarette butts and seal them in a jar for a couple of days. Let your child deeply breathe that air and ask him if he thinks putting that ''stuff'' in his body would make him feel good or bad.

Next, take a fresh cigarette and let him hold it, smell it and look it over carefully to satisfy his natural curiosity. Then take back the cigarette and say, ''If one of your friends tries to get you to try one of these, you are to say, 'No, smoking makes you smell bad and feel bad. Doctors say it makes you sick and I promised my parents I wouldn't.' '' Periodically repeat this procedure until your child can comfortably and confidently recite that statement word for word.

As stated earlier, nicotine and the 2,000 other known and unknown chemicals in tobacco serve as the entrance for virtually all illegal drug use, so teaching your child to say no to smoking is of paramount importance. When your child is about ten, you should borrow a videocassette from the American Heart and Lung Association and let him clearly see the effects of smoking.

Teach your child that when he is offered alcohol in any form he is to say, "No, it's not cool, and my parents would be hurt and disappointed if I disobeyed them and broke the law."

When offered illegal drugs, your child should tell his "friend" that if it takes drugs to be "in," he's going to stay "out," and that means staying out of jail as well. Lovingly but firmly let your child know that if he gets involved in drugs you will still love him, but you will be terribly disappointed. Also let him know *in advance* that if he knowingly and willingly breaks the law even one time, he will suffer the consequences. He will pay the fine and court costs and suffer considerable restrictions in his activities. Be firm, but most of all let him know that you will really be disappointed because you love him so much you would hate to see him jeopardize his health and future.

The Power of Choice

One of the most valuable lessons any parent can teach a child is that every choice has an end result. If you choose to willfully disobey your parents, you have chosen the results of that disobedience. If you choose to stay up late tonight, you've chosen to be sleepy tomorrow. A child should be taught that if he chooses to spend his entire allowance the first day, he will go without any allowance for the rest of the week.

Dr. James Dobson adds that to separate the action from the consequence by giving the child additional money is to refuse to teach him a valuable lesson. Such an approach begun early in life will probably continue throughout life.

Of course we all make choices based on what we know, believe and feel, and in those early years parents do have the greatest input on what their child knows, believes and feels. Having fought on the fringes of the drug war for several years, I can tell you that many parents mistakenly "protect" their children from any painful consequences and thereby create lifetime dependence. Little Charlie shoplifts an inexpensive item (it was "only" 89¢) and it's not worth "humiliating" him by forcing him to return the item to the store owner and apologize. ("He promised he'd never do it again.") Later when "Little Charlie" ("he's really a sweet child") is caught cheating on a test, his parents plead his case with the teacher and again he does not suffer the consequences. Problems are magnified if he's a star athlete because pressures are often brought to bear to make certain his grades are accepted or even "doctored" so that he can remain eligible. He's praised and idolized so frequently that he begins to believe he's simply not vulnerable to the things mere mortals have to deal with. He becomes "reality impaired," and too often the rest of the story is tragic.

A pattern is set when the child is suspended for fighting or smoking pot, but his parents intercede and get him off the hook. His parents pay his speeding tickets. He's bailed out when arrested for drug possession because "basically he's a good kid." The message to the child is clear: go ahead and do what you want to. If you get in trouble, we'll bail you out and everything will be all right. Every choice or action has its consequences and a little "hurting" early in our child's life could prevent tragedies later.

The "Idiot" Drug

In a conversation with Dr. Tennant I asked if cocaine had ever been identified as "the idiot drug." He laughingly replied that he didn't think so, but the name was certainly appropriate because the price of crack can completely wreck an addict's life. The first "high" can cost only $10, but why jeopardize an entire life for a brief "high"? I hope you'll agree that a person in his right mind would not dare to try it even once. Remember Stanley Wilson from Chapter 1 and the story of Len Bias? Len "bought" the idea of getting high and paid for it with his life. Stanley bought the "it won't hurt you" lie and paid for it with his career.

In addition to the millions of kids and young adults who are involved with cocaine, a number of theoretically mature, intelligent thirty-, forty-, and even fifty-year-olds just can't resist the temptation to "try it this one time" with tragic results. Don't do it, dad, even if you could "get away with it." The odds are higher that your child will also try it.

Ironic, But True

An interesting irony about raising positive, drug-free kids in a negative world is that we never have to verbally teach negative, immoral or destructive behavior. It's not necessary to tell our kids that since we smoke they should start smoking even earlier. If we drink, we can expect them to start at an early age. If we use violent, profane and abusive language we don't have to encourage them to do so. Kids are likely to copy our destructive behavior. Eighty-one percent of parents who drink have children who drink, but 72 percent of parents who don't drink have children who don't drink.[15]

However, virtuous, morally sound and beneficial actions usually must be verbally encouraged. If we don't drink or do drugs, we need to warn our children of the misery and destroyed lives drugs and alcohol leave behind. If we don't smoke, we should explain to our children at an early age that we don't because smoking is expensive, unhealthy and socially offensive.

If we don't use crude language, we should explain to our children that we can express ourselves and communicate more effectively without the use of that kind of language. Educated, confident, considerate people simply have no need for such boorish speech.

When you teach your kids what to do, they will probably do it, but if you teach them what *and* why they should or should not do certain things, they will respond far more willingly and are far more likely to heed those verbal instructions and personal examples.

Goals Are Important

From cover to cover we talk about getting your child involved in setting and reaching some worthwhile goals. You can thoroughly cover goal-setting in family conferences, conversations, by reading good literature and by listening to motivational tapes. Start with simple goals, such as being in school every day. As the child advances, his goals will change and mature. Later you will want to explore with your child what he really wants to do in life. Regardless of his choice, discuss and learn why he made that choice and what he believes he must do to reach that goal. If he has a local hero or role model, it would be helpful for that person to talk with your child and share (you might have to do a little prodding!) why a healthy body and mind are essential for reaching the goal in that chosen job, career or profession.

Along these lines, it is critical for you to encourage your child to set high but *realistic* goals, including getting a good education, not just finishing school. The late Clarence Pennington, chairman of the Civil Rights Commission and the second-highest ranking black in the Reagan administration, told me that a black male has over 1,000 times as good a chance of becoming a physician or attorney as he has of making it to the major leagues, N.B.A. or N.F.L. While it's a plus to encourage your child to develop his athletic skills, it's infinitely wiser to insist that he get a solid education.

Most kids today have high financial goals. Since periodic shots of fear motivation are effective, I encourage you, from time to time, to share a newspaper story with your child about the cost of drug addiction. In a matter-of-fact manner, read with him the story of how Len Bias lost his life and a multimillion dollar basketball contract to cocaine. Let him read how Steve Howe *chose* to do drugs and alcohol, and forfeited several million dollars as a baseball player. How the engineer of an Amtrack train *chose* to smoke pot and caused an accident which killed a number of innocent people and imposed on himself a lifelong burden of guilt.

Daily teach your child those values and qualities we discussed in Chapter 3. The bottom line, according to William Lee Wilbanks in a *Reader's Digest* article, is that the first step toward a cure is to remind the addict that he has the power to help himself. We will continue to lose the war on drugs as long as we view addiction as a medical, political or legal problem. It is basically a moral problem. People *choose* to try drugs, which means they have chosen to become addicts.

When we teach our children that they are *personally* responsible for their choices and the consequences of those choices, we've taken a giant step towards raising positive, morally sound, drug-free kids.

Look Forward in Hope, Not Backward in Despair

In 1981, New York businessman Eugene Lange, while making an impromptu speech to sixty-one sixth graders in East Harlem where the drop-out rate was almost 80 percent, challenged students with an offer for a college scholarship if they could complete high school and meet certain other requirements, such as staying off drugs and keeping out of trouble. As of 1989, forty of those students are now enrolled in college. It's true that if there's hope in the future, there is power in the present.

Those kids had a specific goal and the assurance of a college scholarship upon graduating from high school. Mr. Lange also enlists the aid of one responsible person to "be available" to talk with and encourage two of the kids who are striving for that education. Parents, the two keys (1) specific goal, and (2) being available *will* help keep your kids off drugs.

However, keeping your child off drugs will be determined far more by your philosophy of life, your value system and your life-style than by a set of rules or a series of steps.

In the next chapter we look in considerable detail at the things families can do together to stack the odds in their favor for raising positive, drug-free kids.

Time For Personal Evaluation

1. Can you verbalize in one sentence what you can do to raise a positive, drug-free child?

2. Just how serious is the drug problem?

3. _____ % of the illegal drugs in the world are used in the U.S. ?

4. _____ % of the smokers, between ages eleven and nineteen, use illegal drugs?

5. Kids try drugs because they are _____ and _____ the feeling.

6. Kids with clearly defined _____ are less likely to get involved in drugs.

7. We should clearly teach our children that every choice has an _____.

CHAPTER 12

Winning the War on Drugs

> The war on drugs will be won or lost for your child in your home.[1]

The "Ings" of Life

Keeping your kids off drugs can be accomplished by getting close to your kids, as well as your mate, and by practicing a few "ings" regularly.

In other chapters we talked about "hugging" and "talking," but let's examine some others. The first is "praying," here discussed in the context of mealtime. When you pray before you eat, you are "expressing" an "attitude of gratitude." When your children see you expressing your thankfulness to your Heavenly Father for what you have, they will quickly learn that gratitude is a way of life and they will be far more inclined to be appreciative of what they have and less inclined to take everything for granted. They will be more likely to develop the qualities of "giving" and "sharing" because they can see that they have been "receiving."

Second comes "eating," which families should try to do together as often as possible. While "eating," please remember that this family time is for "enjoying" and not for "teaching." The exception to that rule is in the teaching of manners, which are primarily taught by example. Refraining from teaching at the table is "respecting" your child's right to be dealt with as respectfully as you would deal with a friend, associate or employer.

At a later time, in private and mixed in with lots of positive strokes, ideally in a "fun" setting, show your child how to chew without "smacking," to pleasantly ask a family member if she would mind "passing" the bread, and to remove the spoon after "stirring" the tea. Remind your child that during meals there is no "talking" with food in the mouth, that he should not be guilty of "harrassing" a sibling, and that if a trip to the bathroom is necessary, "asking" for permission is required. (No one should *plan* on leaving during the meal.)

During all these "ings" a prime "ing" to keep in mind is "looking." It builds a child's self-image to look him in the eye while you are talking with him. You are delivering the unmistakable message that the most important thing on earth you have to do at that moment is to talk to him. When *he* knows he is important to you, *then* he will listen to any other message you want to deliver. He'll listen when you talk about a good education, moral values, etc., because he knows you want the best for him—because you are giving the best of yourself. These are the major reasons meals should be eaten at the table with no TV viewing.

Walking — Talking — Listening — Thinking — Feeling — Respecting

"Walking" can work some special miracles. A twenty- to thirty-minute walk each evening after dinner gives you time together, contributes significantly to better health and weight control, and gets you away from TV. A casual walk permits you and the kids to talk unhurriedly, which, outside of "hugging,'' is perhaps the most important element in keeping your kids off drugs and out of sexual relationships and trouble. In this relaxed atmosphere with the kids ''sharing'' their hearts and you ''listening,'' a lot of ''learning'' is ''occurring.''

You will come to know what your child is really ''thinking'' and ''feeling,'' and you'll be in a position to do a better job of ''parenting.'' These walks also give you an excellent opportunity to talk about nature: the trees, flowers, shrubs, birds, insects and animals. Over 99.5 percent of all we ever know is learned outside a ''formal'' classroom. Since you have to do some ''learning'' to keep on ''teaching,'' you'll have to keep on ''studying,'' which is excellent ''modeling'' for your kids.

A prime benefit of these strolls is the dramatic impact they will have on your child's self-image. You are spending time with him, listening to him, and talking to him, which means you are ''respecting'' and ''understanding'' him. You, the most important person in your child's life, are demonstrating to him that you consider him ''deserving'' of your respect and your time.

Everyone, including your child, wants to be understood, accepted and made to feel important. When you convey these qualities to your child, he will have little or no need to seek acceptance and recognition among his peers by joining them in sex, drugs, booze or rebellious behavior. Once this habit is established, you will look forward to these leisurely walks with considerable relish. Your kids will be the envy of the neighborhood; don't be surprised if some other children want to join in the walk. *Let them.* You'll have the chance to positively influence them, and your child will gain new friends and respect. The cost is zero.

Incidentally, much of what I'm suggesting is dependent on a reasonably stable work schedule. If mom and/or dad consistently return home from work one to three hours late, then you should prioritize your time more carefully.

Playing — Participating — Singing — Planning

On those occasions when "walking" is out, "playing" is in. If space (and money) are available, activities such as ping-pong, pool, weight lifting, stationary bicycling, jumping rope, etc. can be fun and healthy. Games like dominoes, checkers, picture puzzles, Monopoly, chess, Rook, Scrabble, Trivial Pursuit, Bible Trivia and some other word games are mentally "stimulating" and enable you to do a lot of "communicating."

Technology Can Be a Plus

Under controlled circumstances, many modern technological gadgets can be quite educational and entertaining. For example, my granddaughter, Keeper, received one of the Nintendo systems for Christmas along with a couple of cartridges with some intriguing, educational games. Their proper use promotes togetherness, teaches proper competitiveness and problem-solving, develops the memory and makes for better eye-hand coordination. A Power Pad to go with her World-Class Track Meet cartridge really gives her a marvelous physical workout. You can also buy cartridges of aerobics workouts. The benefits of playing these types of games versus TV viewing are obvious.

An inherent danger is the games' addictive nature; a child can get hooked to the degree of spending *too* much time on them. But parental participation and control set reasonable time limits and nurture your relationship with your child. Again, the more healthy activities you and your child are involved in together, the less likely your child is to get involved in drugs.

Joining, Participating and Growing

Playing should include some kind of "joining" in an organized team sport. Soccer, baseball, football, basketball and other team sports enable your child to compete with kids his own age and size. I love soccer in particular for the little ones. It is relatively safe and fairly inexpensive. Size and strength aren't dominant factors, and the sport develops stamina and coordination while teaching discipline, cooperation and team spirit.

The coach is critical. He/she should give every child a chance to play, and he should emphasize having fun instead of winning. It's infinitely more important for your child to participate in the game and play on a losing team than to sit on the bench for a winning team.[2] Experiencing the disappointment of defeat is the only way your child can fully experience and appreciate the exhilaration of winning. It will also help prepare him for the future. Caution: Remember, parents, it *is* a game and 90 percent of the kids want to play.

You should also gently encourage your child to join organizations such as Cub Scouts and Brownies for ages seven to eleven. "Belonging" to an organization of winners (and Boy Scouts for kids over twelve) boosts your child's morale and introduces him to new friends. In the Scout leader and parents of other group members he will be able to identify other adults as positive role models. Needless to say, you should "check out" any adult you entrust your child to, regardless of the organization. By learning the Scout oath he will acquire some values which have stood the test of time and will help prepare him for the future. Scouts receive tremendous leadership training, and the success in the adult world of those who have gone on to become Eagle Scouts has been well documented.

Church-related organizations promote participation and often offer opportunities for cultivating speaking skills. Your child will receive spiritual direction, meet highly desirable associates, and have a chance to develop intangible leadership qualities. Incidentally, if you are a single parent, I encourage you to involve your child in organizations that have leaders who are members of the opposite sex.

Other marvelous organizations include F.C.A. (Fellowship of Christian Athletes), F.H.A. (Future Homemakers of America), F.B.L.A. (Future Business Leaders of America) and V.I.C.A. (Vocational Industrial Clubs of America). I'm personally familiar with the outstanding National F.F.A. Organization formerly known as the F.F.A. (Future Farmers of America). It offers wonderful training and leadership programs. I've attended its annual convention, met many of its national officers who have attended our three-day BORN TO WIN seminar, and have had the privilege of working with Tony Hoyt, its national director of leadership programs, for several years. I know these kids aren't perfect, but I have yet to see a single one smoke, drink or do drugs. For that matter, I've never heard one of these young people utter a vulgar or profane word. These kids are getting a natural high out of life, so they don't need the deadly artificial high of drugs.

Yes, "joining" the right group can make a positive difference in your child's life, just as "joining" the wrong group can have devastating results. Stay tuned in to your kid's day-to-day activities and friends, for he is positively or negatively influenced by those around him.

The "Ing" of Shopping

Children are fascinated by the external world and learn a lot just by going with us on our rounds. Even trips to the supermarket can be fun and educational, especially when the child reaches the age of twelve. When we point out how the grocery store is organized in an orderly way, we broaden our child's knowledge base and help him to understand that he benefits from order in the world. Since drug abusers seldom have any "order" in their lives, shopping can become a tool for teaching order and its advantages.

Start by going through the pantry and refrigerator and draw up a short list of a dozen necessary items. Explain that you are going to shop for quality at the best price. Teach your child how to select the proper foods, how to distinguish between fresh and wilted vegetables, etc. Show him how you determine the economy of buying a five-pound bag of rice versus a two-pound bag. Explain the difference in cuts of meat and how those containing more fat are not as nutritious as cheaper, leaner cuts. Compare the difference in price between the store brand of beans and a name brand, and stress that often the store brand is just as good, but 5–10 percent cheaper. Show him that by making such judicious choices, you've reduced your grocery bill by several dollars. And since you normally buy five times this amount of items each week, you're talking about a savings of $10. Additionally, by using newspaper coupons, you can save even more. You're not only teaching your child the practical aspects of living, but money management and mathematics. Learning that the choices he makes can have a direct bearing on how well he eats is excellent training for his future.

When you return home, let your child help with "storing," "preparing," and "cooking" the food. From there, "serving" the food, "clearing" the table and "washing" the dishes can become family activities that require only a few minutes.

Be Careful of That Manipulative Two-Year-Old

Warning: If you're not careful, those shopping trips with toddlers can turn into negative learning experiences. Those little guys are enthralled with the "millions and millions" of goodies in a modern supermarket. They want to put half of them in the shopping cart and eat the other half immediately. They discover that the thing parents hate and fear the most is a screaming two-year-old, throwing a temper tantrum and convincing shoppers all over the store that child abuse is taking place right within earshot.

For your sake and your child's, don't let him get away with manipulative behavior. Before going to the store, explain gently but firmly that you are shopping for the family and *you* will choose the items to buy. Occasionally let him know in advance that you will let him *help* you choose one item. *Never* reward obnoxious or disruptive behavior by giving in and giving the child what he wants. By doing so, you'll turn him into a little tyrant (yes, even *your* "baby"), and future trips to all public places will be anything but pleasant. The earlier he learns that good behavior has its rewards and boorish behavior has zero or negative results, the greater your chances of raising a positive child. Undoubtedly the most effective discipline for unruly behavior is abrupt departure. The child values the trip more than the goodies, and a couple of abrupt departures without explanation will quickly solve the problem.

So what do shopping, storing, cooking, etc. have to do with keeping your child off drugs? By themselves, maybe nothing, but as part of a package of positive learning experiences they can be an important component of the overall game plan. You are truly teaching him some important realities of life.

Singing Can Be—and Should Be—Fun

"Singing" is one of the more enjoyable "ings" and can potentially bring families closer together. I know that most families don't gather around the piano or the guitar and sing, but singing together can be lots of fun. You can start with the cheerful, upbeat songs available on sheet music in any music store or the great patriotic songs, or songs of the faith.

Secondly, your family can write its own songs. It's amazing how creative nonmusical people can actually be! Thirdly, buy musical cassettes and sing along with the vocalists. There's also a cappella singing, which often sparks laughter, especially if you have a "ham" or two in the family. These occasions can be hilarious and are another way of getting high on life without the aid of drugs. You can count on the fact that families who enjoy each other and laugh together are supportive of each other and are less likely to do things (like drugs) which would hurt and disappoint other family members.

The wholesome activity of singing together will open the lines of communication about music of all kinds and invariably leads to a discussion of rock music. As stated earlier, many parents have chosen to ignore this music other than to instruct kids to "turn it down." The parents assume peer pressure has a greater influence on their kids than they do, and they want to avoid a confrontation.

At this point I must interject and say that on the important issues, peer influence is grossly overstated. Adolescents *are* more influenced by their peers in fashions, leisure pursuits and other youth oriented activities. But for principles and major issues in life, young people still normally turn to their parents for guidance.[3]

Psychiatrist Ross Campbell says peers become more influential and parents become less so between the fifth and ninth grades.[4] However, in no grade does the influence of peers outweigh parental influence for help and guidance. "To make my parents proud of me" is valued more than maintaining friendships.

Learning About Music

In a nutshell, parents are—or certainly can be—the greatest influence on their children. Therefore, your input into your children's choice of music can affect their involvement in the building-up versus the tearing-down kind of music. Keep an open mind and ask your children why they like heavy metal, etc. and why they listen to it. Most kids can't give a specific reason except that they "just like it," and it makes them "feel good." Drugs and alcohol also make people feel good, at least temporarily, but are certainly not "good" for us. With the door open for discussion, I encourage you to become familiar with the current music your kids are listening to so that you can understand it from their perspective.

Careful, parents. Don't be judgmental because you don't like the appearance of some rock groups. Long hair, unkempt beards and wild clothing are not reliable indications of character. Do listen to the message in the songs, and look at the symbolism on the record covers and at the life-style of the groups. If the message encourages occult or Satanic involvement or anything illegal or immoral, you have a strong parental responsibility to steer your children clear of the rock group and not finance the purchase of their albums or trips to their concerts.

Go with your child to the music store and find the lyrics for the Top Ten tunes on the country and western, rock, pop and heavy metal charts. Read the lyrics with the family and then ask what he's just read and how they make him feel. Are the lyrics positive or negative? Do they build you up or tear you down? In most cases you'll discover that your child hasn't given much thought to the message, but was enthralled with the beat and the sound. At this point you will have laid the groundwork for tuning in your child to the uplifting possibilities of great music.

PLEASE: Don't rush past this last suggestion. Remember that between the seventh and twelfth grades the average teenager will listen to an estimated 10,500 hours of rock music, only 500 hours less than the total time he spends in twelve years of school. Along with harmless tunes, he'll hear such songs as "Sister," a tribute to incest by pop sensation Prince, and Judas Priest's "Eat Me Alive," which describes oral sex forced at gunpoint.

He'll hear songs encouraging or "selling" rebellion,

drugs, suicide, homosexuality, premarital and extramarital sex, etc. Since what we put into our mind affects our conduct, and since the typical teenager listens to these songs dozens, even hundreds of times, their negative influence can be devastating. As a matter of fact, it's a toss-up as to which is more destructive—the music our kids listen to or the TV programs they watch. Throw in the nine hours of MTV which kids view each week, where 75 percent of the music videos have sexual themes and 50 percent have violence,[5] and it's easy to understand why 50 percent of the crime in America is committed by kids between the ages of ten and seventeen.[6]

Introduce your children to the powerful, inspiring, positive music available—music which is "head and heart," not just "body" music.[7] Acquire and read together the lyrics of the Army, Navy, Marine, Air Force and Coast Guard songs, as well as "America the Beautiful," "The Star-Spangled Banner," "Battle Hymn of the Republic," "Amazing Grace," "How Great Thou Art," and "To Dream the Impossible Dream." Then ask the kids how those words and messages affect their "feelings." This approach will prompt your kids to think about lyrics and make choices among all the different kinds of music. Chances are good that they will start "listening" and "benefiting" from better input, especially if you start from their births by playing good music on your stereo or tuning your radio to some of the better stations.

"Planning" and "Studying"

If singing is not your thing or you don't feel inclined to do it every night (you won't), then "planning" is a great alternative. You can plan family vacations or outings, or you can start "imagining" things like space travel. Plan a trip to the library for latest books on the subject. Or plan a trip to a local planetarium or a space center, if possible, to start "viewing" what space is like. By "discussing" and "exploring" your children's major interests and doing some aptitude "testing" to determine any talents and abilities still in "hiding," you'll help prepare them for making future decisions regarding higher education. This is quite important, because over 80 percent of our college graduates, ten years after graduation, are earning their living in a field not directly related to their college majors.

While we are planning, we also need to "sell" our kids on the benefits of higher education, because the need for further education in our high-tech society is increasing yearly. For example, male high school graduates ages twenty to twenty-four earned 28 percent less in real terms in 1986 than their counterparts of 1973.[8] However, a college diploma buys more than ever. The average annual income of a college graduate in 1986 was 49 percent higher than that of a high school graduate. In 1980 it was only 25 percent higher.

The planning process also includes "studying." Any one of the activities we've enumerated will create an environment and establish an attitude which will make studying and preparing for the future "exciting" and "appealing" instead of "boring" or "appalling." "Studying" takes on more and more significance in our increasingly complex world. The average American student spends less than thirty minutes each day in study and preparation outside the classroom. Japanese students, on the other hand, invest approximately three hours each day outside the classroom in study and preparation under the supervision of their mothers. They score significantly higher on competitive tests. You just can't beat one-on-one for learning.

There is no way your child is learning as much while studying if he's listening to the radio or TV. If TV and/or radio helped the learning process, every school in America would require their use in every classroom.

Parental Involvement Is the Key

Parents who exhibit interest and get directly involved with studying and homework positively influence their kids, particularly during the early years of their children's life and formal education. Study habits established early in your child's academic career *will* make a difference later. Open-ended questions about what he's reading, such as "What do you think this means?" or "How do you feel about this?" or "What's happening to her?" or "What is he doing?" will have a bearing on your child's attitude about reading and education. Your personal attention and the example you set of being a consistent reader will set a good example. For additional help, I recommend *Better Grades Easier* by businessman Wayne Knipe. This simple, concise (thirty minutes' reading time) guide costs $2.95 and can be ordered from Taylor Publishing, P.O. Box 597, Dallas, Texas 75221 (214-637-2800).

The Evidence Grows, published by the National Committee for Citizens in Education clearly demonstrates that children whose parents help them at home perform better in school.[9] Kids who are failing improve dramatically when their parents are called in to help. This applies to children at every level of achievement.

> In a world where "good times," "finding yourself," "doing my own thing," and "being free" are placed in front of good grades, this involvement in your child's life will represent a departure from much of today's philosophy. However, I can assure you that the investment in time and energy will bring enormous, long-lasting rewards for both you and your child.

Become "People"-Oriented

Another important "ing" is "visiting." Interacting with relatives, neighbors and friends can teach invaluable social and communication skills while developing closer, more meaningful relationships. Visiting a shut-in or senior citizen will teach your child compassion and patience while simultaneously giving him a chance to soak in the wisdom of the older generation.

Negative visits can be very important, and need only be conducted once. Visit someone with lung cancer or emphysema and let your child see the deadly results of smoking. Go to a drug rehab center and let your child see first-hand what happens to addicts. It will have an impact on him to hear those addicts desperately wish they had never smoked that first joint or tried crack or cocaine "just once to see what it was like."

One of the more meaningful trips your child could take is sponsored by the YMCA and is part of their "A Face-to-Face Aversion" program which takes young people ages thirteen to sixteen—mostly truants and first-time offenders—on field trips to prisons to talk with inmates.

Program founder Lupe Fernandez is quoted in the *Dallas Morning News* as saying, "The program is successful because youths are treated as if they are in prison during their visit to the corrections facility. They go through indoctrination given by the assistant warden and they are told what they can do and what they can't do."[10]

Youths are given a tour of the cellblocks before they sit down to a question-and-answer session with a panel of six to ten inmates. The message is clear: do drugs, drop out of school, and you could end up in the custody of the Department of Corrections. Yes, that's fear motivation, but it's especially effective when kids realize that none of the men and women behind bars ever had the goal of being locked up in prison with thieves, murderers, child abusers and wife beat-ers. They certainly never planned on being in a place where brutal homosexual rape is rampant.

Are drugs and alcohol serious problems? Seventy-nine percent of the women and 89 percent of the men incarcerated in Arizona, according to former Director of Prisons Ellis MacDougall, are there because of crimes committed while under the influence, or because of crimes committed to get the money to purchase drugs or alcohol.

Another educational place to visit is the office of a social worker who deals with teenage mothers. Listen carefully as the social worker describes in endless detail case after case of young girls who "proved their love" or bought the insane idea that "everybody's doing it."

Open those ears wide as you learn just how "glamorous" it is to arise at 6:00 a.m. after being up half the night caring for a fretful baby. Let your teen hear what it's like feeding and dressing that baby, taking him to a day-care center, working all day for minimum wage, and picking up the baby to head home for a bleak supper and a lonely evening. No parties, few friends, no boyfriend (he left before the baby was born because he didn't want the responsibility or he wasn't sure it was his), and little hope for the future. The odds are nineteen to one that mother and baby will *continue* to live in poverty, and the odds are prohibitive that mother and child will end up on drugs or alcohol. Thus the poverty/welfare/addiction chain continues into the next generation.

Let's move on to "riding." An old-fashioned ride to watch God's glorious sunset can be an inspiring experience that draws the family closer. Even a trip to nowhere in particular can be rewarding because it represents quality time together. Schedule weekly "dates" with your child to a destination of his choosing. It's astonishing how even quiet kids will become talkative when alone with a parent in a car with time to relax and share. Try it. You'll learn more about your child and love and understand him more because of it.

Now, if you find all these activities "tiring," let me remind you that outside of eating, I'm only talking about an hour or less each evening for the activity you choose. If you're the typical parent, you spend over three hours a day in front of the boob tube and 70 percent of the time you're watching it because it's "there," not because you're interested. I know you'll agree that investing an hour each day with your child will be tremendously "rewarding" for both of you. This change-of-pace approach to life will reduce the number of times you'll hear your thirteen-year-old complain, "I'm bored." He'll be far more inclined to hit the books more enthusiastically and act like the important member of the family he is. And since positively active kids seldom get involved in negative activities, you're taking another giant step to raise a positive, drug-free child.

I'm not suggesting you do all these things every day or even most of the time. Circumstances vary, and the number and ages of your children will be factors. However, these suggestions increase your options and keep kids busy learning valuable lessons and sharing responsibility for an orderly life.

A couple of final "ings" before we get to the "ending." Especially in the beginning, considerable "disciplining" and "persisting" will be required of you, but when your kids start "observing" how "willing" you are to make them your highest priority, they will reciprocate by "cooperating." Your family will be a "winning" one clearly proving our premise that, "you can have everything in life you want if you will only help enough other people get what they want." Your sacrifices will prevent you from doing any "halo adjusting." Instead, you'll be "shouting" with joy at the delight your children (and later your grandchildren) will bring you. Incidentally, if I had known how much fun grandchildren are, I would have been even nicer to their parents!

Paul Lewis ties it all together in a note to dads, which applies equally to moms: There are two secrets to winning as a dad. When you and I build on these foundations, the rest of fathering follows rather naturally. One of the most indicting cartoons I've seen pictures a young boy with hat, bat and baseball glove in hand standing next to his newspaper-reading father exclaiming, "Play with me, or trade me!"

"Fellow dad, neither you nor I can win unless we both play and pray. These are the two sides of the fathering coin—the secret weapons of the dad who will be effective. All play and no pray builds a fun relationship, but one without depth or backbone. All pray and no play leads to bitterness and rejection by the child of both God and his father. Both must be practiced daily in balanced doses. They're the most important 'work' you or I will ever do."[11]

Time for Personal Evaluation

1. What do you think Zig is really trying to get across with his "ings" of life?

2. Why do you think Zig suggests so many things for the family to do together?

3. Is there a chance we have forgotten how to cooperate, associate and communicate with our families?

4. Who has the greatest influence on a child?

5. What happens when parents get involved in their children's education?

6. What do you think about some of the "visiting" to prisons, hospitals, drug rehabilitation centers, social workers, etc., to see the results of drug abuse?

CHAPTER 11

CHAPTER 13

My Child Is Already Hooked

Perhaps one of the reasons you're reading this book is that you know or fear that your child is already hooked on drugs or alcohol. Your problem is more serious, but it can be solved.

Since getting a child off drugs and/or alcohol is out of my area of expertise, I turned to my friend, Forest Tennant, M.D., America's most experienced and best informed drug authority, for help. Following are some of his invaluable insights.

If you intuitively feel that "something is wrong," but don't quite know what, immediately go down a checklist of symptoms. The signs will be there, especially if your child smokes or is in high school, because approximately 50 percent of all smokers between the ages of thirteen and nineteen are involved in illegal drugs, and 60 percent of all high schoolers are using drugs or alcohol. NOTE: Please do not put this book down and start accusing your child of anything or start searching his room if he smokes. DO calmly and systematically look at everything that might indicate drug or alcohol involvement.

Begin by searching your memory. Has your child changed close friends recently, and if so, do the new friends bother you? Have his sleeping habits changed substantially the last few months? Is he missing meals and other family events more often? Does his mood swing from talkative and outgoing to quiet and brooding?

Does he spend more time isolated in his room, or is he easily offended by any interest on your part about his activities? Has there been a change in his weight or grooming habits? Has he lost interest in a favorite hobby or physical activity? Have his grades declined and has he lost interest in that scholarship? Is he spending an inordinate amount of time listening to hard rock, heavy metal or country and western music?

What about his energy level? Is he too tired to lift a fork to his mouth one day and highly energetic the next? Is his complexion healthy, or rough and sallow? Are his eyes clear, or frequently bloodshot? Do his plans change frequently and exclude other members of the family?

I'm not trying to turn you into a private investigator, but if you're following some of the winning "ings" I covered earlier, you can quickly and easily answer the above questions. If you can't answer all of them, I encourage you to spend about two weeks observing your child(ren)'s behavior and keeping careful notes. Then if you have reason to suspect your child is involved in drugs or alcohol, call the National Clearing House for Alcohol and Drug Information at 301-468-2600 for guidance.

Early detection and treatment dramatically improve your chances of saving your child if he is just getting started on substance abuse, and will save your family untold grief *and* money. Caution: If your child is heavily involved in drugs or alcohol, you need to prepare for one of the most difficult, heartbreaking battles of your life. You must win the war for your child's sake and your family's sake.

Tough Love

The toughest part is accepting the fact that this sobbing, pro-
testing, sullen, often defiant youngster (your "baby") insisting on his innocence is a skillful, bald-faced liar who has
been deceiving you for months, maybe even years. Always
remember that it's not your child who is the problem, but the
drugs in him which are the problem. Your child needs your
total love and complete *dis*trust. Your love must be total and
tough. *Force* yourself to remember that you are talking to a
confirmed liar. Remember that real love demands that you
do the best for your child, and it probably won't be what he
says he wants. You must be gentle, open and firm, always
willing to talk, and committed to verifying everything. I encourage you to seek professional help in reclaiming your
child. You might have to drag your child kicking and screaming into treatment, but good treatment programs get about
the same percentage of uncooperative kids off drugs as those
who are willing to go for help. Keeping them off is another
matter, but right now your number one priority is sobriety.
Once you reach that goal and maintain it for eighteen to
twenty-four months, you can start treating your child like the
normal, responsible person he has become.

In conjunction with entering a professional rehab program, he should establish some good habits and disciplines.
One of the most important is sleeping seven to eight hours
every night at basically the same time. Sleep is the only time
the brain reproduces certain chemicals which are essential
for handling stress.

Your child should eat well-balanced meals with the family
at the same times, if possible. A nutritious breakfast is crucial.

Also, start a disciplined exercise program which gets more
vigorous as your child works his body into shape. He
shouldn't play the hero and start with a marathon. Take the
advice of a skilled physician or follow the suggestions of Dr.

Kenneth Cooper in his book, *The Aerobics Program to Total Fitness.* Exercise activates the pituitary gland and floods the system with endorphins, which are two hundred times more powerful than morphine. It produces a natural high and supplies the body with natural chemicals.

These first three steps will make the substance abuser feel much better physically and make him aware of the importance of his mind and body. They help to establish order, which is prerequisite for whipping the drug problem.

The fourth step is to help your child see that his former drug companions are really his worst enemies. Under no circumstances is he to associate with them, not even to try to get them off drugs. The risk is too high, and your child, at this stage, is far more likely to try drugs "just one more time for old time's sake." As one alcoholic said many years ago, "One drink is too many and a thousand is not enough." It's the same with drugs.

Your child should avoid all areas and circumstances related to his former substance abuse: bars, certain theaters, bowling alleys, restaurants, shopping centers, athletic events, cars, even neighborhoods. Moving may even be necessary; his life is at stake.

Get your child involved in a variety of activities or hobbies that require discipline, time and organization, such as painting, league bowling, chess, church softball, or "back-to-school" programs. They will keep him busy and prepare him for a brighter future.

Next, you need to help him establish a relationship with God. Drug rehab programs such as Alcoholics Anonymous which have a spiritual dimension have a higher success rate. Drugs are supernatural in their power, so a greater supernatural power (God) is needed to reinforce human resources to win the battle. Practice a balanced daily dose of playing and praying. All pray and no play leads to bitterness and rejection in the child, while all play and no pray builds a fun relationship, but one without depth or backbone.

Step number eight is to take inventory of every person your child may have offended, abused, fought with, etc. when he was involved in alcohol and/or drugs. If substance abuse has been prolonged, the list will probably be extensive. Your child needs to apologize to those people, tell them he is now sober and working on a daily basis to stay that way. He should ask for their prayers, support and encouragement—and forgiveness—because he needs everything possible going for him to win this battle.

The ninth step is for him to set some realistic goals for the immediate and future life. One goal should be to stay sober that day. He should set goals in every area of his life: mental, physical, spiritual, social, career, family and financial. A directed life gives him the best shot at whipping the substance abuse habit. As a matter of fact, by following the steps outlined here, he can turn the substance abuse portion of his life into a learning, growing experience.

Step number ten is to reduce stress in his life as much as possible. Don't commit him to a helter-skelter, busy schedule. He should ask close friends and family members to monitor his life in such a way as to let him know when they think he's under too much pressure and to take it easy.

He could set aside some quiet time every day and start the day by reciting the Lord's Prayer. Print it on one side of a $3'' \times 5''$ card and write the Twenty-third Psalm on the other side. He could take a moment during the day to slowly read them, and in the quiet darkness of each evening dwell on the phraseology as he drifts off to sleep.

To separate your child from drugs and the life-style that feeds the habit, eliminate rock, hard rock, heavy metal, etc., as well as country and western music. The former is frantic and clearly identified with drugs. The latter is sad, negative, and identified with drinking. Ditto for violent TV programs and any form of pornography. Substitute soft, gentle melodies with positive, orderly, uplifting lyrics.

The most important step is to enroll your child in a support group such as Alcoholics Anonymous or Narcotics Anonymous. Their support and encouragement will be invaluable. Seeing other people whipping the same problem will give your child confidence that he, too, can win the war against substance abuse.

Seminars, sermons, recordings and books can be tremendously informative and inspiring. Dr. Tennant's research proves that an enthusiastic motivational speaker, preacher or cassette tape activates the brain, which floods the body with endorphins, dopamine, norepinephrine and neurotransmitters. They enable your body to create and store energy, endurance and creativity. The benefits of motivation are psychological *and* physiological.

At this point, you and your child may be convinced that you can win the war, but are concerned that along the way you might lose a battle (have a relapse). You ask, "What do we do then?"

You haven't failed. Your child succeeded in staying sober for so many days, and if he's succeeded for that long, he can succeed, permanently. He should take a deep breath and start over. He'll do even better as he realizes that by winning the battles one day at a time, he will definitely win the war on substance abuse and the game of life at the same time.

Again, though these last three chapters have been on drugs and alcohol, I'd like to emphasize that this entire book was written to help you raise positive, drug-free kids. Now let's move on to another important and challenging step we must take to help our kids become the winners they were born to be.

Time for Personal Evaluation

1. Do you feel like a private investigator, or do you properly feel your concern is for your child?
2. Do you share Zig's belief that despite the nation's drug

problems you can raise your child as positive and drug-free?

3. Will you be able to remember that if your child is hooked on drugs you cannot, must not, believe or trust him?

4. Can you—will you—love your child enough to do what is best for your child to get him off drugs?

5. Would you be willing to move if it were necessary to get your child off drugs?

6. Are you prepared to patiently hang tough and love your child enough to fight battles over his choice of music, TV viewing, friends, etc. in order to do what is best for your child?

CHAPTER 14

Sex

> *If you are still a virgin, you can be like the others any time you want, but they can never again be like you.*
> —Author Bill Sanders

Blessing or Curse

Of all the factors in life, the one with the most potential for good *or* evil is sex. Properly used as God intended for it to be, sex truly brings more pleasure *and* happiness than anything. It brings husbands and wives into a beautiful loving relationship that is almost beyond comprehension. It perpetuates the human race and enables family love to be extended through the generations. Misused and out of control in an immoral way (any sex outside marriage), it brings more grief than any other single factor.

Unfortunately, all sense of sexual sanity seems to have gone by the boards in our media-oriented society. Parents and their children are bombarded from every conceivable angle with sex in advertisements for every product from automobiles to zoos, from coffee to ketchup, and from golf clubs to gulf resorts.

It's difficult to walk into a newsstand and not be hit with

flagrant displays of pornography within easy reach of our children. The suggestiveness of television almost defies belief, whether it's on a talk show, a sitcom, or a movie. Each year there are about 20,000 scenes with suggested sexual acts on TV, all of them without regard to outcome and certainly not to contraception. Kids learn from these that sex is all below the waist.[1] The concept they are selling is: Extramarital sex is fun; everybody's doing it; after all, you only go through life once, so grab all the excitement you can. We see profane and vulgar sexual material on t-shirts, bumper stickers, and almost every other conceivable place. The message is always the same. Sex, any kind of sex, with anybody is the fun thing to do. Almost from the moment of birth, our kids are encouraged more and more to establish "meaningful" relationships (go to dinner first), but to practice "safe sex" and everything will be all right. The daily papers casually report members of the opposite sex living together or taking trips together as if it is the normal, standard, customary life-style. Tragically, when our children are bombarded with the idea that as long as they use birth control, sex is okay, our jobs as parents become increasingly difficult.

For now, let's take a broad look at the entire picture and explore some of the things you can do right now to help insure that your child will grow up to be faithful, first to himself, then to the person he will eventually marry.

Let's start with sex education, which is discussed with more heat and less light than just about any other subject.

Many people honestly feel that sex education is an absolute necessity to prevent or slow down the ever-increasing instances of illegitimate pregnancies, abortions, herpes, AIDS, and venereal diseases. Many others disagree.

Evidence is substantial that in areas where sex education is taught without the attendant moral values, promiscuity, pregnancies, and venereal disease increase in measurable amounts. It is my firm conviction that we need not more information on birth control in the schools but more teaching of moral values and self-control in the home. I also believe that since our kids are sexually stimulated from a very early age by TV, music, and playground gossip loaded with mis-information, sex education *must* be taught from an early age by the parents and only in *rare* circumstances by the schools. For those rare circumstances when sex education in the schools is the only viable alternative, I encourage you to write the Free Congress Foundation (721 Second Street, N.E., Washington, DC 20002) for the booklet *When Schools Teach Sex* by Judith B. Echaniz.

Sex Education Is Taught Every Day

If mom and dad are openly thoughtful and affectionate with each other, evidenced by a little hand holding, expressions of love, and nonsexual hugging, children very early learn that the family is a loving unit, that it's nice to have a mate of one's very own. When loving parents demonstrate kind-ness and caring toward each other, children learn more about the proper attitude and behavior toward the opposite sex than by any other method. Such parents provide an effective life-time laboratory of sex education for their children to observe. This effectively opens the door to teach the kids about sex and the role it plays in their lives. More importantly, it pre-pares the kids to understand that a sexual relationship within the bonds of marriage is a truly beautiful expression of com-mitted love.

I remember one afternoon when my six-year-old son was watching an old, old television movie. The hero and heroine were embracing. As I walked through the den, I saw it and rather facetiously said, "My goodness! That sure is mushy!" Without looking up from the television my son replied, "Huh! You ought to see you and mom!"

To be honest, I would prefer that my son spread the word around the neighborhood that mom and dad are at home hugging rather than that mom and dad are at home fighting.

To the best of my knowledge, my son had never seen me give his mother more than a friendly, quick kiss. But I do know he had seen us hold hands and hug a lot.

I do not believe a child should be permitted to see his parents indulge in any display of affection in which he, himself, cannot participate. Nevertheless, my son had gotten a clear picture that mom and dad were affectionate with each other. It was such a "normal" thing for him to see his parents loving and nonsexually embracing each other that he did not even bother to look up from the television when he made his comment. I believe that's the best way to raise a positive kid who is going to grow up looking forward to a permanent, positive relationship with the girl he marries.

In an article in *U.S.A. Today* Marilyn Elias reports a study done by Utah State University sociologist Brent Miller that involved 1,150 teenagers. He discovered that the more openly parents talked to teens about their sex-related values and beliefs, the less active their kids were in both sexual attitudes and behavior. *Also, if the teens learned the sexual facts from parents, they were significantly less likely to be sexually active than those who learned them from friends.*

Sex Education Starts at Birth

Informally, your child's sex education starts from infancy by the way mom and dad treat each other. "Formal" sex education should start when your child is between the ages of three and five. A marvelous approach is to pick up *Why Boys and Girls Are Different*, by Carol Greene (Concordia Publishing House, St. Louis), and read it to your child in the same natural, animated voice you use when reading other children's books.

A few sessions like this will satisfy childish curiosity and answer any questions the child might have had. This procedure properly sets the stage for more detailed and mature discussions later with no hint of embarrassment for either the parent or child. *Why Boys and Girls Are Different* opens the door of sex education to your child's mind and makes it easier to continue in the months and years ahead with other books, such as *Where Do Babies Come From?* by Ruth Hummell, appropriate for children between the ages of six and eight. When your child is between the ages of eight and eleven, *How You Are Changing*, by Jane Graver, is excellent. Concordia also publishes two books for parents of preteens and teens, *Preparing for Adolescence* by Dr. James Dobson, and *How to Teach Your Child About Sex* by Grace Ketterman, M.D. These books are beautifully and sensitively written. Their approach to sex education demystifies sex and can dramatically reduce the possibility that your children will be sexually active.

Avoiding the Problem

Throughout your child's preteen and teen years there will be many opportunities to share common sense principles and procedures for avoiding situations which can lead to sexual temptation. A few examples: The viewing of sexually suggestive videos, movies, or TV programs can ultimately break down our moral values and weaken our resolve. The use of drugs and alcohol lowers our will power and removes some of our inhibitions. There are, of course, countless reasons not to drink or take drugs, but your child should know that this one is high on the list. The telling of sexually oriented jokes trivializes sexual relationships and puts sex in the category of a sporting event, and should be discouraged. Along the way, you should warn your children that the wearing of revealing or tight-fitting clothes is often misinterpreted by others as an open invitation to "see what you can get away with."

> *When you physically arouse an*
> *appetite you cannot spiritually*
> *satisfy, you are guilty of fraud.*
> —Josh McDowell

Many morally sound, committed young people with strong religious foundations and loving relationships with their parents wind up becoming sexually active and teenage parents, themselves. Why? They erroneously believe that they are always "in control," that their moral foundation is strong enough to withstand any temptation. Over a period of time they start spending more and more time alone with their dates, often ending up parked in isolated spots, which can be life-threatening. All of this time spent alone—parked cars, at the home of a date whose parents are away—is an open invitation for those overly-active hormones to lead from handholding and light kissing to open-mouthed kissing and petting which, if practiced often enough, will lead to sexual intercourse with the boy and girl sharing equal responsibility. Talk to your kids, parents! Tell them again and again never to put themselves in a position to be tempted beyond what they can bear, or raped (date rape is one of the most common unreported crimes in our country).

Play It Safe

In this land of single parents, working mothers, and "too-busy" two-parent families, it is of critical importance to stress that your children should never be alone in the home of a girlfriend or boyfriend whose parents are away—regardless of how innocent it might appear. This includes those times when your son or daughter is baby-sitting and his or her special friend just wants to stop by to "study."

Incidentally, parents, when your child does start dating

and double-dating, you should be prepared to get even less sleep, because you are going to need to stay awake until your teenager comes home. Knowing you care enough and love him enough to sacrifice much-needed sleep until he is safely home will make your child feel loved and secure. It also encourages more responsible behavior on your child's part. If he or she knows you are going to be there to look him in the eye and chat about the events of the evening, chances are greatly improved that there will be no drugs, alcohol, or sexual activity before your child comes home.

Please understand that these procedures will work *only* if you have sold the concepts, life-styles and value system we have covered throughout this book.

One of the biggest benefits of this morally sound, commonsense approach is that it will give your son or daughter the choicest selections for serious relationships which lead to marriage. Interestingly enough, study after study verifies the fact that sexually active guys and gals still want a mate with zero sexual experience. When that "nice young man" from the "good family" looks your daughter in the eye and promises to love her "even more" and respect her "just as much," she could remember that *he's lying*. Nobody who *really* loves you will ever ask you to do anything that is not in your best interests.

You Can't Rush Mother Nature

Between the ages of about six to puberty, according to psychiatrist William McGrath, a child goes through a critical period of latent development.[2] During those years, little boys need to learn how to play little boy games and get along with little boys. Little girls need to learn how to play little girl games and get along with little girls.

Dr. McGrath says it is devastating during that time for children to be artificially stimulated sexually by TV, videos, movies or pornographic materials. Such stimulation forces the child to skip that period of latent development. Tragically, it does not speed the child's maturation process, but in many cases delays and sometimes permanently prevents the child from reaching maturity.

Surely it is no coincidence today that more men and women between the ages of twenty-five and thirty-five are at least partially dependent on their parents than at any time in America's history, because they never grew up or learned to accept responsibility for themselves.

Sexually Ready for the Work World

One extremely important aspect of sexually educating your child, especially your daughter, to the ways of the world concerns the entrance into the world of work. In most cases this involves baby-sitting. On a teen's baby-sitting assignments, mom and dad definitely need to know the circumstances and people involved. You must have a very serious talk with your daughter, regardless of how much you love and trust the person for whom she is baby-sitting. Some men feel an overpowering attraction for young girls, and, if they do not have moral restraints, will rationalize and justify every action they take. With this in mind you need to tell your daughter that there are some men in the world who do not treat young girls with respect. (Let me remind you that by now you will have covered her basic sex education.) Tell her that if anyone says or does anything that makes her uncomfortable, she is to let you know exactly what was said and done. In most cases, parents, you should gently probe the events of the evening when your daughter comes home.

Ideally, from a biological/physiological perspective, mom should talk to daughters and dad should talk to sons. However, when it comes to telling daughters about the way boys "really" are, dad can tell daughters more in a few minutes than mom can all day. For example, most boys in the heat of a passionate seduction effort (which they might but probably don't confuse with love) will pledge undying love and the permanent sealing of their lips. The next day a select few close friends take a sudden interest in dating this "wild passion flower" whom they had never even spoken to before she foolishly believed her suitor of the night before. That is not an isolated incident—that is S.O.P. (standard operating procedure) for most males. The male ego is such that the situation generally occurs even when the guy has been going steady or is even engaged to marry the girl.

Dad can tell his daughter in no uncertain terms that the oldest trick since Adam and Eve is for the boy to challenge the girl to prove her love for him by surrendering her virginity. Any *thinking* girl would know better; but a genuine affection for the boys, fanned by the passion of the moment under tempting circumstances, can cause reason to go out the door if the girl is not forewarned and forearmed.

Because mom understands girls, she can lovingly tell her son how to treat girls to win their love and respect. She can give him the woman's perspective and explain how girls think and feel. Mom can properly caution her son not to become trapped in a relationship that is not healthy.

Virginity is Priceless

From the beginning of sex education for your child, you should stress that sex is a beautiful gift God has set aside for husbands and wives and *only* for husbands and wives. Both boys and girls should be carefully taught and reminded that their virginity is a precious gift they can give to their future spouses. Regardless of what the experts and humanists of the day are inclined to say, premarital sex is not only sin, but it is also irresponsible and definitely not in the best interests of the persons involved.

Because premarital sex and living together before marriage are becoming increasingly popular, your job of "selling" the idea of waiting for marriage before becoming sexually active is a tough one. It is, however, one of the most important jobs a parent has, so prepare your sales talk well! I strongly encourage you to devour a copy of Josh McDowell's book *Why Wait*? It's magnificent and it's loaded with persuasive information to share with your kids before they start dating.

> *Love is not a basis for a sexual relationship. Marriage is.*

The tragedy today is that *many parents never even tell their children that sex outside of marriage is not something "everybody does."* Nor do they tell them that it is absolutely wrong. In many cases they never tell their sons and daughters that, when they surrender their virginity, they are defrauding their future mate and surrendering a part of themselves that is priceless. Tragically, countless parents never even tell their children what virginity is or how it is lost; nor do they mention the possibility of pregnancy or venereal disease.

A psychologist once told me of the tears and heartbreaks of the countless young men and women he has counseled. They took overpowering feelings of guilt into their marriages because they were so "in love" before the wedding they rationalized that premarital sex was not only acceptable, it was also morally responsible and, therefore, not a sin in the eyes of God.

He told me one particular story that made a deep impression on my mind (no names, of course). A beautiful young woman sat in his office one morning and shared how she, in an effort to become popular and to get in with a particular group, surrendered her virginity. The "gang" by whom she wanted to be accepted had clearly stipulated that no virgin would be a part of their crowd. Result: While still a teenager, she surrendered her virginity to a boy she did not even like.

Needless to say, this was not the only boy with whom she became sexually involved. Once the virginity is gone and sexual activity has begun, it is very difficult for a young person to say no.

The psychologist elaborated and pointed out that when the girl was older and fully realized what she had surrendered, she became angry—and even bitter—at the fact that she had never been told what she would be sacrificing. She had exchanged a priceless gift she could have given her husband for the acceptance of a group that was undesirable at best and dangerous at worst. It took her a number of years, during which she often seriously contemplated suicide, to work through the problem.

As a result of this conversation and the other information gathered for this book, I have reached the inevitable conclusion that parents who do not sexually educate their children leave them completely vulnerable to the whims of biology. In a real sense parents are guilty of child abuse—or at least neglect—because the consequences can be so devastating.

Extremely important: If you are a parent who did not properly inform your child, and if your child suffered as a result, don't go on a guilt trip. I believe that you truly love your child and that you did the best you could with what you knew to teach during those years your child needed to be taught. For the rest of you who have small children, the information contained in this chapter can make a tremendous difference in their lives.

The point is crystal clear. If mothers and dads will instruct their sons and daughters by word and deed from the very beginning that their virginity is priceless and that premarital sex is a no-no, many years of grief and unhappiness can be averted. So, parents, *if you do* nothing *in the area of sex education but convince your sons and daughters they should be virgins when they marry, you will have helped them protect their honor and avoid untold grief.* So how, when, and where do you teach your kids the "facts of life"?

Mary Jo Heckinger gives some sound advice on the role of parents in sex education.[3] Ms. Heckinger points out that when a young child has a question, the first step is to ascertain what he really wants to know. The simplest way is to ask the child what he thinks the answer is. This enables you to focus your answer on the information he wants and reveals any of his misconceptions.

She states that scientists say that 80 percent of sexual dysfunction could be avoided if couples had elementary anatomical knowledge, yet most high school students cannot draw diagrams of the reproductive system or adequately explain its function. She maintains that we (parents) need a good dictionary describing anatomical terms, so we can use it when we talk with our children. She also says that boys and girls should be prepared for events they will experience as they change, such as a nocturnal emission or menstruation. Such an event can be traumatic to the unprepared child.

As children become teenagers, it is far more difficult to talk to them. As much as the teenager asks to be left alone, he still needs your support and guidance. He is not completely sure how to stand on his own two feet yet, and he knows it.

Sex Education by Example

Ms. Heckinger stresses the role that God plays in this sex education, pointing out that sexuality is a gift from God to both men and women. In its rightful place it is beautiful and good. One simply cannot tell children for eighteen years that men want what they can get, that all girls are teases, that displaying affection toward the opposite sex is nasty, that intercourse is bad, and then convincingly tell them on their wedding nights that sex is a gift from God. (That approach is both absurd and unrealistic.) I caution you to never even mildly hint that sex is dirty.

Ms. Heckinger emphasizes the importance of the role

model. She observes that if the boy sees that all males open doors for women, then he will open doors for them. If the girl sees females carrying purses, she will do likewise. By watching others of the same sex, children acquire appropriate behavior.

She addresses the issue of exposure of the adult body to children and states that a parent caught in a state of undress needs to react calmly but firmly. Privacy is the issue, not nudity. A parent is well within his rights to state, "In our house we knock on doors before entering. Please go out, and I will be there as soon as I finish dressing." To mimic a screaming banshee and rip the bedspread off the bed will only convince the child there is something terribly wrong with seeing the nude body. How you react will determine your child's attitude about the body later.

Careful Mom—Don't Arouse Your Son

A junior high boy whose mother makes breakfast in a flimsy negligee may suffer guilt feelings because he finds himself responding sexually. Parents should avoid unconsciously seducing their children. Based on her research, psychologist Joyce Brothers has come to the conclusion that some men become rapists as a result of having been sexually overstimulated in childhood by their mothers or mother substitutes.

Wait to Date

Odds are 9 to 1 that a girl who starts dating at age twelve will *be sexually active before she finishes high school. If she starts dating at age sixteen, the odds are 4 to 1 that she* won't *be sexually active when she finishes high school.*

—Josh McDowell

On the surface it might seem that as boys they had been given a great deal of care and affection by their mothers, but they had actually experienced constant sexual frustration. They were continually stimulated but not satisfied; in most cases this seductive behavior by the mother alternated with cruelty, harshness, and beatings. Aggression was often a common occurrence, and the boys grew up with the idea that women had to be taken by force. It is not surprising then that when a rapist marries, he will probably select a woman whose emotional problems are similar to those of his mother.

The normal, healthy feelings of affection between father and daughter and mother and son are vitally important for the mental and emotional health of all parties and are essential for good, solid family relationships.

Mom and Dad's Relationship

Psychiatrist John Kozek noted that many times, as daughters begin to mature and move from innocent adolescence into adulthood, too many parents "lose" their children because of the father's uncertainty in his role.

An FBI study a number of years ago revealed that when the father continues to show normal family affection for his daughter, the number of instances of those girls going astray sexually is dramatically less than it is for the girls who do not have that affection from their fathers. Dr. Kozek made the observation that in our changing society, many times an insecure father with a poor self-image stops hugging and holding his daughter when she begins to mature.

Suddenly, the little girl who was sitting on dad's knee one day is being told by dad the next day, by his body language, to go away. What he's doing is throwing her out to someone who is willing to give her affection—but the wrong kind.

You develop a good level of communication, build a solid relationship, and protect your blossoming teenager from sexual involvement by showing healthy love and affection for her, which she desperately needs. However, dad should be very careful that the affection is in no way of a nature that the child could construe as sexual. If a daughter shows discomfort with any sort of affection from her father, he should discontinue it immediately.

At this critical time parents need to be extremely careful about their daughters' male friends. Many times an eighth or ninth grade girl, who is just blossoming into womanhood, is approached by a junior or senior boy for a date. To begin with, a girl should be at least sixteen before she is permitted to go on a date alone with a boy and fifteen before she's permitted to double-date. Parents should be especially alert to any attention a boy who is three to five years older gives to their daughter when she is twelve, thirteen, or fourteen years old.

The attention from the older boy can be quite flattering, and she may lose her sense of perspective. Incidentally, his attention to her is often a sign of immaturity and a poor self-image on his part. Parents who have a son in the eleventh or twelfth grade, who suddenly takes an interest in a twelve- to fourteen year-old girl, should strongly encourage him to put a stop to that interest. Parents should have a serious talk with him about his sexual role and responsibilities and start regularly spending more time with him.

Realistically, I must warn you that the shy, awkward, stumbling fourteen-year-old boy also poses a tremendous potential risk for your twelve- or thirteen-year-old daughter. Most of that risk is wrapped up in the words *time* and *opportunity*. If they are permitted to spend countless hours together "studying" or watching TV unsupervised, you can count on those hopping hormones in both their bodies to overcome any and all awkward shyness, and a real danger to both the girl and the boy exists and *grows* with every get-together they have. Remember, familiarity and opportunity breed *attempt*. Supervise them, parents—keep them busy—channel their energy into healthy family activities.

Regardless of whether or not you've had a serious discussion about sex with your child, I encourage you to set aside an occasion when mom and daughter or dad and son spend at least a long day together. A hike in an isolated area, a camping outing, a fishing trip, or a long drive where there's no interference or rush of any kind is ideal.

Foundation for Marriage

When my son was sixteen, we spent a long weekend together. He was displaying considerable interest in a pretty young girl. Although he had gone to socials and spent time with other girls in church or in school, for the first time he was showing more than casual interest in one specific girl. We could easily tell, because when the telephone rang no one had to encourage him to answer it. In two fast steps he was there. When he shaved, he was extra careful to get all four of them, and there was a certain hop in his steps that indicated our son was growing up.

With this in mind I scheduled a long weekend with him. We had many beautiful hours of conversation, but to basically sum it up, here are the primary things I shared with my son. (Incidentally, we had pretty well covered the waterfront earlier.) Number one is the fact that premarital sex is a bummer and a losing proposition. First, it is morally and scripturally wrong. God makes no exceptions. He simply says, "Sex outside of the husband-wife relationship is a sin."

God tells us this not because He wants to inhibit us and keep us from having "fun" but because He loves us so much He wants the very best possible life for us to live. The second area I covered was one that he already suspected, as do about 99.9 percent of all young people when those genes and hormones start dancing around. A healthy sexual relationship in marriage is truly one of the most beautiful experiences a human being can have. Movies, television, novels, and magazines have thoroughly sold that idea, and for me to deny the attraction between men and women would have been foolish and would have destroyed my son's confidence in anything I might have had to say.

An important key to being loyal to your mate after marriage is to be faithful to your future mate before marriage.

The third point I made was that *all* successful marriages are built on trust. If he and his girlfriend refrained from sexual activity during courtship and if they were meant for each other and did get married, the inevitable would eventually happen; namely, they would be separated because of the impending birth of his child or because of business trips. If they had refrained from premarital sex, they would have established that trust upon which a successful marriage is built. I emphasize this simply because young people, according to my memory bank and all the information I have ever read, of sixteen to eighteen years old are at the absolute peak of their sexual drives. If they discipline themselves and say no to sex at this point, they will have less difficulty being loyal to their mate once they've made a lifetime commitment.

The fourth point I made with my son was, if this was not the girl for him, it would certainly be marvelous for her to be able to say someday to other people, "One of the really good things that happened to me in my lifetime was the fact that Tom Ziglar was my first boyfriend, and he treated me like a lady." I pointed out to my son that they could be lifetime friends, and he could walk away with an absolutely clear conscience.

None of the Options Are Acceptable

Fifth, I pointed out that when you indulge in sex, whether you are the boy or the girl, not only is it wrong, but once you have a sexual experience, the next thing you have on your mind is to have the second sexual experience. This often leads to promiscuity, and the results from it are devastating.

If pregnancy occurs, a decision has to be made. Should you get married? Should an abortion be performed? Should the baby be born out of wedlock? Since Christians consider abortion to be murder, that possibility would be ruled out. Therefore, another decision would have to be made. Do you keep the baby and attempt to raise it, or do you give the baby up for adoption?

Making these decisions can be extremely painful. With each alternative comes special problems, and there *are* problems with each alternative. Pregnant teenagers have a higher than average amount of health problems, and babies they do deliver have an excessive number of abnormalities compared to babies born to nonteen mothers. Unfortunately, the infant mortality rate is high, too.

I stressed to my son that an unwanted, unplanned pregnancy would totally and completely alter the lives of both teenagers. If he elected to go ahead and get married, he would, in all probability, have to give up his education, his plans for the future, and many of his hopes and dreams. If he elected not to marry the girl, then he would go through life knowing that he had violated a trust.

I pointed out that if they indulged in premarital sex they would probably have intense feelings of guilt and, as a result, would feel compelled to get married. Marriage as a result of guilt does not establish a solid base for a happy, healthy lifetime relationship.

You'll Never Get Acquainted

The other area on which I elaborated at great length with my son was this one: if you get involved in a sexual relationship, you will never really get acquainted with the girl. On the surface this certainly seems like a strange thing to say, but the reasoning is simple and sound.

Once a sexual relationship is started, you will focus on a physical and not a personal relationship, and the chances of the sexual relationship being discontinued are very, very slim.[4] As a matter of fact, when sex enters the picture, all the couple thinks about is getting back together for more sex. (This is particularly true for the boy.) They plan, scheme, and connive every way humanly possible to be off by themselves in private so they can have their sexual liaison. I pointed out to my son that it would probably make a sneak and a liar out of him and seriously affect the beautiful, open relationship he enjoyed with us and the girl's parents.

I also told him that if sex was the major focus of their attention, they would, as a matter of course, eliminate or forsake many of the extraordinarily important discussions upon which a solid marriage is built. They would never get around to asking: Will both of us work, or only one? How many children do we want, if any? What are our philosophies of raising children? How are they similar, and how are they different? Where will we worship?

All in all, it was one of the most important periods of time I'd ever spent with my son, but I repeat, we'd spent countless hours together before then, talking about all the things that concerned him as he was growing up.

One of the most beautiful and moving moments of my life occurred as the weekend drew to a close. My son said to me, "You know, Dad, my idea of heaven on earth takes place every November when I watch you and Mom take off for the three or four days you always set aside for each other to celebrate your wedding anniversary. That's what I want for my life."

Talk to Them, Parents

What all of this boils down to is the fact that to raise positive, moral kids and prepare them for the future, we need to be tuned in and listen to them. We need to be available as often as possible to talk with them.

One important key to communication on any issue or subject, especially the really sensitive issues of our day, is to end every conversation with a comma, not a period. At the end of every discussion on these subjects the wise parent will terminate the session by saying, "I want you to remember that any time you want to continue the conversation, I will be glad to do so; and I promise to give you an honest answer." This approach demonstrates sensitivity and common sense.

The Homosexual Issue

Another major issue that concerns parents today is homosexuality. Many parents want to know what, if anything, they can do to make certain their sons and daughters grow up straight. They are troubled by many of the things they read and hear that are in direct contradiction to each other.

Two books that will be especially helpful to you are *Gay Is Not Good* by Frank M. DuMas and *Growing Up Straight* by Dr. George Rekers. Both are well written, scientifically valid, and full of useful information for parents who want to make certain their kids are never trapped in homosexuality.

The Father's Role

The most critical role in the homosexual issue is that of the father. When fathers are either physically or psychologically absent from the home, their children may suffer major problems in sexual role adjustment. The most frequent family pattern reported by the male homosexual includes a binding, intimate mother in combination with a hostile, detached father. The fathers of homosexual sons are reported to be less affectionate than fathers of heterosexual sons.

In one study of forty homosexual men, not a single man reported having had an affectionate relationship with his father. The fathers of homosexual men have been found to be indifferent and uninvolved with their families. In a majority of cases the fathers had left the decision-making in the home to the mothers. Sons of such fathers often felt that their fathers were critical of their lack of interest in typically masculine activities.

Many homosexual men have reported that their homes and childhood were mother-dominated. In such homes neither the mother nor the father typically encouraged masculine activities or attitudes in the son. Vulnerability to homosexual temptation can also result if the parent tells the child that homosexuality is okay, if your child is taught in a sex education course in school that homosexuality is an acceptable alternate life-style, or, more obviously, if parents involve their children in incestuous, homosexual acts.

I raise the issue of homosexuality primarily to alert you to the dangers and to encourage you never to give up the hope that if your child is involved, he can be helped.

To raise positive, moral kids who are sexually straight, we've got to listen to them and talk with them. We've got to see them as the people—initially little people, young people, and then the teenage people—they are. We've got to understand that they do have sexual feelings at what mom and dad would consider to be a very young age and that they need to be understood, accepted, and dealt with in a loving, positive manner.

Important—Important—Important

Parents, again, I encourage you to read—and encourage your eleven- to sixteen-year-old to read *Why Wait?* by Josh McDowell and Dick Day. Then use that text to open discussions with your son or daughter. It is beautifully and lovingly written and can be tremendously influential in your child's life.

Time for Personal Evaluation

1. Who taught you about sex?

2. How do you want your kids to learn about sex? From whom?

3. What can you as a mom share better with your kids regarding information on sex? As a dad?

4. Armed with factual information, your son or daughter will be better prepared to meet any situation. True or false?

5. Maybe you've made some errors in the way you've taught your children about sex. What can you do to change this? Note again the book Zig recommends.

6. Read again the section on Zig's long weekend with his son. Summarize the discussion they had. Would it be of value for you to have such a time with your son or daughter?

CHAPTER 15

Sex Abuse and Harassment

> Approximately 75% of prostitutes and 70 to 75% of drug and alcohol abusers were abused as children.[1]

Identifying and Helping the Sexually Abused Child

In an unusual way this could be one of the most important portions of this book. It is my hope and belief that this information can save many children from being victims of sexual abuse by alerting you parents or guardians to the problem *and* offering some guidelines to follow. This is important because it is difficult, though by no means impossible, for a child who has been abused sexually to be positive and free of psychological problems. Roughly 80 percent of sexual abuse is perpetrated by someone the child knows—father, stepfather, brother, uncle, Scout master, neighbor, minister, or recreational activity leader. The sooner the abuse is discovered and stopped, the better the chances of recovery. This article from the Sunday, October 28, 1984, *Fort Worth Star-Telegram* is the best I have seen as far as identifying the victim and taking steps to help the child:

Sudden Mood Swings Called Clues to Abuse
by Carolyn Poirot, *Star-Telegram* Writer

The victims often become quiet. Happy, outgoing children suddenly are depressed. They may have nightmares or express fear that they have never expressed before. Curiosity may be squelched.

If children have been sexually abused outside the home, they may not want to go to school or the day-care center and may cry and cling to mother. Or they regress—forget toilet training or begin talking like a baby, therapists and social workers agree.

"Sometimes a child begins kissing with an open mouth or other inappropriate ways or using terms for different parts of the body that he has never used before. Excessive masturbation may also be a sign of abuse," said Ann Clark, supervisor of sexual abuse caseworkers for the Texas Department of Human Resources' Child Protective Services in Fort Worth.

For parents who observe this behavior in their child, counselors advise, "Don't panic." "Stay calm, even if your insides are churning. Speak with a neutral voice in neutral terms. Explosive behavior scares the child," Clark said.

"Parents may act with surprise, anger, disgust or all of the above," said Barney Hisanago, clinical director for the Parenting Guidance Center. "If parents react with shock and surprise, the child may think, 'I did something wrong.' "

"Particularly, a very young child can be so scared by the parents' initial reaction that he will shut it down and not talk about it at all," said Cheryl Dielman, a therapist with the Child Study Center in Fort Worth. "Children are very sensitive to our emotions."

It is natural for the parents to be intensely emotional, and that's the best reason to immediately call the Department of Human Resources or a counseling service to get a professional to talk to the child rather than seeking details themselves, said Alice Wiedenhoff, another counselor with the Child Study Center.

It is most important for families and therapists helping a child to recover to convince the child that he or she is not at fault.

"You have to make them understand that they are not responsible and it is nothing for them to feel guilty about," Wiedenhoff said.

"Tell the child that the adult perpetrator has a problem, that it was the adult's fault and that you and other adults he trusts are going to protect him against it ever happening again. If you can assure the child that he never has to see the abuser again, it will help, although you shouldn't do that unless it's true," the counselor noted.

"To reassure the child, you might tell him, 'This person tricked you and lied to you, and of course you are scared,' " Dielman said. "If a child can really regain a sense that life is predictable and he can trust you and other adults around him to react in a predictable way, it will usually help.

"You have to build their self-esteem. The more they can get a sense of the positive, the more they can let go of what's happened to them. If they can experience success at some task or at school, it usually helps," she said.

"Impact issues of child sexual abuse"—not the abuse itself—is what therapists must deal with. This is the guilt, fear, nightmares, depression, and low self-esteem. It is the feeling in girls that they are "damaged goods" or in older boys that they are going to be homosexuals because of the experience, Hisanago said.

Tell the Kids What to Do

It also is "a good idea to give the child a specific list of people they can talk to if anything like this ever happens again, and put as many trusted relatives and friends on that list as you can so the child knows there will always be someone he can talk with," Hisanago said.

Children experience a kind of catharsis when they can work through a problem by talking or in play therapy, exactly the way adults do in discussing psychological problems with a therapist. "I have one little girl who beats on Bovo (a punching bag doll) and says over and over, 'He was bad, he was bad, he was bad, and if he ever hurts me again, he will get hurt back,' " Dielman said "Another girl I work with whose experience was just horribly traumatic . . . was able to talk about it openly and honestly until finally it was no longer such a strongly emotional issue with her."

While any kind of sexual abuse can be traumatic for a child, abuse outside the family is usually not as destructive, Wiedenhoff said. "They have such ambivalent feelings when it is their father. They hate him but they love him and they're glad he's gone but they miss him. *Often it is the most important person in their lives, the person who always paid the most attention to them who did the abuse.*

"In a day-care or school setting, there is some of that, but you have to look at the whole network. There is usually still a structured family to support and reassure the child. When the abuse is within the family, that structure is usually disrupted," Wiedenhoff said. "In some cases, they lose such a huge part of their family and it's such a disruptive thing in their own little world. I just believe it makes a big difference when they can still trust everyone in their immediate family," she said.

To protect against abuse, children must be taught that certain parts of their bodies are private and special and that others should not touch them there, counselors say. Children need to know the difference between "good touch and bad touch" and be told to "yell and tell" if anyone tries to touch them in the "bad" way. They should know that they can always talk to their parents or other adults about "scary things," such as abuse, problems at school, or "funny feelings," Dielman said.

"So often parents are embarrassed to discuss sexual things with their children," Clark said. "We teach them to respect authority and obey their teachers and caretakers, and in their cases that works against them. We teach them all the good little rules and regulations and we don't teach them what to do if someone touches them inappropriately."

"Children need to be taught that it's O.K. to tell an adult, 'Don't touch me' or 'Leave me alone' in some cases," Wiedenhoff said. All the counselors, however, emphasized the difference between healthy communication and scaring a child.

Who Are the Molesters? Why Do They?

For most of us the thought of a father or other adult becoming involved in a sexual or incestuous relationship with a small child is so repulsive and incredible that it is inconceivable. Who are these people? Where do they come from? What is their profile?

In the May 13, 1984, *Dallas Times Herald*, an article by Joan Sweeney asks the question, "Have you hugged your kids today? If not, a molester will." The article reveals that:

most molesters have very low self-esteem and self-confidence, poor control of their impulses, shallow relationships, and no long-term, gratifying romantic involvements. Many are loners. A majority of the people we see have abused substances, alcohol or other drugs, have had negative experiences with females, humiliating dating experiences or marriages. Some have sexual dysfunction with adult partners. Sex abusers often come from unstable families, lacked consistent fair discipline and love and were abused or neglected as children.

They can be young or old, male or female.

"The average child molester does not use violent threats; he seduces the victim. The sun rises and sets with the child," says police sergeant Joseph Polisar of Albuquerque, New Mexico. "These guys spend hours winning the love and affection of a child." Molesters select a child who is least likely to say no. Almost always the molester will give up on the child who resists. (Parents, note that last sentence.)

"Men in that category often seek opportunities to be with children. They may look for community service or permanent jobs that deal with younger kids in positions of trust—a coach, Boy Scouts, Big Brothers, summer camp counselors," observes Dr. Bruce Gross, acting director of the University of Southern California Institute of Psychiatry at Law and Behavioral Science, who has seen more than a thousand child molesters in twelve years.

"They look like the typical person in the community," he says. "When that type prefers young girls, his opportunities to be with them are more restricted and *he may search out lonely mothers as a way of gaining access to their daughters.*" "Generally he believes he is sharing something good with children," says Dr. Roland Summitt, head physician of Community Consultation Service, Harbor-University, Los Angeles Medical Center. "He is teaching the child to appreciate sexuality. He feels he has given a dimension to the relationship that children are ordinarily denied with adults. He feels his mission is to give children an opportunity to experience sex.

"Whatever the reasons, however, *once a man molests a child it becomes addictive,*" Summitt states. *"Once the taboo is broken it tends to become relentlessly progressive."*

The Molesters Seduce Like This

About 80 percent of all molestation victims know their at-tackers. "It could be your good neighbor or 'Mr. Nice Guy.' He'll say to the parent, 'Why don't you let me help you out? These kids can stay with me for a couple of days.' Once in the pedophile's domain the child is seduced with candy and toys, trips to parks or movie theaters. As the child becomes more comfortable, 'Mr. Nice Guy' may try some tickling, some wrestling, followed perhaps by some 'innocent' fon-dling. The pornography is the next step in the seduction pro-cess. It serves as validation material to lower the youngsters' inhibitions," says Kenneth Lanning of the FBI. (Yes, four-and five-year-olds do experience "arousal" from pornogra-phy.)

"The molester most often begins with photos that are called 'mere nudes.' Pictures of smiling, nude children in non-sexual poses. Mere nudes can include home-made snap-shots of previous victims, nudist colony magazines, sex ed-ucation textbooks, and books such as *Show Me* touted as an educational sex manual for children. That's like their bible," says New York Postal Inspector Daniel L. Mihelko.

"All kids are curious," he explains. "They'll ask, 'How come these kids are naked?' So there's this person whom the child trusts explaining, 'Would I do something wrong? These kids are having a good time. You're as beautiful as they are. Would you like me to take some pictures of you?' " The more children get involved, the harder it is for them to es-cape, experts say. Still some try. That's when blackmail is often used. When pictures are taken, the pedophile will threaten to show them to the victim's parents.

Sexual abuse of the young has reached epidemic propor-tions. What can we as individuals and as a nation do?

As part of your child's sex education, and to help prevent your child from being sexually abused, casually, but specif-ically, instruct your child when he reaches age five to tell you immediately if anyone does anything or touches him in any way that makes him uncomfortable. Emphasize that the child is to tell you even if he is told not to tell. Buy your child a modest swimsuit and teach him not to let anyone see, touch or photograph any part of the body covered by the suit without your permission.

Next, be sensitive to your child's feelings if he/she protests strongly, exhibits fear, or starts to cry when a close friend, neighbor or relative comes by to take the child somewhere for a treat. Almost 50 percent of child abuse cases are incestuous. The pedophile doesn't just want to be with your child, he wants to be alone with your child.[2]

I recognize the danger of becoming paranoid about protecting your child from abuse, and I know that the fear can "rub off" on your child, but your own calm, loving manner can reassure your child fairly easily. However, a child who has been abused often requires lengthy counseling to overcome the truama, so if we parents err, it is better to lovingly err on the side of caution. Understand that the child molester looks like anybody else but is so devious and morally bankrupt that he seeks employment at places like day-care centers and participates in community service where children are involved.[3] There is mounting evidence that he seeks, moves in with, and even marries single mothers for the express purpose of molesting their children. If you question the validity of this finding, let me remind you that children with one stepparent are forty times as likely to be abused as are children raised by their natural mother and father.

Remember Our Goal

As I've indicated repeatedly in this book, we're seeking to raise positive kids who will, in turn, raise positive kids. If moral values are taught from the beginning and a solid bonding occurs between parents and children, husbands and fathers will build winning relationships at home and won't have the inclination to turn to either prostitutes or other women, and wives and mothers will develop normal, fulfilling relationships with husbands and children.

If you are a parent concerned about the safety and welfare of your child and want to do everything possible to protect him or her from child molesters, I strongly encourage you to get involved in the moral climate of America today. Unfortunately, you can be a sound, ethical, moral, law-abiding citizen and still lose your child to a molester or abuser. Parents with young children must guard their children and their relationships in every sphere of life. Great care must be taken to know the people who associate with your children. Also, I strongly urge you to do three things. Number one, as a citizen, make it your business never to trade a second time with any merchant who sells pornography. Write the manager a note, or if your time and courage permit, tell him in a firm but friendly manner why you won't be back. This includes convenience stores, drugstores, grocery stores, hotels, motels, or any other business establishment that sells the pornographic magazines facetiously labeled "adult" magazines.

The evidence is overwhelming that pornography is a causal factor in violence, child abuse, and rape. In a study done by the Michigan State Police involving 38,000 victims of rape, between 1956 and 1979, 41 percent of the victims were raped immediately after the rapist had read a pornographic magazine or had seen a pornographic film or video.

Think pornography is harmless? Would you let your sixteen-year-old daughter date a young man who had been reading Playboy *all afternoon?*

Number two, when you see sexually explicit and suggestive programming on television, write the sponsors of the program, assuring them you will no longer buy their products if they continue to sponsor such pornographic presentations. One letter a *month* by every person who reads this book would have a dramatic impact on TV programming. The sponsor knows that each person who takes the ten minutes to write represents over two hundred who do not take the time to write.

Number three, I encourage you to join the American Family Association, Post Office Drawer 2440, Tupelo, Mississippi 38803. A subscription to its publication costs only $15 a year, and you can learn each month which programs and networks are the most offensive as well as the companies sponsoring those programs. Their efforts have been a definite factor in thousands of merchants removing pornography from their stores and stopping many companies from advertising on offensive TV shows.

In the event you view this as "censorship," let me remind you that we are not denying pornographers the right to publish their magazines or air their TV shows. We *are* denying them our money to pay for their programs on TV. Not only is this procedure clearly within our rights, but it definitely comes under the heading of our responsibility. After all, the child, wife, sister, or mother you save from sexual molestation or rape might be *yours*.

Sexual Involvement Is a No-No

Sexual harassment on the job is a real, and growing, problem. Fortunately, there have been enough laws passed and enough precedents set so that if the harassment becomes too severe, legal relief can be sought. Obviously, though, this eliminates that job as far as your son and daughter are concerned, so handling the problem—short of legal procedures—is the most desirable option. With this in mind, let's take a look at what happens and how we can prepare our kids to handle unwanted and uninvited sexual attention when they enter the marketplace.

Sometimes harassment comes across as subtle, loving, and gentle (the most dangerous kind). On other occasions it is crude, vulgar, and continuous. In *all* cases it must be dealt with, and our children must be prepared for and warned about it. In many instances young (and not-so-young) girls (and boys) are subjected to this sexual harassment by their fellow workers, supervisors, or bosses, in the business, military, industrial, school, and even church worlds. If there has ever been a situation in which young girls need to have their antennas all the way up, their intuition working full force, their answers ready, and their resolve firmly fixed, it's in this area.

Teaching children about this problem should begin as early as the time when your daughter starts talking about her first job, perhaps as a baby-sitter. On her baby-sitting assignments, mom and dad definitely need to know the circumstances and people involved.

Some Specifics

The following tips may be helpful to share with your daughter:

1. When you baby-sit, if someone comes to the home (unless you know him and the people for whom you are sitting have told you he is coming by), *you must not let him in the house unless you call us for permission to do so*. The individual will probably get mad, but he'll get over that, and remember, you are responsible for the child as well as for yourself.
2. During the evening, if anyone says or does anything that makes you uncomfortable, you are to let us know exactly what was said and what was done.

In most cases, parents, you should gently probe the events of the evening when your daughter comes home from a baby-sitting assignment. This can be excellent preparation for your daughter's entrance into the regular business community at a later date. You need to carefully instruct her that if any male member of the house—whether an older brother, husband, uncle, or a visiting neighbor—says anything of a suggestive nature, you are to be told about it immediately. If the person picking her up or taking her home wants her to sit closer or if he tries to put his hands on her or put his arms around her, *she is to tell him that makes her uncomfortable, and then she must tell you.*

If there's any evidence, however slight, of inappropriate behavior toward your daughter, she should not be allowed to have another baby-sitting assignment with that family.

Some Men Are Quite Devious

Entrance into the regular job market is a different matter. Your daughter will be at least sixteen years old, and you can, therefore, talk with her even more openly. By that age she will be more tuned in to her own sexuality and the possibilities that take place in the business world. However, a sixteen-year-old girl is no match for a twenty-one-year-old man and certainly not for a thirty-five or a fifty-five-year-old.

Many times these older guys take a "fatherly" approach and use it as an excuse for the liberties they take and the requests they make. Some of their comments and their attempts at friendship may be parts of this ploy too. Typically one of these men will use a thousand and one "innocent" and "casual" gestures to put his hands on your daughter. A handshake that is three seconds too long. The casual "excuse me" as he "innocently" nudges her or puts his arm around her as he gets off the crowded elevator, walks around her in a narrow hallway, eases past her in the stockroom, encourages her to "have a seat" so he can talk with her a minute, helps her slip on a coat, or numerous other little things to establish a personal relationship.

I certainly don't want to make you or your daughter paranoid about this, but forewarned can and should be forearmed.

Flattery and attention are the prime weapons in the seducer's arsenal. Many young girls are simply not equipped to levelheadedly handle a steady barrage of, "You are really an attractive girl," "That's a beautiful dress," "I'll bet your dad has a baseball bat to keep the boys away from you," "That perfume is absolutely devastating! Aren't you afraid of what might happen when you wear it?" "Please don't be offended, but you could easily go to work for the sweater industry."

This kind of attention, along with the natural concern for her job and "getting along," can seriously impair a young girl's thinking and affect her job performance. (Although our young daughters are far more at risk, I hasten to add that young boys are more and more becoming targets for aggressive females, militant male homosexuals, and older women. They need to be warned of the dangers and taught how to avoid those destructive, entangling relationships.)

At this point, to be fair I must remind you of the obvious. Men in most places are fine, decent, and honorable. They have an interest in your daughter because they work with her as a member of the team and they want to know her as an individual. For your daughter to be unfriendly and suspicious of everyone would be unrealistic and unfortunate. Frankly, the line is sometimes pretty thin between friendliness and familiarity. The best training for being able to distinguish between the two is her relationship with her father. This truly underscores the importance of dad's displaying *natural* parental affection for his daughter and his paying her sincere compliments *all* of her life.

Careful, Daughter

All of this is to say that you should caution your daughter to use care and discretion in her involvements on the job. That does not mean she is to be aloof or unfriendly. It does mean she shouldn't get personally or sexually involved with men who will destroy her values and dramatically affect her life negatively. It also means your daughter should avoid—like the plague—those office flirtations, especially with married men, that often lead to heartbreak and disaster.

With this in mind, you need to have a serious talk with your daughter and caution her that she must be *very careful* to avoid even inadvertently giving a come-on to any of the men around the office. The eyes are the key, and, mom, that's where you can be helpful. Remind your daughter that if she is not careful, she can do a considerable amount of flirting with a glance of her eyes. Also, be sure to carefully supervise the way she dresses. A skirt that is too tight or too short is an invitation to trouble. A sweater that is too tight or a blouse that is cut too low or can be seen through is neither businesslike nor appropriate.

Fathers should explain to their daughters that men are sight oriented, and some of them can rationalize anything. They often have vivid imaginations that permit them to blame the girl for their amorous advances because she was "asking for it." You must keep in mind that there are a lot of guys out there waiting for your daughter. Tell your daughter that seductive behavior and clothing are not appropriate at any time but especially not at the office. That's baiting the hook with the kind of bait that attracts dangerous scavengers. A pragmatic father can give his daughter many invaluable insights into the male psyche.

Be Prepared

One thing your daughter needs to make crystal clear is that it is a very serious matter when an employer or a fellow worker insults her moral character. It is not to be handled lightly or frivolously. Controlled anger is the key. Obviously, a young girl just starting her work career won't have an easy time doing this. That's the reason it is so important you give your daughter that advance warning and as much preparation as possible. You also need to assure her that you support her completely in her desire to avoid sexual advances at the office. If your daughter is unable to stymie the boss's advances with that first rebuttal—and in many cases that will be the situation—the second one should be even more firm.

Another alternative might be to add anger as she tells the boss that she's shocked and can't believe he would do such a thing. If the man is old enough to be her father, she might be able to discourage him by telling him that if he were a little younger, he would remind her of her dad.

Admittedly, all these approaches are difficult because everyone is anxious to do a good job, especially *on that first job*, in order to build a persuasive resumé for the future. That is the precise reason these morally bankrupt men take the liberties they do with young girls. Part of this come-on is to tell the girls that in the "business world," if they expect to "get along," they must "go along." That's despicable and untrue.

To compound the problem is the fact that jobs might be scarce in her area, and she may be working at the only one available. To be subjected to sexual harassment, therefore, is particularly frustrating. In that event the girl should make it clear that if the harassment continues, she's going to take legal action; and if she is fired as a result of that statement, she will do exactly that. I recognize how tough it will be for a young girl to say most of these things to an older man or to her employer. However, whatever the conditions, mom and dad need to be carefully tuned in to all the circumstances, because no job is worth risking the sexual abuse or moral compromise of your daughter.

If You Are a Victim of Sexual Abuse

Finally, I want to write a few words of guidance on that taboo topic—incest. Of all the problems we face in America, incest has got to be at or near the top of the real tragedies. All of us need to recognize the severity of the problem, face the fact that it could happen to our kids, and begin to face the issue in public forum.

In 1984 I started sharing with audiences around the world the ever-increasing incidence of incest and the devastating impact it has on the people involved. In my speaking career, which spans thirty years, I have never touched on a subject that has produced such a response as this one. I've received telegrams, phone calls, personal visits, and letters encouraging me to continue to speak out on the subject. Why? For one reason—there are so many adults who have been closet-victims afraid to identify themselves, hurting but too embarrassed to get help, or not knowing that help is available.

In countless instances after I have covered this subject, a seminar participant has come to me, shaken my hand, looked me in the eye and, with an emotion-filled voice, simply said, "Thank you." Nothing was said in most cases, but I knew, as surely as I know my name, that there was a victim. When I address small groups and can see the face and the eyes of each person, I can, with reasonable certainty, pick out those who have been victimized as children.

I want to mention two specific instances that occurred recently. In Chicago, six women attended the seminar together. On their way home that evening they discovered that three of them had been victims of incest when they were children. This was the first time any of the three had told anyone about being a victim. Each confessed she felt a new burst of hope, combined with a enormous sense of relief and a relieving of guilt, which gave her a tremendous sense of healing.

On another occasion I addressed the subject in a church. One woman who knew me well confessed she was shocked that I brought up such a subject in the church presentation. That evening while having dinner with her husband, she expressed her surprise and said it seemed out of place because in a setting like that there would be few, if any, victims. Things got awfully quiet after her statement; then her husband confessed that when he was six years old, a neighbor had molested him, and this was the first time he had shared that information with anyone.

I'm not naive enough to believe that recognizing the problem will solve it, but I'm realistic enough to know that if a problem exists, it will never be solved until it is acknowledged and addressed. I am now convinced that these and countless other people will be willing to come forth, acknowledge their problem, and seek the help that is available. That certainly is my hope for you if you have been a victim, because your effectiveness as a parent could be affected by that long-ago incident or series of incidents.

> *No job is worth risking*
> *the sexual abuse or moral compromise*
> *of your daughter.*

You Must Take Action—Now

Along these same lines, if your spouse is sexually abusing your child and you know it but have never been willing to admit it, you have the strongest possible moral obligation to face that issue immediately and decisively. Surely the protection of a helpless child is of paramount importance in anyone's life. If you fear for your own safety, I plead with you to call for help. The court systems, as well as your minister or an attorney, can give you the advice you need to protect your own life and to prevent the further destruction of your child's life. You're dealing with a person with a sick mind who is going to continue to abuse your child unless you take action. It is in his best interests as well as in the child's best interests. Realistically, if this is your situation, you do not have a "family" at this stage of the game. With help there's always the chance that you can have that family. I encourage you—take action and *do it now*. You owe it to your child, yourself and your mate. You also owe it to any number of unknown children, because when your daughter either moves out or grows up and puts a stop to the abuse, your mate will probably seek out other children to abuse. Still later he will turn to his grandchildren.[4] Stop him now.

If you are the one guilty of child abuse, spouse abuse, or sexual crimes toward others but most especially toward children, I want to say this and communicate it with as much love and gentleness as I possibly can. At the same time I want to be forceful, dogmatic, and persuasive on *your* behalf.

In plain, simple language you are a sick, miserable human being. Not only are you permanently scarring the life of the child, but you are doing enormous damage to yourself. I encourage you to seek professional help immediately. Chances are a thousand to one that you know you are wrong; you've faithfully promised yourself you're going to stop it; chances are that you've made an honest effort to stop, but just as you cannot remove your own tonsils or appendix, neither can you heal yourself in most cases of this terrible sickness you have.

I encourage you to finish this paragraph, then go to the telephone, and call for help. There are any number of sources of help, and many of them are free. Your county mental health association, for one, will have someone who can work with you. Ideally a Christian psychiatrist or psychologist is the one you should see, but you desperately need help and you need it *now*. Do it before you further destroy the lives of those whom you *profess* to love. If you really do love them, you will get that help now. Otherwise you will continue to be a miserable, destructive human being. Remember, there is a God. He loves you and wants to help you. He can and will do exactly that, but He often helps through trained counselors. Find one.

Parents, make sure your children are protected. Keep informed and involved, and give your kids a solid moral foundation.

There Is Another Side

Child abuse, especially sexual abuse, by a parent, relative, or trusted family friend, is devastating. Our children must be protected from the child abuser. However, there is mounting evidence that thousands of people have been falsely accused of this monstrous crime with calamitous results. For this reason I encourage you to explore accusations of child abuse cautiously. You simply can't believe everything you read in the papers, hear on TV, or learn via neighborhood gossip.

Important: If the child makes the accusation or there is evidence that abuse is taking place, I encourage you to quickly notify the proper authorities so action can be taken. *However*, to help you keep your objectivity, I encourage you to read *The Child Abuse Industry* by Mary Pride.

Many innocent victims of sexual abuse harbor undeserved feelings of guilt, believe they are "damaged goods," and give up in despair. However, I like to state emphatically that there are few, if any, hopeless situations, but there are lots of people who lose hope in the face of the situation. Following is a truly inspiring story which offers hope to anyone who has been abused, sexually or otherwise.

Mamie Claire Darlington was one of nine children and her

dad died when she was just three years old. She was sexually abused by men who were close friends and neighbors. Tall and skinny, she had buck teeth and a pug nose which restricted her breathing and caused her to turn bright red at the slightest frustration or embarrassment. Her sister, Martha Ann, who was closest to her in age, was poised, bright, beautiful and popular, so sibling rivalry was fueled and it doesn't take much imaginaiton to guess whose self-image suffered. Material goods were scarce for all the Darlington kids, who even had to wear dresses made from flour sacks.

Despite all those obstacles, Mamie is a winner because she had a mother who, with God's help, raised her on faith and hard work. She worked her way through college, added a few pounds to her slender frame, had corrective surgery on her nose, trained and performed as a model, and decided it isn't where you start, but where you finish that counts. It isn't what happens to us, but what we make of what happens to us, that makes the difference. Today, thanks to indomitable will, this mother of three (who lost her husband to a massive heart attack when her children were eight, six and five) is a beautiful, confident, loving, dynamic individual who heads our "I CAN" program, which is currently taught in thousands of schools in all fifty states and is positively influencing millions of kids to become better students. Her influence on our educational system and her book, *I CAN. YOU CAN TOO!*, is proof positive that Miss Mamie McCullough, the "I CAN" Lady, is a role model and example that clearly proves that you and your child, regardless of difficulties in the past, can make your future bright.

Time for Personal Evaluation

1. What are some of the characteristics displayed by a sexually abused child?

2. How can you mothers and fathers better work together to protect your children from child molesters?

3. Who are the most common offenders among child molesters?

4. If you have a daughter, what specific tips does Zig recommend that you share with her to protect her in the job market?

5. As a parent, you may be the secret victim of child abuse. Would it help you to share that information with someone? Your spouse? Your minister? A professional therapist? What does Zig recommend doing?

For information on the "I CAN" course, write the "I CAN" Lady, The Zig Ziglar Corporation, 3330 Earhart, Suite 204, Carrollton, Texas 75006

CHAPTER 16

Forgiveness—The Ultimate "Positive" in Life

> *Forgiveness takes the burden of hate, guilt and bitterness off your back and, with the lighter load, you can climb higher and faster, and be much happier in the process.*

Since we dealt with sexual abuse in considerable detail in the last chapter, we need to look carefully at what will be the ultimate solution for you if you have been a victim. Since it is extremely difficult to feel good about yourself in sufficient measure to successfully parent your children if you bear deep emotional hurts that have trapped and stymied you psychologically over the years, what's the solution for you?

Forgiveness! Surely the most important, difficult, and dangerous act in life is that of forgiveness. The Bible is clear on the subject: "For if you forgive men their trespasses, your heavenly Father will also forgive you. But if you do not forgive men their trespasses, neither will your Father forgive your trespasses" (Matt. 6:14–15).

Forgiveness gives you a clear path to the love and power of your heavenly Father, *and* it clears the air and opens the communications door to the person who has abused or offended you. If there is hatred, resentment, or bitterness between you and a relative or former friend or between you and your abuser (I'm assuming you are now an adult), you can completely free yourself *only* through forgiveness. Read on.

In 1982 I received a lengthy Christmas greeting from a man who was bothered with a problem. In his letter he stated that when he and I "had our two serious altercations," he had been completely convinced I was 100 percent wrong. Now he was writing that over the years, he had come to realize that he was the one who was wrong. He stated that he wanted to clear the air and set the record straight so he could go on with his life. He asked forgiveness, acknowledged the error of his ways, and signed his name. Unfortunately, he did not give his address. How badly I wish he had; because if my life depended upon it, I cannot recall either the man or the incidents he wrote about. Yet, these incidents were obviously important in his life. I'm delighted he wrote the letter, because now he is free.

If I were to single out one thing from this entire book that I believe will enable you to do more with and for your children and your career while giving you peace of mind and helping you enjoy life more, it would be this: Forgive those who have abused you in any way, shape, form, or fashion. That includes rape, beatings, assault, incest, slander, gossip, and a host of other things. You could forcefully argue that anyone who did those terrible things to you doesn't "deserve" to be forgiven, and you could well be right. However, you deserve the best treatment for yourself, and to forgive others is best for you. In some cases you will want to seek out the people in life you feel have wronged you. Ask each individual to forgive you for what you might have done to him. Then assure each one that you certainly have forgiven him. I might say in advance that this is perhaps the most difficult thing you will ever undertake. I also say it is the most important single thing as well as one of the most dangerous things (I'll explain why it's dangerous in a couple of pages) you will ever do.

In other cases, when distance or accessibility are factors, or if any physical danger is involved, you will want to contact the person via the phone or a letter to ask for forgiveness and to forgive.

In still other cases, you will be wise to simply ask God to forgive you and for you to forgive that person in your heart for whatever wrong he/she may have done to you. In all cases, you will want to be very careful not to harm innocent people, such as an unsuspecting parent or spouse. However, you need to forgive, regardless of the offense.

A Tough One to Forgive

When I speak to general audiences, I say, "You need to forgive those who have hurt, offended, or damaged you in your lifetime *regardless* of the offense." Of course the list of offenses could be mind-boggling—abandonment, theft of goods, infidelity, defamation of character, and on and on. Statistics indicate that incest and other forms of child abuse would show up on such a list for many people.

Thousands of adults bear deep scars from wounds inflicted on them in childhood. There's a great need for inner healing. In my experience in dealing with victims of incest or sexual abuse, regardless of whether the incident took place fairly recently or forty years ago, I have never talked with anyone who did not weep bitter tears of remorse, anger, hurt, and frustration.

Forgive Yourself

If you are a victim, regardless of the crime perpetrated on you, you need to learn how to forgive. More specifically, if you are an incest victim, I encourage you to do two things. First, and by far the most important, you must *forgive yourself*. As a child you did nothing to encourage it. You were an innocent victim. (Some experts say as many as 34 percent of the women and 15 percent of the men are victims.[2]) *Forgive yourself*. If you have any feelings of guilt, they can, in virtually every case, be traced directly to the seeds planted in your mind by the perpetrator of the crime.

Forgive the Other Person

The second thing you need to do is to *forgive the person who victimized you*. This is a tough, tough thing to do, but it is a must if you are to be free to be the best you *and* the best possible parent you can be. The odds are great that you will. If you find it impossible to forgive yourself and the person who victimized you. Therefore I encourage you to seek professional help to resolve the problem. The change in your life can be dramatic. I urge you to seek that help.

Both steps of forgiveness are tough and dangerous to take. The reason they are tough is obvious—your emotional involvement and the fact that you probably feel the offender should be seeking forgiveness from you. But let me remind you that as incredible as it may seem, *in the eyes of the other person, you are probably at least partially to blame* for whatever happened.

They are dangerous because when you forgive the abusive relative, the abusive spouse, the trusted "friend" of the family, or whoever the offender may be, you are saying, "I now accept full responsibility for my future, my behavior, and for my success or failure. I no longer blame you for the fact that I'm not doing well, that I'm broke, drinking too much, on drugs," or whatever your particular problem happens to be. When you accept this responsibility for your own behavior, and subsequently your own success, you have taken your biggest step toward freedom, individual growth, and personal success.

You might also accomplish two other worthwhile objectives. First, your forgiveness could well enable the other person to face the awfulness of his deeds and seek forgiveness from you and his other victims (if any). Thus you will have freed one other person to reach his full potential. Second, you will be protecting your own child or children. A high percentage of child abusers and perpetrators of incest were victims themselves. As much as the victim hated the act of being victimized, it nevertheless made the strongest possible impression on his mind, and his chances of doing the same thing to his child are frighteningly high.

Yes, forgiveness is practical, psychologically sound, and important to your physical and mental well-being. In my own life a classic example occurred some twenty years ago. I had a serious disagreement with a close friend over a substantial sum of money. We both thought we were right. When collection efforts failed, I filed a lawsuit which was my "legal right."

In retrospect, I made a serious error since I did not try hard enough to resolve the matter outside the courtroom. Also, I exercised extremely poor judgment and a lack of compassion by telling mutual friends about how my friend had wronged me grievously, especially since the delay in getting my money had nearly forced me to sell our home. It was a bitter pill. The matter was finally settled out of court to our mutual satisfaction and advantage. Needless to say, however, scars remained because the hurt had been so deep.

A couple of years later, God turned my life around. He became real to me, and I was born again. For the next several months it seemed that every time I opened my Bible, it fell to the spot that clearly told me that if I did not forgive others, my heavenly Father would not forgive me. I was still hurt, resentful, and bitter toward my friend-turned-enemy. However, as I strengthened my walk with the Lord and pursued His work, encountering those forgiveness verses finally caused me to take action.

Figuring that everyone would be in a forgiving mood on Christmas Day, I finally called my former friend. We had a pleasant visit, and I acknowledged the error of my ways and asked him to forgive me for the things I had said and done. He cheerfully accepted my apologies and forgave me for what I had done and the healing started almost immediately.

> *Forgiveness is tough, dangerous & exciting. Tough because of our human nature. Dangerous because it forces us to take responsibility for future progress. Exciting because it frees us to become our best self.*

Since that Christmas Day the relationship between my friend and me has grown steadily. Today he is one of my closest friends and trusted advisers, and he has been enormously helpful to me on numerous occasions.

In fact, a few months after that Christmas phone call, based on his recommendation I secured a series of speaking engagements with a major corporation that would pay a considerable amount of money. Further, officials of the corporation asked if they could pay me in advance for the entire series so that they might include the fees in their present budget, rather than in the next year's. That was the only time in my speaking career when any company volunteered to pay me in advance. That payment saved me a tremendous amount of stress and difficulty, because I was operating on a shoestring and having a difficult time financially.

It's important for you to understand that if you seek forgiveness for selfish reasons or for what you expect to gain, then it becomes a sham and a farce. My benefits were enormous, but they came as a result of obeying God and learning to forgive.

If you have a real or an imagined difficulty with a friend or a loved one, regardless of the harm or damage inflicted upon you, I urge you to forgive that person and ask him or her to forgive you for anything you might possibly have done. It's the best possible thing you can do for both parties. Not only does it clear the relationship between you and God, but it also opens the door for healing and reconciliation with the offender.

Time for Personal Evaluation

1. Is seeking forgiveness a principle practiced in your family? If it isn't, what steps can you take to make it so?

2. Zig says seeking to forgive others is dangerous. Why?

3. Zig says seeking to forgive others can offer major benefits. What are they?

4. Is there someone you need to forgive now? Your child? Your spouse? What is stopping you from doing this?

5. Not only does forgiveness clear the relationship with you and the person who has offended you, it also opens the door for _____ and _____ .

CHAPTER 17

Discipline—The Key to a Positive Kid's Greatness

> *Remember: When you discipline your child to do the things that he needs to do when he needs to do them, you are preparing him to be able to do the things he wants to do when he wants to do them.*

Discipline: "training or experience that corrects, molds, strengthens, or perfects."

A Truly Handicapped Child

Handicapped children come in many forms. For example, Freddie is a seriously handicapped child. I met him a number of years ago when I was in a home in South Carolina making a call on his family to sell a set of cookware. Just looking at him, you would seriously question my observation that he is handicapped. He was a precocious nine-year-old with beautiful blond hair and blue eyes. He was a little large for his age, and his dad said he was a "natural athlete." He made good grades in school and gave every indication of being a bright student. Yet I can honestly say he was one of the most handicapped youngsters I've ever met. He was handicapped behaviorally.

Freddie was rude, thoughtless, selfish, demanding, and

inconsiderate, and he had a temper he used to manipulate and intimidate his family. At school he was not popular with his teacher or his classmates. When his parents visited friends, he was not exactly welcome because he took over and got the lion's share of whatever the host and hostess offered in the form of refreshments. He took the kids' toys and demanded to have his own way in everything. Later on in life when Freddie goes out to get a job, he's probably going to be faced with the same basic rejection he gets now when he goes places.

However, it's not Freddie's fault. He is simply doing exactly what he's been taught to do. His parents have indulged and spoiled him, maintaining they love him so much they just can't say no to him. By not saying no to his whims, demands, temper, boorishness, selfishness, and thoughtlessness, they're forcing the business, academic, and social communities to say no to the son they seldom said no to as he was growing up. How tragic, especially since Freddie, like *all* kids, really wanted to be loved enough to be disciplined.

I believe it is human nature for all of us from time to time to resist authority. At each stage of a child's life, he is going to take those steps of resistance. As a parent interested in raising a positive child, you need to understand that his resistance or rebellion does not mean he wants to win or that he wants you to surrender to him. He is simply testing you. What he wants is reassurance that you are firm and strong but still loving. He needs and must have boundaries within which he can operate and a loving authority to whom he can go with the confidence he's going to get the direction necessary to succeed in life.

As parents we ought to remember that when our child is being obnoxious and is apparently testing us just to see how far he can go, in most cases the reason is not to cause trouble or hurt us. According to author Fred Smith, it is because the child is hurting. Understanding this fact will help us to love our child even when he is acting unlovable.

Security Through Discipline

If you won't let your child open his mouth one day, but permit him to get away with murder the next day by talking back and being "sassy," you create incredible inner turmoil and problems for him. Dr. Bruno Bettelheim, the world-famous psychologist from the University of Chicago, says that any time a parent permits a child to talk back or put the parent down, to belittle or degrade him, serious damage is done to the child. The child's security is wrapped up in a parent he can trust and look to for strength and guidance. When the child belittles or degrades the parent, the child has no one to look up to. Consequently he loses his security.

One of the saddest things about overt permissiveness, when a parent lets a child "run loose" and do everything he wants to, is that it sets up expectancy in the child's mind that others should and will treat him the same way. That is both unreasonable and unrealistic. When an overindulged child visits or goes to play in other homes, and especially when he gets into school, he is going to have a "long row to hoe" as we would say down home.

This is certainly poor preparation for survival in our world today. Over the long haul, this leads to serious problems for both child and parents because many of the parents' best friends will not welcome the intrusion into their home of a little monster (as they see him) who is destructive, selfish, bad-mannered, and ill-tempered and who abuses their own children. This causes the undisciplined one to feel rejected and certainly damages his ego and self-acceptance.

Discipline and order are part of the natural laws of the universe. The child who has not been disciplined with love by his little world (the family) will be disciplined, generally without love, by the big world.

Parents—Not Buddies—Badly Needed

Some parents work hard at becoming their children's "buddies," permitting the children to call them by their first names and treating the children as equals. In reality, there is nothing equal about a five-year-old and a thirty-year-old.

The obvious question is, If you become a pal to your child, when the need arises for you to discipline, instruct, or require certain conduct and performance from your child, why should he obey a pal's orders? After all, you're equal. At least that's the view you've created in his mind by becoming his buddy instead of his mom or dad—the one he can look to for protection, counsel, guidance, and loving discipline.

What Is Discipline?

Discipline is teaching a child the way he should go. And the secret to having a disciplined child, according to Dr. Howard Hendricks, is to be a disciplined parent.[1] Discipline, therefore, includes everything you do to help your child learn. Unfortunately it's one of the most misunderstood words in the English language. Most people generally think of it as punishment or as something unpleasant. However, both Greek and Hebrew words denoting discipline include the meaning of chastening, correction, rebuke, upbringing, training, instruction, education, and reproof. The purpose of discipline is positive—to produce a whole person, free from the faults and handicaps that hinder maximum development.

One of the synonyms for discipline is *education*. The word *discipline* comes from *disciple*, who is "a follower of a teacher." A disciple should not follow his teacher out of fear of punishment, but out of love or conviction. Certainly positive, loving parents will want their children to follow them and their rules because they love and trust them, rather than because they fear them.

> *The child who has not been
> disciplined with love
> by his little world
> will be disciplined,
> generally without love,
> by the big world.*

The reality is that whether you do or don't discipline your child, you educate him to a particular set of values. Realistically, if you don't administer loving but fair discipline to the child, you can be certain society sooner or later *will*, but not always in a loving, fair manner. Perhaps that's the reason a 1980 Gallup Poll revealed that over 90 percent of the graduating high school seniors wished their parents and teachers loved them enough to discipline them more and require more of them. Maybe these young people instinctively knew that in the real world they would be entering (where the report card is a paycheck), they were going to need the knowledge, confidence, and discipline they had not received while they were in school. They knew that winners are not developed on feather beds.

Discipline—Wanted, Needed, and Demanded

I love this thought: "No man ever became great doing as he pleased." Little men do as they please; great men submit themselves to the laws governing the realm of their greatness.

When you teach a child discipline, you are giving him one of the most important tools for his future success and happiness. Instinctively children seem to know this. For example, in families where there is a divorce and the child is given a choice of which parent to live with, he almost always chooses the parent who is the disciplinarian—the one who has been the most firm and demanding of him. The child *knows* that real discipline is an expression of love and is in his long-range best interests.

The disciplined person is the one who does what needs to be done when it needs to be done. He is a practical pragmatist who does the things necessary and not just the things he wants to do. Show me someone who has accomplished anything of any significance, and I will show you a disciplined person.

None of Them Are Happy

One summer when the Redhead and I were in Colorado on a "working vacation," we happened to see a well-known interviewer and commentator on TV. At that time this person undoubtedly knew more celebrities in Hollywood than anyone else. The discussion was about the death of comedian Freddie Prinz, whom some of you will undoubtedly remember. Freddie had just taken his own life, and the commentator was asked, "Do you know of any other superstar in athletics, music, entertainment, the television industry, or movies who might also be in danger of either deliberately or accidentally taking his own life?" After a moment's reflection, she answered with one of the saddest statements I've ever heard. "I don't know of anyone who is famous and in these fields who is not in danger of either deliberately or accidentally taking his own life, because I don't know a single one who is happy."

That's really tragic, isn't it? In most cases these people have more money than they can use, often spending more on a wardrobe in a month than the average person will spend in a span of years. Private jets take them anywhere they want to go; they receive an enormous amount of publicity; many of them have so much charisma they have to hire bodyguards to keep members of the opposite sex away from them. They're idolized and eulogized on a daily basis, and yet not a single one is happy. It becomes more evident every day that what you have is not going to make you happy—*it's what you are*. That's why in *Raising Positive Kids* I stress repeatedly that the character qualities you teach your children are far more important than the "things" you give them.

Some Practical Tips for Parents

Mrs. Johnson came into young Billy's room to find him bandaging his thumb.
  "What happened?" she asked.
  "I hit it with a hammer."
  "But I didn't hear you cry."
  "I thought you were out."—A. H. Berzen*

This little "funny" is so true of life. To raise a positive child, parents and grandparents need to ignore the child occasionally. I'm comfortable with the statement that virtually all parents have observed that when little Johnny or Mary falls, if mom and dad rush forward to pick him or her up, extend all sorts of sympathy, offer reassurances that everything's all right, and kiss away the hurt, they establish a pattern. Every time anything happens, little Johnny and little Mary cry, and mom and dad are on their way to raising a crybaby who will be dependent on them for too long.

Don't misunderstand. If your child falls and really *is* hurt, then obviously he needs your attention. But with our four, I can tell you their mother and I have seen them on many occasions "hurt" themselves. As we watched from the corners of our eyes, it was obvious that their reaction—crying and demanding attention or going on about their business—was entirely dependent upon whether or not we rushed forward to kiss away their hurts. I'll admit that after our first one, we became a little more discerning with the other three.

*Reprinted with permission from The Saturday Evening Post Society, A Division of BFL&MS, Inc. © 1984.

One little technique we developed was to watch the immediate reaction of our little girl. If she couldn't decide whether to laugh or cry, we would say, "Come over here and I'll pick you up." If she got up and came to us, we were comfortable she was going to survive.

On one memorable occasion when granddaughter "Sunshine" was four years old, she was crying about some imagined physical or emotional hurt. I took a very large mixing bowl from the cabinet and told her that her tears were far too valuable to lose and she must put all of them in the mixing bowl. We both got tickled, so that ended the tear-collection process.

Another event that begs to be ignored is the childhood squabble. When your child and another child get involved in one of the 28,211 squabbles they're going to have, you should usually maintain a discreet distance, assuming they are of roughly the same age and size. I'm not talking about permitting your child to injure or mutilate another, nor am I talking about permitting your child to be injured. I'm simply saying that when two four-year-olds have their differences about playing with a toy or being first in the sandbox, they are inevitably going to have countless little altercations. If parents get involved, the incidents are blown out of proportion, and the kids may stop playing together. Both of them, as well as their parents, lose as a result.

You might well ask, "How can you tell when to pick your child up when he falls?" or "How can you tell when is the time to intercede in childhood squabbles?" Those are questions no book can answer for you. You have to rely on that plain common sense and instinctive judgment God gives you as parents. Obviously, as you and the kids get older, you will become more adept at making the decisions that are best for you and your child.

Don't Be a "Upas Tree" Parent

Though the advantages and benefits of mom's staying home to raise the children have been dealt with at length, I want to stress that she needs to teach the children to be self-sufficient and not completely dependent on their parents. The worst possible mistake parents can make is to devote all of their time, attention, and energy to the children. That's what "upas tree" parents do. Let me explain.

The upas tree grows in Indonesia. It secretes poison and grows so full and thick that it kills all vegetation growing beneath it. It shelters, shades, and destroys. "Upas tree" parents smother their children, and although they don't actually choke off life itself, they effectively hinder growth and keep their children "babies" all their lives. Here's an example of how to be a upas tree parent.

Because of space limitations and because of their desire to be available to take care of the new baby, many young parents place the crib in their bedroom. Also, some couples make the mistake of starting to put their babies in bed with them "for the night." Both actions are unnecessary unless the baby is sick or extremely fretful and the mother feels the baby needs the comfort and reassurance of her presence. Among other things, there is always the danger that mom or dad will roll over and injure the baby. Whether anything happens physically or not, if this situation continues, it will destroy the normal life-style and relationship between husband and wife. (P.S.: I'm not talking about the small child getting up in the early morning hours and occasionally sneaking into bed with mom and dad for some extra snuggling and hugging.)

Of considerable significance is the fact that the child will grow accustomed to sleeping with the parents and will soon be unable or unwilling to sleep anywhere else. When this happens, you, your child, and your marriage are facing a rocky road ahead, which means the little one has to get out of your bed and bedroom.

It is true that your child might not sleep as well the first night he is alone, but it is also true that by the fourth or fifth night he will sleep pretty well. And you will sleep much better, which will make you better parents.

Start the Teaching Process Early

Start teaching your children to do things at an early age, provided, of course, there is no physical danger involved, such as using a knife, a power lawn mower, or some other potentially harmful tool. But things like sweeping the floor, taking out the trash, making the bed, and so on are appropriate activities for youngsters.

Frankly it would be much simpler for you to go ahead and do those things. You can do them much better and faster, and actually with less effort than it takes to spend some time persuading and teaching the child how to do them. The problem is that a four-year-old is often unaware of his limitations, and at that stage of the game he believes he can do just about anything and is anxious to give it a shot. When you put the child aside and say, "Here, let dad or mom do it," you are sending a message.

The message is, "You can't do it very well, but dad or mom can." You will probably need some time to convince him of it, but by the time the child is nine or ten years old, you will have totally convinced him that you are much better at doing everything than he is. As a result, the child not only will "let" you do everything but also will obstinately refuse to help you around the house. Either that or he will do it so grudgingly that you come to the conclusion that you were right all the time. Of course, you will send a child into the world both unprepared and unwilling to tackle anything difficult or distasteful.

You raise positive kids by teaching *and* requiring them early on to do the *little* things around the house. Step by step they naturally progress into accepting more and more responsibility until the happy day arrives when they will be able to do many things better than either parent. That's when you will know that discipline pays.

A Small Child Said It Best

If you don't let me help when me ain't no help,
me ain't gonna help when me could be some help.

Double-Barreled Burden

"It hurts me worse than it hurts you!" That statement has been handed down through the generations. No doubt many a kid has heard that and wondered to himself, *Oh, yeah? Well, why don't we just trade places for a while!* When they're on the receiving end of such consolation, you can bet that kids aren't feeling sorry for their parents, but it is one of the toughest parts of parenting. I call that dilemma the "Double-Barreled Burden." It's like a double-barreled gun that shoots in both directions. You've got to think about it before you start shooting.

The way you reprimand your kids is a very sensitive aspect of parenting, because the method you use will have an effect on their esteem. You should reprimand and criticize the action, not the person who committed the action. When you have an understanding with your kids, they know what's expected of them. If they don't do what's expected and agreed upon, they expect, even demand, a reprimand. Not to follow through is to weaken and negate the possibility of future effective follow-through in regard to your other requirements. When kids do something wrong and get by with it, they feel guilty. The only way to relieve that guilt and to reinforce your authority and your rules is to deal effectively with the problem.

Should You Actually Spank Them?

Speaking on parental discipline, Billy Graham once told of the time his two-year-old son spat at him in a fit of anger. He said, "I don't know where he learned such an ugly habit, but one thing I know for certain: If that boy chews tobacco when he grows up, he'll swallow the juice. After what I did to him, he'll never spit again."

Question: Is physical discipline (spanking) necessary?

Answer: Yes, it is, for several reasons. Primarily, children between the ages of about two and eleven live out a decade in life when they lack the maturity to listen to, understand, and responsibly follow their parents' instructions. Part of the fabric of humanity is a matter of individual will. Kids come into the world, into the family, and into society without any controls on that will. One of the most significant aspects of maturity is learning to be self-controlled or self-disciplined. A young child simply will not have this kind of maturity. Discipline literally means "to train," and youngsters need a lot of training; most of it should be of a verbal or spoken nature, but some of it will have to be a firm, physical nature.

As a rule of thumb, when your child is "willfully disobedient" toward you, that's when physical action is necessary. It could be the swiftest, surest way to get your message across. If a child continues approaching something of danger after several verbal warnings about the danger—playing in the street, standing on chairs or on top of kitchen counters, climbing on the roof of the house, playing with matches or with household appliances—then it is imperative that you react swiftly. A little heat on the bottom should instantly communicate what you mean.

Kids will "ask for it," but they don't always understand what they are asking for. It might take a few instances of willful disobedience, followed by instant corrective action, before they understand and follow your parental guidance. You must not fail to give them what they're asking for. It is critically important that you give your kids a spanking if they challenge you. You must realize that your decision to spank will be met with protest. You must also realize that kids don't always want what they're asking for, but they usually need it.

Psychologist James Dobson in *The Strong-Willed Child* points out that many times our children will test us to see what the boundaries are. He says, "This testing has much the same function as a policeman who turns doorknobs at places of business after dark. Though he tries to open doors he hopes they are locked and secure. Likewise a child who assaults the loving authority of his parents is greatly reassured when their leadership holds firm and confident. He finds his greatest security in a structured environment where the rights of other people (and his own) are protected by definite boundaries."

Dr. Dobson lays out some carefully thought-through guidelines as far as corporal punishment is concerned. He says that a child should not be spanked for behavior that is not willfully defiant. Childish irresponsibility is very different from willful defiance and should be handled more patiently. He firmly believes a spanking is to be reserved for use in response to willful defiance whenever it occurs. It is much more effective to apply it early in the conflict while the parents' emotional apparatus is still in control than after ninety minutes of scratching and clawing. In fact, child abuse is more likely to occur when a little youngster is permitted to irritate and agitate and sass and disobey and pout for hours until finally the parents' anger reaches a point of explosion where anything can happen and often does.

In response to the effectiveness of discipline, Dr. Dobson says, "If punishment doesn't influence human behavior then why is the issuance of speeding citations by police so effective in controlling traffic on a busy street? Why then do homeowners rush to get their tax payments in the mail to avoid a 6 percent penalty for being late? If punishment has no power then why does a well-deserved spanking often turn a sullen little troublemaker into a sweet and loving angel?"

The first book ever written on the family specifically advocated spanking as a method of discipline and demonstration of our love. Proverbs 13:24 (NIV) says, "He who spares the rod hates his son, but he who loves him is careful to discipline him." Proverbs 29:15 (NIV) says, "The rod of correction imparts wisdom, but a child left to itself disgraces his mother." Let me remind you that the rod in the Bible was primarily used to protect, rescue and guide the sheep.

Use with Care

When approaching corporal discipline, you must recognize first of all that spanking is only one means of discipline. It should be used with careful discretion, primarily when willful disobedience is involved. When there is a need to spank, the way you do it is also important. Never spank your child when you are angry. Kids can and will do things that will make you absolutely furious. *That's not the time to spank them.*

My good friend psychiatrist John Kozek suggested that if you are overly angry because of your child's disobedience and it calls for a spanking, wait a few moments to calm yourself. You need to be certain that the intensity of your discipline fits the offense and that it's not related to the intensity of your anger. Dr. Kozek recommended that, if possible, the other parent should be present and your discipline should be followed by expressions of love with lots of hugging and holding and explanations of the reasons for the spanking. This is probably the most important thing to convey to your kids—that you love them—and because you love them and because of their disobedience, you discipline (spank) them.

Your spanking conveys a message of care, concern, and love and helps them to eliminate feelings of guilt. Psychologists will tell you that guilt is very destructive, but it is harmful only if it is not dealt with. When a child rebels or disobeys a parent, there is a feeling of guilt, and the guilt is real. The spanking will serve to remove the guilt, and as Chuck Swindoll says, the child's tears flush out his guilt and clear his conscience.

But how often do your spank? How often is it needed? There will be periods in the growth and development of your child when you will have to spank more than at other times. As he reaches grade school age, if proper discipline has been administered in the early years, the need to spank diminishes. That need is something for the parent to decide; no one can really judge but you.

However, let's think about some reasonable guidelines. Until children can understand your words and can comprehend your "redirection" of their close calls with danger and difficulty (about fifteen to eighteen months of age), your maturity as an adult must prevent you from taking physical action.

Be Careful How You Discipline

The "shaken-infant syndrome" is now being reported around the country. Parents, otherwise well-meaning in their behavior, have shaken their infants so severely that brain damage has resulted. Usually the parents are trying to stop their infants from crying or to punish a baby for a perceived misdeed, which most often is merely childish clumsiness. Not only are such efforts fruitless with infants, because they are too young to understand what is required of them, but the tragedy could have been averted if parents understood more about what to expect from young children. Shaking a baby is not discipline—it is abuse.

Infants are going to cry when they're hungry, hot, cold, uncomfortable, wet, or sick. Toddlers are going to be clumsy. When a child spills, damages, or "destroys" something because of childish clumsiness, spanking is only confusing, because it is for the wrong reason. You don't spank because a kid has black hair and not brown hair, or because he has freckles and not dimples. Neither do you spank a child for an accident.

But what if it's dinner time and two-year-old Billy won't stay in his chair? An appropriate application to the backside should do the job, especially if you leave the ruler or other spanking object in plain view of the child.

That raises another important question concerning what you will use to spank your child. A very definite rule is that you use a "neutral" object such as a light ruler or yardstick rather than your hand. The main concern is that it must not be a heavy object that would cause injury. That would be a tragedy. The object used must deliver enough "warmth" to the backside that it does what it is intended to do. As the old saying goes, "No pain, no gain."

When the need to discipline comes, it is imperative that you use not your hand but a neutral object that will not be associated with you personally. If the situation is really critical (as with a small child and immediate danger) and you must use your hand to quickly swat him a time or two to get his attention, that is fine. However, when disciplinary action is seen as necessary for repeated or serious defiance of parental direction, then a more "formal" approach, meaning privacy with the child in the home and with appropriate disciplinary action, is the course to take.

As a child approaches kindergarten and school age, he

continues to need to be disciplined for his willful disobedience, but he also needs to be instructed about the motivation behind his behavior. Other means of discipline, such as restrictions and deductions of allowance and other privileges, become more effective.

But remember that corporal punishment is just one method of discipline. Spanking is more effective for some children than for others.

Discipline can also include a "time-out" when you take the child to a separate room and require him to stay there quietly for five to fifteen minutes, depending on his age.

An open, loving relationship between parent and child makes many rules unnecessary and the other rules easy to implement.

Careful about the When and Where

Another thing about the way you use corporal, "of the body," discipline is that you never strike a child, young or old, upon the face. If you've ever tried to pet a "whupped dog," a defenseless, cowering critter that was regularly slapped by his master, then you understand why slapping a child will literally destroy the spirit rather than channel and redirect the spirit, which is what appropriate discipline does. The interesting thing about it all is that the body is equipped with a sensitive but naturally well-padded "point of disciplinary contact." That's right—the backside is the place to deliver the discipline called for.

The sweet joys of family life will be wisely salted from time to time with some form of firm, corporal discipline. It is a part of the normal way of life and parenting. It is to be used sparingly, with very careful restraint, and stopped when the child is about ten or eleven years old. Child discipline revolutionaries will cry that such things strike at the foundation of a child's personality. However, just as a master's chisel strikes to carve the rough edges off a block of stone to ultimately reveal his masterpiece, so the brief shock of corporal discipline tears your child away from his immaturity and selfish recklessness and propels him toward the toughness and maturity needed to face a negative world and win!

The Most Important Paragraph

Sometimes there is a thin line between spanking and child abuse. If you ever get carried away and so completely lose control that you spank (beat) your child too hard, you *must* forever abandon corporal punishment as a method of disciplining your child. If his body (bottom) carries welts, bruises, cuts, or abrasions an hour later, you have overdone the punishment. Obviously you *never* physically discipline your child if you've had *any* alcohol or done *any* drugs.

"Permissive" versus "Authoritarian"

In his book, *How to Make Your Child a Winner*, Dr. Victor Cline, a professor of psychology at the University of Utah in Salt Lake City, states that a major disaster occurred in a large number of American families starting in the 1950s. Called by many names, most frequently "permissiveness" and "family democracy," it was a noble experiment based on the mistaken notion that young children are basically wise and good and perfectly able to determine their own destinies. Exerting control over your children was called "authoritarian" and "antidemocratic." Spanking, even in love, was seen by certain "experts" as a form of child abuse. Being a good parent meant letting your kids "do their own thing." Dr. Cline states he is in complete disagreement with almost all of those premises of the fifties. He points out that by setting reasonable limits on your child's behavior and enforcing them, you're helping your child establish his own inner controls over his antisocial impulses.

James Dobson states "It is certain that I will make mistakes, but I cannot abandon my responsibility simply because I lack infinite wisdom and insight. Besides, I do have more experience and a better perspective on which to base decisions than my children do. I've been where they're going."

In a series of studies conducted by psychologist Stanley Coopersmith, he found children with high self-esteem have parents who run a tight ship with a clearly defined and comprehensive set of rules, zealously enforced. These findings suggest that parents who have definite values, who have a clear idea of what they regard as appropriate behavior, who make their beliefs known to their children are more likely to rear children who value themselves highly, develop their own sense of ethics, and have greater respect and affection for their parents.

If parents don't assume this responsibility, if they don't set and consistently enforce reasonable limits, the child is apt to interpret this as parental indifference. This makes the child anxious and reduces his capacity to develop inner controls.

Parents, Discipline Yourself

In many ways, discipline is the fundamental quality upon which all notable achievement rests. It takes discipline to discipline our children when we're tired and it would be less fuss to let it slide—but love demands that we say no to that impulse and do for our child what is best for him.

It takes discipline to save a portion of your income, and your financial future hinges upon that habit. It takes discipline to say no to drugs and to alcohol, but that "no" plays a major role in your happiness and length and outcome of life. Discipline is required to back away from the table when you crave that second or third portion, but your health and self-respect often depend on it. Discipline is required to get you and the kids out of bed on Sunday morning and to go to church when you would prefer to sleep, but the example you set could well determine your child's eternal future.

Fortunately, discipline can be taught and the best way is by example, and the best time is when the kids are young. The responsibility is enormous, but the opportunity to give our kids a leg up on life is awesome.

Some Do's and Don'ts From the Kids

In the business world, it's a given that the people doing a job on a daily basis know some specifics about doing that job which the people who are supervising or observing the job do not know. Using that yardstick, surely kids can give us some guidelines to help us be better parents. Here's an example which appeared in an Ann Landers column[2]:

"The Rev. C. Galea was assigned to the Guelph Correction Centre for boys for his summer work. He asked the boys for clues as to why they had ended up in that institution. He then asked them to draw up a code for parents, zeroing in on specific areas where they had failed. Here is what emerged.

1. Keep cool. Don't fly off the handle. Keep the lid on when things go wrong. Kids need to see how much better things turn out when people keep their tempers under control.

2. Don't get strung out from too much booze or too many pills. When we see our parents reaching for those crutches we get the idea that nobody goes out there alone and it's perfectly O.K. to reach for a bottle or a capsule when things get heavy. Children are great imitators.

3. Bug us a little. Be strict. Show us who's boss. We need to know we've got some strong supporters under us. When you cave in we get scared.

4. Don't blow your class. Stay on that pedestal. Don't try to dress, dance or talk like your kids. You embarrass us and you look ridiculous.

5. Light a candle. Show us the way. Tell us God is not dead, or sleeping, or on vacation. We need to believe in something bigger and stronger than ourselves.

6. Scare the hell out of us. If you catch us lying, stealing or being cruel, get tough. Let us know WHY what we did was wrong. Impress on us the importance of not repeating such behavior.

7. When we need punishment, dish it out. But let us know you still love us, even though we have let you down. It will make us think twice before we make that same move again.

8. Call our bluff. Make it clear you mean what you say. Don't compromise. And don't be intimidated by our threats to drop out of school or leave home. Stand up to us and we'll respect you. Kids don't want everything they ask for.

9. Be honest. Tell us the truth no matter what. And be straight-arrow about everything. We can take it. Lukewarm answers make us uneasy. We can smell uncertainty a mile away.

10. Praise us when we deserve it. Give us a few compliments once in a while and we will be able to accept criticism a lot easier. The bottom line is that we want you to tell it like it is.''

Discipline is necessary and good. You can't raise successful children without it, but discipline should not repress or tyrannize. Discipline should lead to powerful habits of direction, work and good judgment. Good discipline produces strength, not weakness; creativity, not banality; responsibility, not self-indulgence. It can also help shape the character out of which a capacity to love, lead and accomplish can emerge.

> *Character is the ability
> to carry out a good
> resolution long after
> the excitement of
> the moment has passed.*
> —Cavett Robert

Time for Personal Evaluation

1. Zig uses Freddie Prinz as an example. Why?

2. Give Zig's definition of discipline.

3. What is a "upas tree" parent?

4. What is Zig's position on spanking? According to Zig, what is the most important paragraph in this book?

5. Do you agree with the quote by psychologist James Dobson? Why?

6. Zig says that discipline should not _____ or _____. Good discipline produces _____, not weakness; _____, not banality; _____, not self-indulgence. Do you agree?

CHAPTER 18

Positive Persistence
Produces Positive Kids

> The conditions of conquest are always easy.
> We have but to toil awhile, endure awhile;
> believe always and never turn back.
> —Simms

You Gotta Hang in There

All children need to learn the story of the Chinese bamboo tree. My friend Joel Weldon, an outstanding speaker from Phoenix, Arizona, tells the story. The Chinese plant the seed; they water and fertilize it, but the first year nothing happens. The second year they water and fertilize it, and still nothing happens. The third and fourth years they water and fertilize it, and nothing happens. The fifth year they water and fertilize it, and sometime during the course of the fifth year, in a period of approximately six weeks, the Chinese bamboo tree grows roughly ninety feet.

The question is, Did it grow ninety feet in six weeks or did it grow ninety feet in five years? The obvious answer is that it grew ninety feet in five years, because had they not applied the water and fertilizer each year there would have been no Chinese bamboo tree.

All of us have had those "Chinese bamboo tree" experiences. We might have had a difficult assignment in geometry, physics, or chemistry. We worked and could not get the answer. We worked again and no answer; again we worked and still no answer. Finally, we tell the teacher with a big grin, "Teacher, I've figured it out! The book is wrong!" The teacher looks at us, smiles, and says, "Give it one more shot." This time when we go back, we come up with the answer. As a matter of fact, the answer, once we've found it, is so simple and obvious that we're astonished we did not discover it before. I might point out that we came up with the answer not because of our intellectual brilliance but because of our persistence.

Discipline First—Enjoyment Later

For twenty-four years, by choice, I weighed over two hundred pounds. I say "by choice" because I have never *accidentally* eaten anything. And when I *choose* to eat too much today, I have *chosen* to weigh too much tomorrow.

At age forty-five, I chose to do something about my weight and physical condition. I changed my eating and exercise habits, got down to 165 pounds, and my whole life changed. Now I'd like to point out that the months required to lose the thirty-seven pounds were ten of the toughest months I've ever experienced. For nine of those ten months I really hated jogging, but I hated being out of breath and out of shape even more. (I might point out that until I started jogging, my idea of exercise was to fill the tub, take a bath, pull the plug, and fight the current.)

Today I jog an average of five times each week. I feel better, have more energy, and can do things I could not have done when I was twenty-five years old. My love of, and enthusiasm for, jogging is so great that I have jogged with the temperature as much as *forty degrees below zero* outside. (Of course, I was jogging *inside*—wouldn't want to mislead you!) I lost that 37 pounds in ten months by losing one and nine-tenths (1.9) ounces per day. I wrote *See You At The Top*, a 384-page book which has sold over 1,500,000 copies, by writing one and one-fourth pages every day for ten months.

You raise positive kids in a negative world, build a magnificent marriage, move to the top in the business world, become an honor student or a well-conditioned athlete by the series of little things you do every day that move you closer and closer to your objective. It's not the big earth-shattering things you do which will ultimately produce positive, drug-free kids. It's those little daily displays of care, affection, positive input, direction, discipline, love, time, interest, concern in your child's life which will make the difference.

To raise positive kids I believe one of the most important lessons we can teach them is persistence. Many times our kids are simply going to have to "suck it up and tough it out." They have to get their homework assignment whether they are inclined to do so or not. They'll have to go to school whether they really are feeling on top or not. Please don't misunderstand. I'm not talking about a child who is sick with a fever or a child who is really ill. I'm talking about the countless instances when all of us, including our children, want to quit just because we don't really want to do something or because we don't feel 100 percent.

Do It Anyhow

Every successful man or woman I've ever known did many things when not feeling 100 percent. The interesting thing is that often when we start doing something we don't feel like doing, after just a few minutes we like doing it. The message is both simple *and* profound. Logic will not change an emotion (feeling), but *action* will. This is a valuable but difficult lesson to teach our kids, and it's one that requires loving persistence on our part.

Anyone who utilizes his ability to the utmost will do so

only because he understands that a disciplined, persistent individual is the one who ultimately gets things done. It is inevitable that all of us are going to suffer frustrations, defeats, and setbacks. We can take a lesson from the great inventor Charles Kettering, who suggests that we must learn to fail intelligently.

> *Logic will not change*
> *an emotion,*
> *but* action *will.*

He observes that once you've failed, you should analyze the problem and discover why you failed. He believes each failure is one more step leading up to the cathedral of success. "The only time you don't want to fail is the last time you try," he says. When you do fail, you need to honestly face defeat. You never fake success. *When you fail, don't waste that failure.* Learn all you can from it, because every failing experience can teach you something, and in reality you haven't failed if it has. Above all things, you never use failure as an excuse for not trying again. After all, the first time your toddler falls, you certainly do not say, "You've had it! That's it! Keep your seat for the rest of your life."

Take One More Step

You may not be able to reclaim the loss, undo the damage, or reverse the consequences, but whatever your failure has been, you can be like that toddler and simply stand up and make a new start. But this time you will be a wiser, more sensitive, and more determined individual. *Knowing how to benefit from failure is the key to success,* and if your kids see you benefiting in your life on a daily basis and growing from your failures, they certainly are going to be encouraged to give it another shot. Persistence is one quality you'll always find in successful people.

Another classic example is that of explorer Fridtjof Nansen. He and his companion became lost in the Arctic wasteland and soon ran out of supplies. They ate everything they had, including the dogs and their harnesses. As they trudged on across the empty, bleak, and frigid terrain, with no evidence whatsoever of another living human being within hundreds of miles of them, Nansen's companion gave up, lay down in the snow, and died. However, Nansen's will was such that he was simply too strong to concede defeat. He kept thinking, *I can take one more step, just one more,* which is exactly what he did. He kept stumbling on until he literally stumbled into the American expedition that had been sent to look for the lost explorers.

The message is clear—when you keep going on or even stumbling on, you never know what you'll stumble onto. This is exactly what Nansen did. Obviously, you're not going to stumble onto anything when you are sitting down.

A wise man once observed that the persistent pursuit of knowledge and growth cannot be separated from the pursuit of happiness. Since happiness is everyone's objective, that persistent pursuit certainly rates high in the qualities we must teach our kids if we're going to raise them as positive, productive individuals.

Set the Example, Parents

It's old, but true: Quitters never win, and winners never quit until the job is complete. Unfortunately kids don't come equipped with persistence. Many are naturally quitters. They'll tangle with something until they tire of it and then leave it. That's the way toddlers and young children are. However, when they're old enough to begin having responsibilities like putting away their toys, helping keep things straight in the house, taking out the trash, making their own beds, helping mom with the dishes, and doing the 101 different chores around the house, parents can begin building an attitude of persistence.

> *There are very few problems that pure, dogged persistence won't eventually solve.*

It's extremely beneficial when parents see to it that their kids do what they're supposed to do, when it needs to be done, and that the task is completed and done well. If kids get out of their responsibilities early in life, regardless of the reason, they will try to get out of them from then on. At this point parents are establishing a habit, and it's not a winning one.

Parents, you must apply your parental insistence if you're going to instill persistence in your kids. Obviously, your kids are not going to be overly enthusiastic with your tactics, but they will look back and thank you for the rest of their lives.

Many years ago Calvin Coolidge said, "Nothing in the world can take the place of persistence. Talent will not. Nothing is more common than unsuccessful men with talent. Genius will not. Unrewarded genius is almost a proverb. Education will not. The world is full of educated derelicts."

When you teach your kids the value of persistence, they might temporarily pause, but they won't stop short of their goals. They'll keep after them and, in the process, will discover that there are very few problems that pure, dogged persistence won't eventually solve.

Time for Personal Evaluation

1. In your own words, describe the story of the Chinese bamboo tree.

2. What is the lesson we can learn from Charles Kettering? Have you seen this lesson effective in your life? How can you teach it to your child?

3. Zig thinks kids don't come equipped with persistence. What does he suggest parents do to combat this problem?

4. When was the last time you insisted that your child keep working on a difficult task? Was it tough on you? Zig says it's worth it. Do you agree?

CHAPTER 19

Real Love

> *Love never reasons, but profusely gives—*
> *gives like a thoughtless prodigal, its all—*
> *and trembles then lest it has done too little.*
> —Hannah Moore

A "Special" Little Boy

Many times parents are not blessed with that beautiful, healthy, mentally alert, bouncing baby boy or girl. Instead, in many ways they are even more blessed with a child who has some problems of one kind or another—physical, mental, emotional. Some are minor; some are serious. In my book *See You at the Top*, I gave the vivid details of a young boy with cerebral palsy. His parents, Bernie and Elaine Lofchick of Winnipeg, Canada, are now like a brother and sister to me. Thirty doctors said there was no hope for their son, David, and advised them to put him in an institution for his own good and for the good of the "normal" members of the family. The Lofchicks, however, found another doctor who was oriented toward solutions, not problems. He was the world-famous Dr. Pearlstein from Chicago.

Bernie was able to get an appointment when a little boy from Australia cancelled his, and they went to Chicago for the examination. The examination itself was very comprehensive. Dr. Pearlstein spelled out what would be required if they expected David to make the progress he knew David could make.

One of the things required was that when David was about two years old, they had to put heavy braces on his legs, and each evening they had to be made progressively tighter. Consequently the pain steadily increased. On many occasions as mom or dad started to put the braces on, little David would protest.

Now I want you to clearly see the picture. David was a beautiful little boy—coal black hair, olive complexion, beautiful green eyes. With tears in his eyes he would plead, "Mom, do you have to put 'em on tonight?" Or, "Dad, can't you leave 'em off this one time?" Or, "Do you have to make 'em so tight?" Surely every parent alive can relate to the situation and understand the difficulty of Bernie and Elaine Lofchick's position. But they loved David so much they said no to the tears of the moment so they could say yes to the laughter of a lifetime.

Today "Little David" is twenty-nine years old. He weighs about 195 pounds, has a barrel for a chest, and is the number one condominium salesman with the number one real estate firm in Winnipeg, Canada. He is an outstanding young man in every respect. He is happily married and the father of a beautiful, healthy daughter and a handsome, robust son.

Needless to say, there are going to be many, many instances as you raise your positive kids, when it would be easier and less hassle to simply give in to their demands. On many occasions it will be easier to plop the kids in front of the television set or let them eat the junk food.

Later it will be easier to allow them to stay up until ten instead of having to explain why they need to be in bed by nine. Still later it will be easier to let them start dating early and stay out until an hour you know is too late just to avoid the hassle—so they can be "like all the other kids." However, real love demands you do what is best for your children and not necessarily what they wanted you to do.

Real versus Counterfeit Love

By far the most important single ingredient in the formula to raise positive kids in a negative world is deep, genuine love. Kids need to clearly understand the difference between real love and the counterfeit love they often see on television.

Several years ago, the Redhead went to the bank with a deposit. As you know, when tellers count the money, they really get after it. They pop those bills out so fast I'm mystified as to how they know how many they've actually counted. As a matter of fact, I'm always afraid they've given me too much, so I recount to make certain they've not overdone it.

On this day as the teller was counting the money, she suddenly stopped, reached down, and picked up a twenty-dollar bill and said, "Mrs. Ziglar, this is a counterfeit bill." She recognized the counterfeit instantly, because in most banks they will not let a teller even touch a counterfeit. That way when a counterfeit appears in a stack, the teller can instantly, without looking, tell the difference by the "feel."

Yes, there's a difference between real and counterfeit money, and there's a vast difference between real and counterfeit love. The counterfeit variety is often depicted on television and in dime-store novels. In an hour's encounter boy meets girl, they go to dinner, establish a "meaningful relationship," fall madly in love, and go to bed. They make every effort to depict this as the real thing, pointing out that there is nothing morally wrong with any facet of a relationship, provided it is "meaningful."

The dictionary says, "Love is the tender and passionate affection for one of the opposite sex." Obviously real love goes considerably beyond tender and passionate affection. When the child sees what real love is, when he clearly sees that "for better or worse" positively means that if mom or dad becomes ill, the faithful mate looks after the other one, whether the illness involves a few days in bed or whether it's a permanent, crippling, disabling injury involving years of loving treatment and care, then the chances of raising a positive child are dramatically enhanced. Why? Because the child sees genuine love in action. There is nothing more powerful!

Demonstrating Love

Several years ago I remember chatting with my son, and I asked him, "Son, if anybody should ask you what you like best about your dad, what would you say?" He pondered for just a moment and said, "I'd say the thing I like best about my dad is that he loves my mom." I naturally asked why he would say that, and he responded, "Well, Dad, I know as long as you love Mom, you're going to treat her right; and as long as you treat her right, we'll always be a family, because she sure does love you. As long as you love each other, Dad, and treat each other right, I'll never have to make a choice of living with you or living with Mom." Of course, I had no way of knowing it, but that very day one of his closest friends had been given that choice. The need for parents to demonstrate their love for each other before their children is so important. If they truly do love each other, they'll be thoughtful and considerate of each other. Not only will they benefit, but the children will benefit enormously.

> *Love—real love—demands that you do*
> *what is best for your child,*
> *not necessarily what your child*
> *wants you to do, or what is easiest for you.*

Even as I sit here in our home writing these words, I'm in East Texas at Holly Lake. This is where the Redhead and I come to relax, and it is where I do most of my writing. Tonight is extremely foggy. Our son is with us. He and my wife had planned to have dinner and take in a movie in Tyler, which is about thirty miles from where we live, since I was busy writing. However, as the day progressed, fog set in, and by the time of departure, it was extremely heavy.

My son was all gung-ho for going, but my wife was apprehensive; and to tell you the truth, I was more than apprehensive, so I asked them not to go. Had the trip to Tyler been an emergency, perhaps I would not have felt so strongly. However, with so much at stake on a foggy night, I simply could not bear to see them leave. Now I certainly did not encourage them to stay home because I'm a killjoy or because I was envious of the fact that they would be relaxing and having a nice time. Far from it! I get extreme pleasure out of the enjoyment my family has. However, I love them far too much to watch them pull out of the driveway into a foggy night with unknown dangers and drivers on the road. It occurs to me that this is love in action. Where the rubber meets the road in everyday life, parents must demonstrate love.

Hugging and Kissing

Probably the most misunderstood area for most parents, particularly fathers, centers on the amount of affection they should give their children. I cannot begin to tell you the number of men and women, forty, fifty, and sixty years old, who have told me during the course of our BORN TO WIN seminars that they cannot ever remember their parents telling them they loved them and hugging or kissing them, even when they were children. Tragically this often means that these people are not showing love and affection with their own children and grandchildren, and this is a sad situation.

Fortunately the no-hugging chain can be broken. Although they were never hugged and kissed, many parents recognize the void it created in their own lives, and consequently, they've determined to break that chain. Slowly but surely many of them are now learning to show affection and appreciation for their children. It is something that certainly can be learned.

Fathers and mothers need to kiss both sons and daughters. A popular misconception that many ''macho men'' have is that if they show affection for their little boys, particularly after they get past the toddler stage, it will increase the chances of their becoming homosexuals. Actually, the exact opposite is true. Dr. Ross Campbell, a psychiatrist who specializes in working with children, says that in all his reading and experience, he has never known of one sexually disoriented person who had a warm, loving and affectionate father.

The need for affection doesn't end when we become adults. One psychologist says we need four good hugs a day to be healthy. Studies by the University of California, Los Angeles, Medical Center and the Meninger Foundation, Topeka, Kansas, showed that *hugging relieves many physical and emotional problems and can help people live longer, maintain health, relieve stress, and promote sleep.*

I'm seldom so bold as to say, ''We did this one right''; but in the area of hugging, if there has ever been a family that has done it right, it has been our own. Because of this huggin' habit the Redhead and I have, our children have picked it up. The result? A strong emotional closeness that increases as the years go by.

Love Can Make All of Us Winners

I'm convinced that love, and the demonstration of that love, is the answer to many problems that might and do exist in the family today. In fact, love can do what nothing else can.

At one of our BORN TO WIN seminars in Dallas, a young man and his wife were with us from Tennessee. He was astute financially and quite successful, but he had a problem—he could neither read nor write. Since part of our BORN TO WIN class involves writing good things you notice about others on what we call our "I Like" note pads, this young man was at quite a disadvantage. On the third day of the class, he stood up to speak to the group and said, "I've got something to confess to you. All of you have been sending me these wonderful notes telling me of many good things you see in me, and they have really been encouraging; but I haven't been sending any notes to you. My wife has been reading mine to me because I can neither read nor write." And with that, he broke down and wept.

Spontaneously from the people who were gathered for the seminar, a young man from Malaysia, a big strapping Texan, a woman from Australia all simultaneously rushed to the young man, embraced him, and wept with the emotion of the moment. The class arose as one and gave a standing ovation to the young man from Tennessee *and* to the three who had gone forward to assure this young man of his worth and their respect for him as a human being. I only wish that the United Nations could have witnessed that inspiring scene of love and caring shared by the four people from three continents, three countries, and three faiths as they affirmed and encouraged one another.

Love is the highest, purest, most precious of all spiritual things. It will draw out from men their magnificent potential. In practical terms, it instills the will to persist when the going gets so tough that any "reasonable" person would quit. We see this love demonstrated many, many times when a child is seriously ill or terribly injured in an accident and mom and dad lovingly invest countless hours over a period of months—even years—in an effort to comfort him and hopefully restore him to mental and physical health. Time after time, love is the determining factor.

The Real Authority on Raising Positive Kids

In many ways, I suppose, I'm ending this book in a most unusual fashion. I've shared data and material collected out of my own life's experiences and observations; and after talking with countless mothers and fathers over a period of many years, I've quoted numerous "authorities" on the subject of rearing children. I've given data that supports the things I've had to say, and I hope and believe I've given you some valid guidelines that will enable you to deal more effectively with life yourself and to give your children a better shot at being positive, drug-free winners.

I must confess, however, that when the book was 95 percent complete as far as the accumulation of all the data, I visited with an expert on raising children who can definitely teach all of us a number of lessons.

Love Comes in Many Shapes and Sizes

Her name is Thelma Boston, and I first met her on Friday, December 21, 1984, although I had been hearing bits and pieces about her over a period of several years. In September 1969, Thelma's husband was murdered, and things looked pretty bleak. However, Thelma is truly one of the most remarkable people I've ever seen. In every sense of the word, she is the Mother Teresa of South Dallas when it comes to pure love and total faith. Thus far, Thelma has had a hand in the rearing of some two hundred foster children, and in December 1984, she had fourteen in her home. The children Thelma gets are those nobody else wants. Some of them are severely retarded mentally, and others have physical problems that would break your heart.

However, when Thelma gets these kids, miracles take place. Many of them come from a background of extreme abuse—physical, sexual, psychological, and mental. They're both male and female and represent the black community, the white community, and just about everything else in between.

Twenty-two-year-old Jonathan, who has the mental alertness of a nine- or ten-year-old, is an example of one of these needy "children."

Jonathan had established quite a reputation in twenty foster homes, and nobody wanted him—but that's the kind of kid that Thelma seeks. It wasn't his mental alertness that caused him to be unwanted. Lots of kids who function at much lower levels than Jonathan are accepted at other homes. Jonathan was unwanted because he did things that are socially unacceptable. "Little" things like waking up in the middle of the night, walking over to his roommate's bed and spitting or urinating in his face. "Little" things like choking the neighbor's cat to death. In short, Jonathan was not the kind of child who would be welcome in most homes. Now he is one of Thelma's miracle boys.

Then there's Marco Evans. Marco is a teenager who is about three feet tall. He's in bed most of the time because his physical condition doesn't give him many options. His bones are extremely soft, and he cannot stand. Marco is a bright, articulate boy who reaches up and grabs the heart of everyone. The influence he has, and the respect he enjoys from the other kids, is remarkable. As you watch Thelma talk to him and you see his bright-eyed optimism, you can't help but be encouraged and excited.

"Just Love 'Em and Trust the Lord"

In talking with Thelma I asked how she managed to work these miracles. Without any show of anything other than modesty, grace, and faith, Thelma said, "I just love 'em, and I trust the Lord."

When you try to pin the accolades on Thelma, she just smiles and says, "No problem. The Lord's taking care of everything." Yes, the Lord does take care of everything, but in the case of these "special" kids, He is doing it through the loving heart and arms of a remarkable woman who demonstrates that love combined with faith is an unbeatable force in raising positive, drug-free kids in a negative world.

> Love can do
> what
> nothing else can.

I tell this story because, when you look at your child I'm going to tell you that regardless of his mental, physical, and emotional condition, the odds are enormous that at least one of Thelma's kids is infinitely worse off, and yes, each one of them is responding to her love and faith. I'm not even hinting that it's easy to do what Thelma has done and is doing, but when you look at all the kids in the Thelma Boston Home it's clear to everyone that the biggest winner there is Thelma. The exhilaration that comes from winning is tremendous, but it is a pale shadow when compared to the feeling you have when you can take a child and make his life richer and more meaningful, almost regardless of any problems he might have.

If your child doesn't happen to be normal and healthy in every way, I ask you to consider the miracle of South Dallas and Thelma Boston and take hope. If she can give faith, hope, and love to two hundred youngsters who have been abused or neglected and who are retarded or handicapped in some way, then surely there is much you can do to give your child the love, commitment, and affection that will ease his burden through life and help make him a winner. In the process, the biggest winner will be you.

That's where this book ends—by urging you parents to use your special glasses which I fitted you with in the first chapter to *look again and see what that special child of yours can be in the future, with your prayerful and patient help, with positive input, and with that God-given love that can overcome any obstacle.*

Time for Personal Evaluation

1. Remember the Lofchicks of Winnipeg? Zig describes them in this way: "They loved David so much they said no to the _____ of the moment so they could say yes to the _____ of a lifetime."

2. Describe the difference between real and counterfeit love.

3. Are you a "hugging" family? If not, is it because your parents never practiced hugging with you? Zig says it is critically important for a child's well-being. Do you agree?

4. Remember the young man from Tennessee in the BORN TO WIN seminar? What was his problem? How was real love demonstrated to him?

5. You have a special child, unique in many ways. What can you do to demonstrate real love to that child on a long-term basis?

Don't stop. The epilogue is significant.

Epilogue

Many of you may wonder what our children think about what I have written. With that in mind, I asked them for suggestions and comments about the things we did that they felt were effective and those that they believed were ineffective.

We Did Some Things Wrong

1. *A no for no reason.* The big winner for being most ineffective was our too-frequent tendency not to give them a reason when we gave them a no. On many occasions our answer was, "Because I said so." If we could do it over, that's one we would change.

2. *Too few family outings.* They expressed disappointment over the fact that we did not do more things together as a family. They specifically mentioned going on picnics, attending athletic events such as baseball or football games, or going camping.

3. *Little follow-up punishment.* Too often we did not follow up with some kind of punishment when they failed to do the few chores we had assigned to them. All of them pointed out they would have had more opportunities for growth and better preparation for life if they had been given more responsibilities around the house.

4. *Inadequate warnings about sexual harassment.* Another area in which we really goofed with our girls was that we

did not prepare them for the sexual advances they received as they grew up and went to work.

5. *Insensitivity to the effect of relocation on the family.* One of the worst things we did was to move frequently from one city to another. Some moves were necessary, but several of them could have been avoided had I been more sensitive to the needs and feelings of my daughters. In retrospect, I would include my family in making the decision, and it would be made in a loving, not a dictatorial fashion.

6. *Handling of financial difficulties.* Until our youngest daughter was about seventeen, we were often on a financial roller coaster and frequently in a feast-or-famine situation. However, we never discussed or admitted to them that we had money problems. It wasn't until years later that we learned the girls had been deeply troubled during those times. They thought we were going to lose everything. A little honest dialogue would have alleviated most of their fears.

We Did Some Things Right

We were delighted that the list of things our kids felt we did right was substantially longer than the list they felt we "goofed" on.

1. *Same ordering privileges.* Interestingly enough, one of the things they appreciated most was the fact that when we ate at a restaurant, we always gave them the same ordering privileges we had. If we ordered steak and that's what they wanted, they ordered steaks. This communicated to them the value and worth we felt they had and did wonders for their self-images.

2. *Teaching the absolutes of right and wrong.* For example, their mother would not lie for them if they didn't want to talk to someone who called or came by. Also,

the day each child reached the age of twelve was the day
we started buying that child an adult ticket to the movies.

3. *Not using improper language.* They all felt that not being allowed to use, and not ever hearing us use, cop-out
words like *stupid*, *dumb*, *hate*, or *yuk* was important.
Also they never heard us curse or use filthy language.

4. *Teaching them courteous responses.* Teaching them to
respect their elders, including us, with courteous "Yes,
sir" or "Yes, ma'am" answers, along with generous
use of please and thank you, has been extremely helpful
to them.

5. *Respecting ourselves and others.* Never seeing us drunk
or out of control was especially important to the girls,
and Tom most appreciated the affection and appreciation
we demonstrated for each other. Respecting other races
also rated high on their list of things we effectively taught
them.

6. *Insisting on personal responsibility.* Our middle daughter, Cindy, was especially pleased that we made her feel
responsible for always doing her homework and being
on time—and that after the first year of college, she was
permitted to make her own choice regarding the rest of
her education.

7. *Sensible dating restrictions.* We would not let them date
anyone we felt would not be in their long-range best
interests just because "others were doing it." We always felt they should never date anyone they would be
unwilling to marry and have as the father or mother of
their children.

8. *Taking the time to listen.* Daughter Suzan especially appreciated the fact that we either had the time or took the
time to talk when she needed or wanted to talk.

9. *Showing no favoritism.* Treating all of them equally,
showing no favoritism, was high on their list. The girls
smilingly point out that Tom was the exception, since
he was the only child we took overseas. (Tom came

along ten years after our youngest daughter, and the girls were already married when we took him on those trips.) They emphasize, however, that it's still not too late.

10. *Displaying love and affection openly.* Easily the most important thing to them was the fact that we openly displayed our love and affection for each other and made them feel comfortable that mom and dad respected and loved each other.

11. *Raising them in the church.* Seeing each one of our children, and now our grandchildren, come to know Jesus Christ as Lord and Savior was by far the most important thing we did right. Since all of us are going to be dead longer than we are going to be alive, and since the Bible clearly says there is a heaven and a hell, where you spend that eternity is important.

12. *Gave them unconditional love.* Our unconditional love for them in equal amounts was never seriously questioned by any of our children, and we are grateful for that because love truly is the most powerful force for good and for raising positive kids on the face of this earth.

Families can and should be a tremendous source of love, inspiration, and enjoyment. Here's hoping and believing that *Raising Positive Kids in a Negative World* will help you and your family as you grow together.

Endnotes

Foreword
1. Zodhiates, Dr. Spiros, *Family Happiness is Homemade* (Carol Stream, Illinois: Family Concern, Vol. 12, No. 11, November 1988).

Introduction
1. Ketterman, Dr. Grace H., *199 Questions Parents Ask*, pp. 11–12, (Old Tappan, New Jersey; Fleming H. Revell, 1986).

Chapter 1
1. Ryan, Michael, *Parade*, pp. 10–11, (Reprinted by permission of the author and the author's agents, Scott Meredith Literary Agency, Inc., 845 Third Avenue, New York, New York 10022; December 25, 1988).
2. *San Francisco Examiner*, January 23, 1989.

Chapter 2
1. Watson, Dr. Marvin; former President, Dallas Baptist University, Dallas, Texas.
2. *Albuquerque Journal*, February 17, 1989.
3. *The Dallas Morning News*, December 26, 1988.
4. *Good News*, p. 12, January/February, 1986.
5. *Journal of the American Medical Association*, October 7, 1988.
6. *San Francisco Chronicle*, January 22, 1982.
7. *Executive Digest*, March, 1988.
8. *Dallas Morning News*, 1988, Associated Press Release.
9. *American Journal of Orthopsychiatry*, February, 1989.
10. Seligman, Martin E. P., "Boomer Blues," *Psychology Today*, pp. 50–55, October 1988.
11. *Dallas Morning News*, March 21, 1985.

Chapter 3
1. Kirby, Dr. William E., Texas State Commissioner of Education.
2. Family Concern, September, 1984.

Chapter 4

1. Strack, Jay, *Drugs and Drinking*, p. 122 (Nashville, TN.: Sceptre Book, Royal Publishers, 1979).
2. Johnson, Wendell, *People in Quandaries*.

Chapter 5

1. *Dallas Times Herald*, May 15, 1982.
2. *Dallas Times Herald*, July 2, 1988.
3. *Signs of the Times*, April, 1984.
4. Family Concern, August, 1984.

Chapter 6

1. *U. S. News & World Report*, April 30, 1984.
2. *These Times*, February, 1984.
3. Strack, Jay, *Drugs and Drinking*, p. 122 (Nashville, TN.: Sceptre Book, Royal Publishers, 1979).

Chapter 7

1. "Korn/Ferry International's Executive Profile: A Survey of Corporate Leaders in the Eighties." Korn/Ferry International, New York, New York, 1986.
2. *Child Protection Guide*, p. 29, National Child Protection Program, Renod Productions, Inc., Santa Rosa, California, 1988.
3. Conn, Harry, *Four Trojan Horses of Humanism*, p. 7 (Milford, MI.: Mott Media, Inc., 1982).
4. Light, Paul C., *Baby Boomers* (W. W. Norton & Company, 1989)
5. *Christianity Today*, August 10, 1984.
6. *Christianity Today*, August 10, 1984.
7. Campbell, Ross, M.D., *Your Child and Drugs*, p. 30 (Wheaton, IL.: Victor Books, 1988).
8. *Houston Post*, September, 1984.
9. *Atlanta Journal*, April 27, 1984.
10. *Christianity Today*, May 18, 1984.
11. Hampton, Ruth, *Family Happiness is Homemade* (Carol Stream, Illinois: Family Concern, Vol. 12, No. 11, November 1988).
12. *U. S. News & World Report*, p. 74, November 14, 1988
13. *American Way*, April, 1982.

Chapter 8

1. Campbell, Ross, M.D., *Your Child and Drugs*, p. 62 (Wheaton, IL.: Victor Books, 1988).
2. Strack, Jay, *Drugs and Drinking*, p. 97 (Nashville, TN.: Sceptre Book, Royal Publishers, 1979).
3. Andelin, Helen, *All About Raising Children* (Santa Barbara, CA: Pacific Press, 1981).

Chapter 10
1. Whiston, Lionel, *Family Happiness is Homemade* (Carol Stream, Illinois: Family Concern, Vol. 13, No. 1, January 1989).
2. Campbell, Ross, M.D., *How To Really Love Your Child*, p. 53 (Wheaton, IL.: SP Publications, Inc. 1977).
3. *U. S. News & World Report*, November 12, 1984.
4. Dobson, James, M.D., *Focus on the Family*, Vol. 13, No. 2, p. 21 (February, 1989).
5. *The Atlanta Journal and Constitution*, January 18, 1989

Chapter 11
1. *Dallas Morning News*, February 6, 1989.
2. *U. S. News & World Report*, p. 50, February 6, 1989
3. Page, Clarence, *Chicago Tribune*.
4. U. S. Surgeon General's Report.
5. *U.S.A. Today*, February 24, 1989.
6. *U.S.A. Today*, "USA Snapshots," Roper Reports, spring 1988 survey
7. *The Dallas Morning News*, March 18, 1988.
8. Strack, Jay, *Drugs and Drinking*, p. 35 (Nashville, TN.: Sceptre Book, Royal Publishers, 1979).
9. *The Dallas Morning News*, March 18, 1988.
10. *Floria Times Union*, September 15, 1988.
11. *The Atlanta Journal and Constitution*, September 5, 1988
12. *Journal of the American Medical Association*, October 7, 1988.
13. Campbell, Ross, M.D., *How To Really Know Your Child*, p. 20 (Wheaton, IL.: SP Publications, Inc., 1987).
14. Campbell, Ross, M.D., *Your Child and Drugs*, p. 15 (Wheaton, IL.: Victor Books, 1988).
15. Strack, Jay, *Drugs and Drinking*, p. 44 (Nashville, TN.: Sceptre Book, Royal Publishers, 1979).

Chapter 12
1. *The Family in America*, Vol. 2, No. 7, July, 1988
2. National Youth Sports Research, *Family Happiness is Homemade* (Carol Stream, Illinois: Family Concern, Vol. 12, No. 11, November 1988).
3. *The Family In America*, January, 1989.
4. Campbell, Ross, M.D., *Your Child and Drugs*, p. 21 (Wheaton, IL.: Victor Books, 1988).
5. Strack, Jay, *Drugs and Drinking*, p. 98 (Nashville, TN.: Sceptre Book, Royal Publishers, 1979).
6. *U.S.A. Today*, July 21, 1988.
7. *Texas Business*, pp. 5–10, July, 1987.
8. *Fortune*, p. 50, November 7, 1988.
9. Hume Educational Services, 835 Franklin Court, Box 105627, Atlanta, Georgia 30348-9966.

10. *Dallas Morning News*, January 22, 1989
11. Lewis, Paul, *Family Happiness is Homemade* (Carol Stream, Illinois: Family Concern, Vol. 13, No. 1, January 1989).

Chapter 14

1. Chassler, Sey, *Parade Magazine*, p. 16, December 18, 1988.
2. McGrath, William B., M.D., *The Heart Does Not Speak English*, p. 27 (Phoenix: O'Sullivan Woodside & Company, 1975).
3. *The Lookout* (Cincinnati, Ohio, The Standard Publishing Company, 1980).
4. McDowell, Josh, *Family Happiness is Homemade* (Carol Stream, Illinois: Family Concern Vol. 12, No. 4, April, 1988).

Chapter 15

1. *Child Protection Guide*, p. 5, National Child Protection Program, Renod Productions, Inc., Santa Rosa, California, 1988.
2. Ibid.
3. Ibid.
4. *The News & Daily Advance*, Lynchburg, VA., February 9, 1989.

Chapter 16

1. *Child Protection Guide*, p. 4, National Child Protection Program, Renod Productions, Inc., Santa Rosa, California, 1988.

Chapter 17

1. Hendricks, Dr. Howard, *Family Happiness is Homemade* (Carol Stream, Illinois: Family Concern Vol. 13, No. 3, March, 1989).
2. *Dallas Morning News*, December 31, 1988.